Nonlinear Psychoanalysis

Nonlinear concepts from chaos theory, complexity studies, and fractal geometry have transformed the way we think about the mind. *Nonlinear Psychoanalysis* shows how nonlinear dynamics can be integrated with psychoanalytic thinking to shed new light on psychological development, therapeutic processes, and fundamental psychoanalytic concepts.

Starting with a personal history of the author's engagement with nonlinear dynamics and psychoanalysis, this book describes how his approach applies to diagnosis of psychological conditions, concepts of normal and pathological development, gender, research methods, and finally the theory and practice of psychoanalysis and psychodynamic psychotherapy. This book is full of new ideas about the basic nonlinear processes of human development, nonlinear views of gender and fundamental psychoanalytic processes like working through, and the nature of the therapeutic process as conceptualized in terms of the theory of coupled oscillators. Galatzer-Levy questions many standard psychoanalytic formulations and points to a freer practice of psychoanalysis and psychoanalytic thinking. His new approach opens the readers' eyes to ways in which development and treatment can occur through processes not now included in standard psychoanalytic theory. The book not only provides useful theories but also helps readers take note of commonly passed over phenomena that were unseen for lack of a theory to explain them.

Galatzer-Levy brings an unusual combination of training in psychiatry, psychoanalysis, and mathematics to this unique study, which summarizes his forty years of exploration of nonlinearity and psychoanalysis. *Nonlinear Psychoanalysis* will appeal to psychoanalysts and psychotherapists as well as students of nonlinear dynamics systems.

Robert M. Galatzer-Levy, Clinical Professor of Psychiatry and Behavioral Neuroscience at the University of Chicago is also a faculty member of the Chicago Institute for Psychoanalysis. He practices child, adolescent, and adult psychoanalysis and psychiatry in Chicago.

Psychoanalysis in a New Key Book Series
Series editor: Donnel Stern

When music is played in a new key, the melody does not change, but the notes that make up the composition do: change in the context of continuity, continuity that perseveres through change. Psychoanalysis in a New Key publishes books that share the aims psychoanalysts have always had but that approach them differently. The books in the series are not expected to advance any particular theoretical agenda, although to this date most have been written by analysts from the Interpersonal and Relational orientations.

The most important contribution of a psychoanalytic book is the communication of something that nudges the readers' grasp of clinical theory and practice in an unexpected direction. Psychoanalysis in a New Key creates a deliberate focus on innovative and unsettling clinical thinking. Because that kind of thinking is encouraged by exploration of the sometimes surprising contributions to psychoanalysis of ideas and findings from other fields, Psychoanalysis in a New Key particularly encourages interdisciplinary studies. Books in the series have married psychoanalysis with dissociation, trauma theory, sociology, and criminology. The series is open to the consideration of studies examining the relationship between psychoanalysis and any other field—for instance, biology, literary and art criticism, philosophy, systems theory, anthropology, and political theory.

But innovation also takes place within the boundaries of psychoanalysis, and Psychoanalysis in a New Key therefore also presents work that reformulates thought and practice without leaving the precincts of the field. Books in the series focus, for example, on the significance of personal values in psychoanalytic practice, on the complex interrelationship between the analyst's clinical work and personal life, on the consequences for the clinical situation when patient and analyst are from different cultures, and on the need for psychoanalysts to accept the degree to which they knowingly satisfy their own wishes during treatment hours, often to the patient's detriment.

A full list of all titles in this series is available at:
https://www.routledge.com/series/LEAPNKBS

Nonlinear Psychoanalysis

Notes from Forty Years of Chaos and Complexity Theory

Robert M. Galatzer-Levy

Routledge
Taylor & Francis Group
LONDON AND NEW YORK

First published 2017
by Routledge
2 Park Square, Milton Park, Abingdon, Oxon OX14 4RN

and by Routledge
605 Third Avenue, New York, NY 10017

Routledge is an imprint of the Taylor & Francis Group, an informa business

British Library Cataloguing-in-Publication Data
A catalogue record for this book is available from the British Library

Library of Congress Cataloging-in-Publication Data
Names: Galatzer-Levy, Robert M., 1944– author.
Title: Nonlinear psychoanalysis: notes from forty years of chaos and complexity theory / Robert M. Galatzer-Levy.
Other titles: Psychoanalysis in a new key book series; v. 36.
Description: Abingdon, Oxon; New York, NY: Routledge, 2017. | Series: Psychoanalysis in a new key book series; 36 | Includes bibliographical references and index.
Identifiers: LCCN 2016057099 | ISBN 9780415508988 (hardback) | ISBN 9780415508995 (pbk.) | ISBN 9781315266473 (e-book)
Subjects: | MESH: Psychoanalytic Theory | Nonlinear Dynamics | Psychoanalytic Therapy | Human Development
Classification: LCC RC506 | NLM WM 460.2 | DDC 616.89/17—dc23
LC record available at https://lccn.loc.gov/2016057099

ISBN: 978-0-415-50898-8 (hbk)
ISBN: 978-0-415-50899-5 (pbk)
ISBN: 978-1-315-26647-3 (ebk)

Typeset in Times New Roman
by codeMantra

For Jeanne, for forty years of chaos and so much more

Contents

Introduction

Mathematics, Psychoanalysis, and the Human Sciences

Though this introduction comes at the beginning, it is nearly the last piece I wrote for this book. As I prepared it, my mind wandered. I browsed the Internet. It had been years since I had looked at my father's writing, and, since it was his 111th birthday, I Googled him. I knew my father had an enormous influence on my personality and thinking. I am, after all, a psychoanalyst. Later you will see that I also knew that some of my interest in nonlinear systems theory is a reaction to his linear worldview.

Today, a major chunk of his publications is available online, including one on the chemical embryology of the chick embryo, published in 1952 (Levy, 1952). I remembered seeing this paper long ago. It stuck out in my mind because it started with the chemical pseudo-equation,

$$\text{Egg} + O_2 \text{ -> BaBy Chick} + CO_2 + \text{side products}$$

The equation typified my father's sense of humor, gentle understatement, and irony, but the capital B as the third letter of *baby* always puzzled me. Was it subtle humor or a typographical error? Perhaps that it stuck out in my recollection was kind of screen memory standing in place of what came next. I firmly believed my father had no notion even of the types of problems that nonlinear systems theory would come to address. Yet it was there in this paper written when I was eight years old, right after the baby chick equation. He asked, how could it be that an apparent violation of the second law of thermodynamics, the chemical system consisting of the egg and oxygen, could become vastly more ordered, developing into the incredibly complex structure of a baby chick from far less ordered components? In other words, he saw and struggled with a major element of nonlinearity, the concept of emergence, the appearance of complex order apparently from nowhere. Remember, the paper was written before it was clear how DNA communicated genetic information. He was trying to understand how nonlinear complex processes emerged from linear chemical ones. But even more surprising to me was the realization that my story of coming to think about nonlinear systems theory had to be revised, made more complex, and made even less linear than I had thought it to be.

The chapters in this book provide a history of my efforts to bring a nonlinear point of view to psychoanalytic thinking or, to put it better, show how my attempts to make greater sense of psychoanalytic phenomenon and ideas led ever more naturally to a nonlinear world view. In this foreword, I try to give an idea of how my thinking developed and the intellectual context in which it emerged.

A psychoanalyst looking back on more than forty years of an intellectual adventure almost reflexively asks how and why he did it. He easily traces some of its origins to those common roots of scientific investigation in the mysteries of his own body and the bodies of others: the transformation of food to excrement, the mysterious sounds emanating from the bedroom next door, the at the same time intense and vague desires to see and feel. Yet this account, though thoroughly convincing in some ways, leaves open the vast question of why the young boy's future researches take the form that they do. So it is without discarding an appreciation of the infantile origins of my investigations that I search for additional sources in more unique life experiences than in the ever-curious mind of my still much-alive three-year-old self.

I grew up in a world where science and rationality were venerated above all else. Though I was a year old when Hiroshima was destroyed by the work of the most brilliants minds of the century, and in a year in which millions of Jews were murdered using technology and ideology based in scientific thinking, the world in which I lived was inhabited by people who believed, above all else, that a scientific approach would result in unimagined material happiness and, more important, rational and peaceful living.

This worldview was firmly located in my father, a professor of biochemistry at New York University, and his two laboratories—one at the university, where I spent Saturday mornings from the time I was seven until sometime in high school, doing various tasks around the laboratory and absorbing its atmosphere; the other in Woods Hole, Massachusetts, a summer colony for biological and oceanographic researchers, where the postwar enthusiasm for science extended far beyond the walls of the laboratory into the mess hall where scientists and their families ate together and endlessly discussed science and how a rational world could be built on scientific principles, and to Stony Beach where the same scientists continued their debates knee-deep in the temperate waters of Buzzard's Bay, or the sidewalks, insofar as they existed, where graduate students seemed literally to dance around Otto Loewi, the Noble Prize–winning discoverer of acetylcholine, the first neurotransmitter. Though I knew that some people lived in different worlds—my mother's family was composed of successful small-business men and my father's included people in professions other than science—it did not occur to me until sometime in my late twenties that I might live in any other sort of world, and, in fact, although the superficial reality is that I live in the world of a psychoanalytic practitioner, I continue to experience myself as living largely in the world that surrounded me as a boy and young adolescent.

This world had its limitations. First, it had no place for the more direct forms of sensual pleasure. Sublimation was the name of the game, and for a young man this does not work particularly well. In addition, it had no place for my mother's neurotic, but in some ways realistic, concerns about money, a constant source of tension as she compared my father's modest academic income to that of her businessmen brothers and brothers-in-law. These factors, combined with a particularly unfortunate roommate assignment, left me sufficiently miserable during my freshman year of college that I went to the NYU student mental health service for help, where I had the good fortune to be listened to carefully for a few sessions and then, to my amazement, to be referred to a psychoanalyst. It did not occur to me until many years later that I was part of a huge wave of nice Jewish boys from New York who were being similarly referred. The referral was particularly successful because it hit at just the right moment. The introductory psychology course I was taking at the time, taught by a newly minted PhD, Philip Zimbardo, who was to go on to become one of the leading social psychologists in the country, included reading fascinating clinical material from a schizophrenic patient. This experience has stayed with me as a conviction that the best source for ideas and the most convincing tests of those ideas derive from studying individuals and particular situations in depth, and that, while it is sometimes possible to come to useful generalizations about people and their situations, theorizing that fails to again and again return to particular circumstances is at best likely to become sterile and at worst to blind investigators to the richness and complexity of the actual situations with which we deal. As I try to show in this book, a nonlinear worldview addresses the tension between particular situations and general theories in a fruitful way because the theory points to particulars and, for the investigator immersed in a nonlinear worldview, everyday experiences repeatedly cry out for a nonlinear understanding.

My sophomore year in college seemed to provide a wonderful mix of intellectual stimuli. In addition to Zimbardo's course, I came across several books by Theodore Reik, whose writings seemed to support my intuition that everything convex was phallic; everything concave, vaginal; and everything flat, the denial of these two wonderful possibilities. At the same time, a course in differential equations and Agnew's text on the subject convinced me not only of the beauty of mathematics but also the appropriateness of spending my life studying it. A required English literature course with Edwin Miller demonstrated that English literature, at least to 1750, was best understood as an exploration of castration anxiety, a point that the professor seemed to repeatedly illustrate by placing his hand and crossing his legs in a manner that suggested an ongoing personal familiarity with the issue. But among all of this, the analysis probably should be given first place in shaping my future life.

I was extraordinarily fortunate in my first analysis in ways that I only came to understand many years later. I thoroughly enjoyed the experience of exploring my own psyche in the presence of someone who appeared consistently interested (as indicated by the scratching of his pen on a notepad) but whose silence and lack of intervention left me feeling for many years that youthful opportunities had been missed to discuss some of the difficulties I faced. This negative assessment of the analysis was supported by an unresolved transference, only worked through years later, in which I saw my analyst

Dr. William Frosch as a representative of conventional moral values. At the same time, I felt that he had not adequately confronted some of my own more problematic dynamics and that, if he had, I could have been spared a certain amount of misery. Indeed, one of his rare interventions along this line opened a path of investigation that was life transforming.

The analysis took place in the mid-1960s when boys letting their hair grow long occupied a remarkable amount of energy. One Monday morning, I came to my session bitterly complaining, as I often did, about my mother who mistreated me during our alternate Sunday afternoon get-togethers at my parents' house, visits rationalized as necessary to get my laundry done.

"Now she's going on and on about how I need to get a haircut. I'm not going to get one, no matter how much she fusses about it. She's not going to control me!"

Frosch asked, "Don't you see that she's controlling you just as much if you avoid getting a haircut because of her demands as if you get one because she demands it?"

The interpretation not only struck me as accurate, but it led to a long, fruitful, and practical exploration, a major outcome of which I regarded for many years as the most useful result of the analysis—I was able to go to medical school, even though my mother wanted me to.

My first experience of analysis more or less coincided with my graduate education at the Courant Institute of Mathematical Sciences at New York University. Although the analysis succeeded in freeing me to the extent that I was able to go to medical school despite my mother's wishes that I do so, much analytic time was devoted to my peculiar notion of free association, which was to be allowed to talk about whatever I wanted to talk about at whatever length I chose. The trait of loving the sound of my own voice served multiple functions of narcissistic display, an opportunity to think aloud about matters that concerned me, and a defense against the emergence of more troubling material that might have come forward had I been less committed to talking in this coherent, intellectualized way. One day, as I lay on the couch describing a particularly challenging problem in group theory, a very abstract, powerful, and advanced topic in pure mathematics, my analyst dared to interrupt with what I now regard as a reasonable inquiry, "What is a group?"

I immediately responded through emotionally, if not physically, clenched teeth, "A group is a set with binary operation, such that ..." and proceeded to rapidly recite the postulates of group theory. I don't remember whether I literally said or just thought, "There. Now are you satisfied?" And I don't recall whether we analyzed this intense emotional response subsequently, though I have returned to this episode repeatedly in my thoughts, but it has largely been to criticize then-orthodox psychoanalytic technique and to remind me of the narcissistic world of the late adolescent boy in all its intensity, glory and maladaptiveness.

What I failed to recognize until recently, despite having discovered elements of the thought both in further psychoanalysis and self-analysis, was that at heart, the problem lay at having discovered something of extraordinary beauty, namely mathematics, and at the same time having realized the extreme difficulty of sharing this discovery with others. I realized that I was far from alone in this quandary. I believe that much of the difficulty analysts encounter in reading Bion derives from his internal frustration and anticipation of incomprehension for his deeply mathematical way of thinking. I also recognized the same central problem in the writing of British mathematician G.H. Hardy. Though his conflicts concerning it reached a far more profound level, Hardy's (1967) *A Mathematician's Apology* is a beautiful little book that comes as close as anything I know to showing the mathematically unsophisticated reader the intensity of the pleasure that can be derived from the study of mathematics. Hardy had himself been a major creative mathematician, a beautiful expositor of mathematical ideas, and a mentor of other great mathematicians. But like many mathematicians, age brought with it an increasing incapacity to do new mathematical work on the level of his youth, and with that came a profound and tormenting depression. His colleague, C.P. Snow, a physicist and novelist now best known for his book *The Two Cultures* (Snow, 1961), suggested that Hardy write a book about the appeal of mathematics as a means of working through his depression. The effort, *A Mathematician's Apology*, while leaving us with a wonderful book, did not relieve Hardy's depression, and he killed himself shortly after completing it.

Having the advantage of personal analyses and examination of the problems facing Bion and Hardy, though certainly not their intellectual capacities, I hope I have largely transformed the frustrated rage of my nineteen-year-old self into something that will be more useful to you, my readers: a comprehensible description of certain mathematical ideas that I believe can inform and enrich psychoanalysis.

Many years, two analyses, and a great deal of thought later, not to mention the development of my own thinking about analytic process, I have come to think of that first analysis quite differently and much more positively than I once did. I was given the opportunity to explore my own psychology in depth in a manner that supported a lifelong curiosity about and valuing of psychological processes and a personal recognition that such an investigation can be life transforming, even though the particulars of the process may not lead to specific desired changes and its specific outcomes may remain unclear. It was not until many years later in the context of studying Winnicott and later Bion that I was able to understand how the muddle of free associative analytic process could be transformative in the way I had found it to be during this first analysis and not until the study of nonlinear dynamics had provided its conceptual tools that I was able to think clearly about how this odd process could have worked so well for me.

One of the frustrations of writing about nonlinear dynamics system theory, teaching it, and talking about it is the frequency with which many colleagues don't "get it," something that is, on the one hand, hardly surprising but, on the other hand, can be more than frustrating, especially when those colleagues can exercise a certain amount of power in where and when I can teach or publish about these ideas. There seems to be, at least among a few, a certain narcissistic resistance, probably similar to that which I imagined in my first analyst, feeling humiliated and embarrassed to not get it. They turn around and attack the ideas and myself as their representative. Sometimes, this actually becomes amusing, as when a leader for an international journal expressed a profound skepticism about the possibility of using mathematical ideas in psychoanalytic thinking, because several years ago he had attempted to read Bion's *Transformations* and found it too difficult to understand.

In the paper *What Kind of Science Is Psychoanalysis?*, Bertram Cohler and I (2007) argued that psychoanalysis is a human science—that is, it is a science devoted to the study of meanings and personal motives as they emerge in narratives. We joined a large group of analysts who had been influenced by such philosophers as Ricoeur in recognizing that psychoanalysis is a form of hermeneutic study that searched for personal meanings through methods similar to those developed in Christian, Jewish, and other religious communities for finding further and deeper meaning beyond the plain text of sacred writings. Freud (1905a) himself noted that his case descriptions had a novelistic-like quality, and it is apparent to most serious students of psychoanalysis that the hermeneutic dimensions of Freud's work rather than, say, the metapsychological theories appear to have held up best. (Freud's developmental theories occupy a position somewhere between the traditionally scientific and the hermeneutic in that they make claims beyond dissecting the patient's narrative while, in large measure, building on those narratives.)

On one hand, Freud's general ideas of unfolding development analogous to the late nineteenth century embryologist's views of organismic development continue to be valued, albeit with markedly different content and emphasis than Freud's initial proposals; on the other hand, their primary use in psychoanalysis as an element in the hermeneutic uncovering of the analysand's personal narrative has grown ever less satisfactory because developmental ideas tend to transform from suggestive road maps that suggest paths of explorations to rigid rules of normativity, deviation from which demands active intervention.

Colleagues have repeatedly inquired how claims that nonlinear dynamic systems theory can inform psychoanalysis can be put in harmony with assertions about the hermeneutic nature of psychoanalysis. In fact, they worry that the nonlinear dynamic systems theory approach, like Freudian metapsychology, ego-psychology, and other overarching psychoanalytic theories will interfere with an interpretive stance by tying analytic thinking to highly abstract ideas and discouraging confidence in the analyst's spontaneous responses to the patient.

These seem to me to be reasonable concerns but ones that arise not so much from a misunderstanding of nonlinear dynamics as from a misunderstanding of tools that can assist the hermeneutic venture. Powerful hermeneutic procedures often emerge from their recognition of the possibilities of satisfactory stories that are different in kind from the ones that were previously available. Thus for example, by introducing the idea of unconscious mentation, Freud developed an explanation of how dreams, symptoms, parapraxes, and jokes could be explained in a satisfactory narrative way through the introduction of that idea that part of the story is barred from awareness. We see the same thing in traditional science where, for example, the experimental findings regarding the nature of light could not be integrated into a coherent narrative until it was recognized that the apparently unresolvable problem that light sometimes behaved as if composed of particles and sometimes of waves could be integrated into a single description in what came to be called quantum mechanics. Although I did not appreciate it at the time, my concurrent analysis, which was, in fact, a hermeneutic exploration of personal meaning, and the education I was receiving in mathematics created what would ultimately be an extremely useful tension between seemingly opposite worldviews, a tension I now believe can be in large measure resolved through nonlinear dynamic system theory.

For those accustomed to thinking of mathematics primarily as the language of the empirical sciences with their focus of prediction and control as opposed to grasping the meaning of phenomena, it may appear that mathematics and hermeneutics are poles apart. I hope to show that this apparent contradiction grows from a misunderstanding of how mathematics can inform a worldview. On the one hand, I hope to show that the possibilities suggested by nonlinear thinking suggest ways of thinking about psychological phenomena that are hard to come to without this point of view. Complementary to this idea, I hope to show that much psychoanalytic thinking is already, in fact, permeated with mathematical ideas that gain a significant portion of their force because they are implicit, seem commonsensical, and therefore go unquestioned. These ideas usually derived from a linear worldview. For example, when a clinician asserts that a small event cannot have caused a major personality change so that the patient's association of the event with the change in personality must be a disguise for some more profound happening that is barred from awareness (as for example occurs with screen memories), that clinician is implicitly using a linear model of causality in which effects are assumed to be proportionate to causes. The clinician has a highly mathematical idea about how the world is ordered. It seems so obvious that it does not even invite question much less an exploration of whether it reflects a very dubious theory of the mathematics of the real world. The study of nonlinear ideas both opens up possibilities for an enlarged psychological worldview and, at the same time, brings into focus and questions assumptions that are usefully questioned and lie hidden because they seem so "obvious."

One of the great advantages of a good mathematics education is that it includes a liberal dose of information about how thinking and logic can go awry. The concept of "rigor" in mathematics reflects a preoccupation with demonstrating the validity of theorems and proofs often by pointing out where implicit assumptions have been made that could potentially lead the mathematician astray. Additionally, since a major part of mathematics is showing how one has reached a conclusion, good mathematics teachers are forever pointing to students' failures in this regard. An episode from early in graduate school years has stayed with me and is often a point of reference in my own thinking.

My friend, Arnold Rosner, who later became a composer, and I took a course together in advanced calculus. Our teacher, a fascinating but somewhat strange man with a French accent, Jean Van Heijnoort, who was at that point in his career a major contributor to the history of mathematical logic but earlier on had been Leon Trotsky's bodyguard, had asked Arnie to do a problem at the board. A long tradition in mathematics invites replacing tedious computations with the statement "it is obvious." When this phrase appears in the writings of substantial mathematicians, it can usually be translated as "if you do a long and tedious computation, you will, in fact, find that what I am asserting is true." In any case, Arnie came to a point in working the problem in which he felt he could say of the next step "it is obvious."

Van Heijnoort interrupted him in a gentle, thoughtful tone of voice and lovely French accent, "It is not obvious."

Pause.

"It is not obvious at all. In fact, it is not so!"

This episode became the basis of a sort of mantra that Arnie and I shared for the next fifty years until his recent death, "It is not obvious. It is not obvious at all. In fact, it is not so" became both our more or less automatic responses when assertions were made with great assurance but without a firm basis. I continue to find the memory of the episode one of the most useful heuristics in a variety of situations.

A friendly word to the reader: Many of the central ideas in this book come from mathematics, and explaining them well requires using some mathematical concepts. I have tried my best to explain these ideas as they arise in plain English, assuming that the reader has little knowledge of mathematics. However, I know that some readers will be put off by anything resembling formal math, and short of a thoroughgoing analysis, which, unfortunately I cannot provide as a supplement to this book, they will continue to feel only discomfort in the face of mathematics. While I encourage such readers to try to explore the mathematical portions of this book, if this does not work, I suggest skipping over them and trying to get the gist of what is being said. You will not be able to have quite as precise an idea of what is going on as the mathematical reader, and you will have to simply trust me that what I say about the math is accurate and, at this point in time, factually no longer the subject of controversy.

I first encountered the term *nonlinear* while in graduate school. Many faculty members at NYU's Courant Institute of Mathematical Science were studying natural systems that were not adequately described using the standard *linear* differential equations of classical physics. They were having little success in working with the resulting equations. The solutions could not be written out as even complex formula, and the partial solutions that were found were often physically implausible.

The term *nonlinear* has an unfortunate history that reflects the supposed obviousness of a linear worldview. A differential equation is an equation that relates various rates of change to one another. A *linear* equation is one that can be written in a certain form (as the sum of dependent variables and their rates of change multiplied by constants). For example, one of Newton's laws of motion, F = ma, says that the force applied to a body is equal to the body's mass times the acceleration. It is the central equation of Newtonian physics. Acceleration is the rate of change of the velocity and velocity the rate of change of position. F = ma is a linear equation because the only dependent variable in it, acceleration, is multiplied by a constant (the mass of the body). Linear equations are so named because they have the same form as the equation of a line in analytic geometry. (Remember, y = mx + b.) Variables are only multiplied by constants.

Nonlinear equations arise often in the study of natural systems. A nonlinear equation involves multiplying terms that include derivatives and the dependent variables. An example is the equations for the motion of an object on a surface when friction is taken into account. The friction term is proportional to the square of the velocity (the velocity multiplied by itself) so that the equation is nonlinear, because a rate of change is multiplied by itself.

The difference between a linear and nonlinear equation is its form, nothing else. Please notice that linearity in this sense and sequential (in the sense of being in a line) may be related, but they are not the same. Linear systems can be complicated and certainly not result in straight line–like sequences, although the term *nonlinear* is now commonly used for any situation in which the sequence of events does not seem to follow a simple rule.

In any case, linear equations have many "nice" features. The most important is that their solutions are characterized by the fact that small differences in the parameters of the equations result in small changes in their solution. For example, if a rocket is launched with slightly more force, we expect it to go slightly farther, not take some entirely novel path.

Nonlinear equations often do not have this quality. Slight changes in initial conditions or parameters can result in major changes in the solution. This is not simply a matter of mathematical formalism. Consider the experience of pushing a heavy object against friction. When you apply force to it initially, the object does not move. This phenomenon continues until a certain critical point is reached when the object starts moving, a qualitative change, and the force needed to continue or change its movement changes but slightly. Thus, although nonlinearity has a profound effect on the qualitative properties of differential equations and the physical situation they represent, it is in no sense mysterious, has nothing to do with lines, and has nothing to do with being non-sequential. Unfortunately, as the term has gained in popularity, it has come to be used in all these ways. This misapplication confuses things.

Nonlinear differential equations eluded solutions that could be written down exactly in terms of straightforward equations. Furthermore, the nonlinear elements that were introduced by virtue of the presence of more than two interacting bodies could not be worked out, except as "perturbations" of a linear equation sometimes. The equations led to predictions that were clearly physically impossible, such as infinite velocities, so-called "singularities." Huge amounts of mathematical effort were devoted to trying to fit an essentially nonlinear world into linear mathematics. When the approximation of nonlinear systems by linear ones was good enough, as it was for most of planetary physics, hugely successful science resulted, but, as it sometimes failed, it became evermore clear that something new was needed. If instead of asking where the planets would be in a hundred years, a problem that could be solved using the methods of linear differential equations, one asked whether the solar system would continue indefinitely (assuming the physical properties of its components did not change), the problem exceeded the capacities of the best twentieth century mathematicians. A new mathematics was needed to answer such questions. At the point I left mathematics, everyone knew that these were very tough problems. There were some technical advances in the field but nothing like a comprehensive forward move into a promising general approach. There were beautiful, highly theoretical developments, but no one saw where they would lead.

As my formal medical studies were nearing an end, I was lucky enough to come across French mathematician René Thom's first steps into this nonlinear world, a world that was to blossom intellectually in the following decade as the result of the convergence of two seemingly disparate mathematical developments, one being the rapidly emerging capacities of computers that made calculations routine that had never before been possible, and the other the application of topology, rubber sheet geometry, the study of those qualities that remain unchanged in a geometric object when it is stretched but not cut or pasted.

Many of the ideas that were to become nonlinear dynamics systems theory had been foreshadowed by the great French mathematician Henri Poincaré and some of his students, but without computers it was basically impossible to even begin to explore elementary nonlinear configurations. As computers became available, mathematicians, beginning with Benoit Mandelbrot, were able to produce amazing graphics that allowed them to literally see something of the nature of the nonlinear world. In a similar way, from the other end of mathematics but also originating in the work of Poincaré, conceptions from a field called *differential geometry* allowed for very high-level abstractions about the nature of dynamical systems, systems that change with time, abstractions that showed that nonlinear systems could, in a fundamental sense, not be understood as simply deformed or perturbed linear systems. Just as a donut cannot be reshaped into a sphere, no matter how one squeezes or pushes it (at least without cutting or pasting the donut), so, too, the forms represented by various different types of nonlinear equations cannot be transformed into those represented by linear equations.

Thom claimed that his new mathematics was a mathematics of forms and that it was relevant to biological morphogenesis. I well remember the thrill of coming to these new ideas one lovely summer day on the sun porch of my parents' summer cottage in Woods Hole and wondering whether, after all, I hadn't made a mistake in leaving mathematics for medicine. It would be another six years before I actively pursued this explicit connection, but Thom's book had a more immediate emotional impact by reinforcing my sense that a great deal was not known, a great deal remained to be learned, and that much that the authorities say "ain't necessarily so." The book had much of the same effect on me that aspects of Freud's experience with Charcot seem to have had on him. In particular, Thom's vision of a whole new world of mathematics would later remind me of Charcot: *la théorie, c'est bon, mais ça n'empêche pas d'exister* ("the theory is fine, but it doesn't prevent something from existing").

I have yet to recover from the transition from NYU's Courant Institute of Mathematical Science to Washington University's Medical School. Washington University had then and continues to have what is generally regarded as one of the best medical schools in the world. Yet, to a young man coming from a graduate mathematics program, the difference in attitude among the faculty both toward students and their subject could not have been more profound. The faculty at Courant, perhaps humbled by the fact that most mathematicians do their best work in their twenties, treated the students as colleagues. The Washington U. faculty, though thoroughly benign in their attitudes, were clear that they knew far more than the students and expected to be treated with unquestioned authority. More difficult still was an attitude that, despite the fact that medical research is an ongoing enterprise, the faculty seemed to feel that there was a body of information that students needed to absorb to become good physicians and that questions about the validity and appropriateness of the information they provided seemed to them at best irrelevant and at worst invitations of an inappropriate defiance on the part of students.

Embarrassingly for me, the son of a biochemist, the introductory biochemistry course seemed particularly unrelated to anything I could find interesting. The "Krebs cycle," the means by which cells transform chemical energy to do work, had recently been elucidated, and we learned about this process in excruciating detail with no attention being paid to such questions as how it fit within the actual biology of organisms, nor how it had been elucidated, nor its relevance to clinical medicine. It became emblematic for me of a central problem in medical education that I think continues to be a problem not only in medicine but also in fields like psychoanalysis with educational models that are derived from medical schools. The questions that had been central to my mathematics education, such as, "How is it that we know what we claim to know?" and how some particular piece of knowledge informs our general understanding of the subject, seemed simply irrelevant to my medical school professors who were anxious to pass along "facts" about the human body and its function with little or no regard for any other considerations. Even when, as in some of the pharmacology and medicine courses, an effort was made to provide explanations for phenomena in terms of available theories, it was extremely rare that this was accomplished with even a modicum of rigor, nor was this failure seen as a problem or a push toward a better understanding, but instead, our teachers seemed to regard it as intrinsic to the subject matter. When, as a second-year medical student, it occurred to me that the subject matter that was foundational to medical practice probably belonged to the social rather than the biological sciences and I wrote a rather grandiose and scathing critique of our education titled "The Basic Medical Sciences and the Sciences Basic to Medicine" for the student newspaper, I was met with total silence, so that I do not know to this day whether my essay was so appalling or simply so uninteresting to the faculty and my fellow students that it called for no response at all.

My first year of medical school I returned to Woods Hole, a place where I had spent all but one of my summers, where I had the delightful experience of being a course assistant in the physiology course.

Part of the course was being taught by Sydney Brenner, who was then continuing to work in the mode of molecular biology, though at the same time moving toward the study of the organization of nervous systems, work for which he was ultimately to win the Nobel Prize. Sydney and I got along famously, in part because he thoroughly enjoyed vigorous and skeptical exchanges and because I found it absolutely delightful to once again be dealing with a really bright person. For him, as for many researchers at the time, the question of how the now better understood molecular biological mechanisms of inheritance could translate into the complex systems of organisms remained a central puzzle, and it was because in part that I was puzzling over this question that I happened across René Thom's (1975) startling *Structural Stability and Morphogenesis, An Outline of a General Theory of Models,* a masterpiece not only of mathematical but also conceptual thinking that introduced the ideas of catastrophe theory in a rigorous mathematical way, showed their application to the problems of embryology, and demonstrated that the linear worldview was not the only one available for thinking about the world.

Surprisingly, at Washington University, one area where the unthinking attitude of certainty did not reign was in the Department of Psychiatry, then headed by Eli Robbins. Robbins held a violently anti-psychoanalytic view that perhaps originated in the failure of psychiatrists to diagnose his own demyelinating condition. Robbins and his colleagues recognized that the paradigmatic methods of medical research based on well-defined diagnostic entities could not be applied using the conceptualization of psychiatric disorders derived from psychoanalysis and similar depth psychological investigations. By defining psychiatric conditions based on etiological considerations, psychiatry had gotten itself into a circular position where clear investigation was impossible and was often replaced by speculative psychologizing.

Robbins and his colleagues set out to replace this diagnostic muddle with definitions of conditions based on syndromes of observable signs and symptoms as a foundational step toward research into these now clearly defined diagnostic entities. The "Research Diagnostic Criteria" (Spitzer and Robins, 1978) they developed for severe psychiatric illnesses moved toward this end at times with surprising results so that, for example, the empirical observation that men with same-sex desire seemed to not share any other symptoms led the group to expunge homosexuality from its diagnostic categories. Furthermore, when applied to clinical populations seen in psychiatric hospitals, the new diagnostic nomenclature helped distinguish between several conditions, all presenting with severe symptoms and each having a different prognosis and treatment that had previously been easily confused with one another. This "neo-Kraeplinian" approach to psychiatry engaged and impressed me as it did many others. Unfortunately, its transformation into a series of American Psychiatric Association books, DSM-III, DSM-IV, and most recently DSM-V, diluted the approach and corrupted it to meet the administrative needs of insurance companies and the wishes of the pharmaceutical industry so that much that was useful in the approach has been lost to psychiatry. However, although I would not recognize it until many years later, the approach has a fundamental foundational flaw, namely that it fails to recognize that the behavior of complex nonlinear systems can very seldom be encompassed in the type of sharp descriptive catalog that the Washington U. group and the DSM authors attempted. In fact, only in recent years has it become clear that despite some dramatic successes in applying such an approach to medicine generally, the whole paradigm is probably seriously inadequate for general medicine for reasons that are apparent only from a nonlinear systems dynamic point of view (West, 2006).

From Washington University, I went to the University of Chicago Psychiatry Department, in large measure because Eli Robbins had told me that, except for Washington University, there were only two tolerable departments of psychiatry in the country, Stanford and the University of Chicago. The latter, he said, was unfortunately "contaminated" by a faculty that included many psychoanalysts. Since secretly I wanted to study psychoanalysis, I, of course, chose the University of Chicago and landed there at a moment when Heinz Kohut's *The Analysis of the Self* had just been published.

Although we did not recognize it at the time, 1971 was in many ways a turning point in American psychiatry, and the department's recently appointed chair, Daniel X. Freedman, was a pivotal figure in this transition. Freedman, whose training had included graduation from a psychoanalytic institute, was dedicated to the development of a biological psychiatry founded in the role of neurotransmitters in psychiatric illness. This approach found intellectual, not to mention financial, support from the findings of the previous two decades that pharmacological agents could significantly diminish the symptoms of psychotic disorders. It initiated a research program that remains vigorous to this day of attempting to find explanations for psychiatric conditions in the realm of neurotransmitters. This program, which strikes me forty-three years later as having achieved remarkably little beyond its own self-promotion, struck me then as simply intellectually unpromising. As a graduate student in mathematics, my particular interest had been mathematical logic and the *theory* of computation. It seemed clear to me that, while the brain might not function in a similar fashion to human designed computers, it could not fail to be a computer of some sort. My study of computational theory made it clear that the most important features of a computer relate to the abstract processes that it instantiates and only secondarily to the mechanics of its instantiation—that is, whether a computing device has the capacity to add two numbers is of greater importance in thinking about it than whether it does this by using mechanical gears or electronic signals or hydraulic devices. Furthermore, if one thought of the brain as the product of an evolutionary process within a biological organism, it seemed equally clear that it was very likely that the same components would be used for multiple conceptually unrelated purposes. Just as a nail can be used to put together a shipping crate or the roof of a house, so, too, the same neurotransmitter can be used to stimulate emotional discharge or the coordination of motion or cognitive processes.

From this point of view, what I thought of as "the search for gold in them there hills"—i.e. the attempt to find neurotransmitters and their variation linked to specific psychiatric disorders—always struck me as unpromising and intellectually nearly vacuous. What I found particularly annoying was the prestige that this approach tended to be provided by the fact that its pursuit in a traditional laboratory with the technology of chemistry setting seemed to mark it as "scientific." I must admit to a similar pessimism about more recent developments in neuroimaging. The analogy would go something like this: Whereas the neurochemist grinds up parts of the computer and tries to infer interesting things about its function from its chemical makeup, the neuroimager takes X-rays of the same part and tries to infer how it works from the resulting radiographs. While functional neuroimaging that follows changes over time is clearly more promising in this regard, neuroimaging at this point in time is both so slow, compared to the processes that are of psychological interest, and involves such large areas of the brain, compared to the fine structure that would correspond to the detailed neuro-processing that the psychoanalyst would like to understand, that one cannot help but feel that it will be a very long time before such research contributes very much to our understanding of psychological functioning. This is particularly so since that functioning is almost certainly nonlinear, which means that the types of changes that would have to be captured through such investigations would have to be extraordinarily data-rich to provide the desired information.

While both my psychoanalytic and neuroscience-oriented teachers were themselves involved in developing new theories, much like my medical school teachers, they seemed committed to communicating known truths to psychiatric residents and later to psychoanalytic candidates. This knowing attitude is, to my mind, one of the major interferences with the development of new knowledge in our field. As a teacher, I have learned that it is not simply a function of the educator's narcissism and commitment to his or her own ideas. People who are responsible for the care of individuals in distress very much want to know how to do it right and more than invite their teachers to take a knowing attitude.

The psychoanalytic world as it appeared to the eyes of a candidate beginning training in the mid-1970s in Chicago was very appealing. Heinz Kohut was among several very smart and thoughtful people who taught us and whose ideas were both fresh and exciting and brought with them the excitement of discovery. Candidates, though not necessarily encouraged themselves to do research, could not help but feel that psychoanalysis was a discipline that was rapidly changing and demanded the development of new thought. In retrospect, I think I mistook the part for the whole, believing that the enthusiasm for research and discovery I saw in some of my teachers and classmates represented an overall view of the field and failing to recognize that many in it basically adopted the medical model of the transmission of authoritative knowledge, even if at times that knowledge was newly discovered. Within a few years of the publication of Kohut's work, for example, there emerged a group of dogmatic Kohutians who knew the truth as manifest in the gospel according to Heinz.

As if enacting some sort of repetition of *Paradise Lost*, Kohut's most brilliant student, John Gedo, put forward a competing vision of psychoanalysis with a brilliance and enthusiasm rarely seen in our field. Gedo was in some ways a particularly attractive figure to me, not least because we shared a New York Jewish background in some detail. One of his books is dedicated to J.E.R. who said, "T'ink, boys, t'ink." J.E.R. was John. E. Richie, a professor of chemistry at New York University who taught the rigorous quantitative analysis course that John and I both took, though twenty years apart. Richie's enthusiasm for encouraging us to "t'ink," a product of a strong Italian-Brooklyn accent, evidently stayed with both Gedo and myself, and it represented a spirit that I continue to long for in our field. Thinking is hard, fun, and rewarding. (Our shared background did not always have such a happy dimension. I had gone to John for private supervision, and one afternoon while squinting because of the sunlight that was coming from the window behind him while simultaneously not finding what he had to say about the patient terribly helpful, John commented to me, "You look like some disapproving medical school professor." I didn't have the heart to tell him at the time that this was at least in part because I looked very much like my father who had indeed been John's professor of biochemistry at NYU.)

Although my thinking about nonlinear dynamics in psychoanalysis had proceeded far enough that I wrote two papers on related topics while I was in analytic training, the focus of my intellectual efforts increasingly shifted toward clinical issues and an understanding of received psychoanalytic theory. At this point, I did not have a rich enough understanding of psychoanalysis nor of nonlinear dynamics to accomplish very much by way of integrating the two studies. What struck me again and again was the way in which mechanistic psychoanalytic theories, while providing an explanatory outline for the phenomena observed in clinical psychoanalysis, seemed to simultaneously fail to capture central elements of the analytic experience while forcing narrow and limiting views of analytic process on practitioners. It was as if psychoanalysis was being forced into an ill-fitting corset, which, at the same time, constricted and distorted the human form it clothed. Partial answers to this tension were provided by the work of analysts like Winnicott, who used a combination of evocative language, tolerance for a "muddle," and an appeal to "common sense" psychology to underscore central but complex psychological ideas while avoiding distorting abstractions. Yet as attractive as I found such formulations, these essentially romantic notions left me thoroughly uncomfortable and longing for greater clarity.

It was at this point that I had the great good fortune, along with many psychoanalysts, to be introduced to the research on infant and early childhood development that was emerging from direct observational studies involving the emotional life of children. Most striking was that, unlike traditional psychoanalytic studies that were shaped primarily by an effort to fit infant and child observations into the developmental framework that derived from reconstructions of the development in the analysis of adults, these newer studies introduced genuinely novel ideas about human emotional development. What was more, those ideas supplemented and clarified the emerging field of self psychology. Self psychology grew out of the observation that a significant group of analytic patients responded poorly to interpretations based on classical conflict models of mental functioning but did respond well to interventions focused on issues of the coherence and aliveness of the self. These issues appeared in analysis and daily living in relation to persons who were used to maintaining experiences of coherence and vigor, selfobjects in Kohut's (1971) terminology.

It was my great good fortune at this point to start working with Bertram Cohler, whose combined career as development psychologist and psychoanalyst had led to a deep engagement with precisely these issues. As well as sharing a fascination and commitment to an expanded vision of psychoanalysis both in its intellectual and practical dimensions, Bert and I remained fascinated with the question of how to retain the richness of psychoanalytic understanding epitomized in a clinical encounter with some sort of coherent theoretical stance. Our effort resulted in the concept of "essential other," an appreciation of the lifelong need for the support of the self through relationships to people, institutions, and objects in the environment. Our book, *The Essential Other: The Developmental Psychology of the Self*, attempted to provide a life course developmental description of how the self emerges and evolves in a complementary way with the environmental surround.

During this period, I studied human development carefully and consistently found that developmental studies shared certain problems. In retrospect, these problems pointed toward nonlinear concepts, but at the time, they simply appeared as difficulties, and my view of those difficulties was primarily that it was important to acknowledge them. My initial response was to think that these difficulties arose from the particular theory. If, for example, her data failed to support Margaret Mahler's concept of separation-individuation, as it did not, I thought of the problem as arising from the specific theory in question. It took about two decades for me to realize that the difficulty might come from the picture of development implicit in many of these theories rather than the particulars of the theory itself. All the theories of development that I studied shared an idea that an underlying developmental program exists, although what that program is and even the psychological area that it is intended to explore varies greatly between developmental theories. Furthermore, the extent to which the theories incorporate variation and environmental influences varies substantially. Thus, for example, Freud's idea of a line of development of the libido, which was systemized by Abraham (1924), concerned itself with the changing nature of desire and its consequences as the individual matured. Only a single pathway was normal and desirable, and a variant development was conceptualized as a deviation from this pathway. Environmental influences played a distinctly secondary role. In contrast, Bowlby's (1969, 1973, 1982, 1988) attachment theory focused on the child's need for physical and psychological proximity to caretakers, erotic desire, and its transformations taking a distinctly secondary role. Environmental influences were treated as much more important, but the theory was built around a vision of normal caretaking, albeit normal caretaking as underlined by the effect of the deprivation from such caretaking caused in young children.

The relationship of the two theories to data was also strikingly different. Freud's theory was developed with minimal reference to any observation of children but instead reflected the reconstructions that occurred in the analysis of neurotic individuals. While Freud (1900, 1905c) argued convincingly that normal and neurotic development were essentially the same and different only in terms of quantitative factors, the fact remained that his data about normal development could reasonably be critiqued because it was derived with work from neurotics. The studies of the attachment theorists, though far more empirical, also tended to rely on data derived from sources other than the observation of normal infants, such as the dramatic effects associated with disrupting the child's relationship to its caretaker or studies of animal populations.

Other developmental studies, like the work of Jean Piaget, shared the problem that while they were, in fact, conducted within particular cultures, despite their richness and depth, the question remained of to what extent they were properly applied to people from other cultures. Was the charming and thoughtful inquisitiveness evident in Piaget's Swiss subjects a general quality of children of the age he studied, or did it derive from the peculiarities of the safe and prosperous environment enjoyed by these children? I sought for answers to these and similar questions in the context of the many interesting theories that were then available. Cohler and I attempted to develop what I continue to believe is a very useful point of view in thinking about development with our idea of the essential other. This idea had many advantages, including an attempt to account for the sources of variation in human development in the varied relations to people that were experienced.

As satisfying as this work was, it left open for both of us a question that we were only able to formulate in retrospect. The question only deepened as a result of our studies of same-sex desire. These studies, like the studies that led to the essential other, suggested that, on the one hand, human development must have certain underlying themes and structures and, at the same time, that it was sufficiently complex in a way we did not understand and sufficiently diverse that any mechanistic description held little promise.

Sometime in the late 1990s, two things occurred to me. One was that there is a nonlinear worldview that the results of the study of nonlinear systems suggest seeing the world and all sorts of phenomena in a different way. Benoit Mandelbrot was the first to point this out in what has now become commonplace—that natural phenomena from clouds to trees to the airways of the lung have a fractal structure, a geometry that is fundamentally different from the geometry of lines and figures that dominated Western thought since Pythagoras. These ideas reshaped the way we think about length and dimension and gave us a whole new conceptual world for shape and form. At the same time, nonlinear thinking transformed the way we think about how systems evolve from an image of smooth transitions to one ordinarily involving radical jumps in transformations. Similarly, it changed the way we think about systems interacting with such possibilities as very slight interconnections profoundly transforming both systems, and, finally, a concept of emergence, the appearance of qualitatively new phenomena when elements that individually did not even suggest the phenomenon are brought together to a new whole.

At this point, it became obvious to me, as I hope it will become obvious to the reader, that the field of psychoanalysis, dealing as it does with complex interactive systems, was in need of reconceptualization within this new worldview. The series of chapters in this book that develop these ideas with regard to development and therapy, the heart of the volume, basically became obvious to me with this shift in worldview, but it would be only gradually that a group of colleagues came to similar conclusions. Unaccustomed to thinking of mathematics as a way of widening one's vision, many psychoanalysts equated the use of nonlinear dynamics systems theory with a mechanical worldview. Others, remembering the horrors of high school and college mathematics, were simply repelled by the notion of bringing mathematical ideas into humanistic psychoanalytic discourse, and still others, who were in a continuing recovery phase from postwar metapsychology, were loath to think that any general theory might expand psychoanalytic thinking.

Mathematics, Applied Mathematics, Metaphor, Analogy, and Hand Waving

To understand the influential challenge posed by attempting to use concepts of nonlinear dynamic systems theory, we must explore the role of mathematical ideas in science generally. Although there is some controversy about it, mathematics (sometimes called pure or abstract mathematics) is a group of studies that examines the consequences of starting with the group of assumptions and examining those propositions that can be derived from them using formal logic. Doing mathematics may be motivated by any number of factors, such as the belief that studying a particular system will lead to beautiful results or the anticipation that those results will be helpful in some practical problem. But its essential features are that it is based on the manipulation of strings of symbols according to pre-defined logical rules.

Therefore, in Kant's classification, all mathematical statements are analytic—that is, they must be true by virtue of the underlying logic independent of qualities of the external world. For example, the entire statement "all rodents are mammals, and all mammals are vertebrates, therefore, all rodents are vertebrates" is true because the form of the argument, independent of its content, makes it true. One could substitute anything for rodents, mammals, and vertebrates without affecting the truth of the statement. Empirical evidence is wholly irrelevant to the truth of such statements, however, notice that the statement is not "all rodents are vertebrates." That conclusion can be reached only on the assumption or demonstration of the first two elements of the analytically true statement.

Because writing out the analytic statements that are the true content of mathematics would lead to hugely unwieldy and incomprehensible text, a mathematical tradition dating back at least to the Greeks omits the first clause of these arguments and describes their conclusory portion as true statements. Thus, most of us learned that the area of the square on the hypotenuse to the right triangle is equal to the sum of the areas to the squares on the other two sides, a statement which is neither true in itself nor empirically true of the external world. What is true is that, under the postulates of Euclidian geometry, "the area of the square on the hypotenuse is et cetera." It is no wonder that mathematicians chose this shorthand. Written out in full, even the simplest mathematical statements become absurdly long and tedious. When mathematical philosophers Whitehead and Russell set out to fully delineate the logic that leads to elementary arithmetic, they required a major part of the first volume of their three-volume tome *Principia Mathematicia* to reach the point of proving that $1 + 1 = 2$.

It was not until the middle of the nineteenth century that mathematicians recognized the significance of the analytic nature of their discipline. Starting in the early nineteenth century, a new kind of rigor emerged in mathematical arguments that emphasized the contingency of conclusions on their underlying assumptions and the logic by which those assumptions were manipulated. For example, by exploring the possibilities of substituting other postulates from Euclid's fifth postulate (that one and only one line parallel to a given line runs through a given point not on the original line), mathematicians discovered new geometries of enormous intellectual and practical significance. It would take us too far afield to describe the consequences of the careful study of how mathematical assumptions shape the statements that are often treated as their conclusion. But it could be reasonably argued that few other intellectual developments have so profoundly shaped the way we think about the world. If it was easy for generations of mathematicians to forget that true mathematical statements are merely elaborate tautologies, and are highly contingent on the assumptions underlying them, it is no wonder that consumers of mathematics easily forget this, too, and treat conclusory statements as though they were the full mathematical proposition. However, they are not, and as we will see, considerable confusion can be introduced into discussions by assuming that they are.

If true mathematical statements are merely the product of the manipulation of symbols according to logical principles, it is utterly remarkable that such manipulations lead to predictions about a means for dealing with the external world. The field of applied mathematics involves the application of mathematics to real-world situations, and its effectiveness has been the hallmark of the stunning intellectual success of the modern era.

The study of nonlinear dynamics began in pure mathematics with the work of French mathematician Henri Poincaré who was probably the deepest mathematical thinker of the twentieth century. Since Newton and Leibniz discovered calculus, mathematicians have struggled with finding the means to solve differential equations, equations which relate the rates of change of variables and from which one wishes to extract descriptions of how those variables themselves actually change with time. For a limited class of differential equations, it is possible to write an explicit formula for their solutions in terms of time, although this is more often than not impossible. When it is possible, finding the formula may be very difficult and, even when the formula is found, its significance may remain obscure.

Poincaré introduced an entirely novel approach to the study of differential equations. He recognized that it was the qualitative features of the solutions that held the greatest insight into the differential equation. Thus, he addressed questions, like whether differential equations had solutions that were stable over time; whether the solution eventually fell into a periodic mode; and whether small changes in the initial state of the system tended to damp out, continue as small changes in the solution of the equations, or result in differences in the solutions that grew ever greater with time. Poincaré was able to show that these questions could be approached by using the then novel branch of mathematics called topology, which studies the properties of forms that do not change even though the object is stretched or compressed in various ways.

Studies by Poincaré and his followers went to a beautiful theory, the qualitative theory of linear ordinary differential equations. Linearity in this context refers to how the differential equation being studied relates to the rates of change that are its terms. To be linear, an equation must express the relationship of these rates of change in terms of sums and differences of those rates multiplied by constants. If the equation involves terms in which the function or rates of change of the function are multiplied by one another, or have any other more complex relationship than they do in the linear case, the equation is called "nonlinear." The beautifully clear and simple results that had allowed the categorization of linear differential equations were not only un-generalizable to nonlinear equations, but students of the field were able to show that many nonlinear equations had qualitatively different features than linear equations. The further development of these ideas was largely put on hold until it became apparent that the study of nonlinear equations was absolutely essential to solving real-world problems—problems of applied mathematics.

Applied Mathematics

Applied mathematics is the study of how mathematics can be used to describe and understand phenomena in the real world. The enormous success of this effort, starting in the sixteenth century, transformed the Western view of the world, changing what it meant to understand a subject and allowing unprecedented capacities to predict and control a wide variety of phenomena. Large segments of disciplines ranging from the physical sciences to economics and sociology are, in fact, the studies of applied mathematics.

To explore some of the features of applied mathematics, let us look at a mathematic application familiar to everyone—the everyday financial exchanges in which we all engage. These exchanges involve the application of arithmetic through activities like making change from a purchase or calculating an overall price when the group of items is purchased together. For these activities to be successful, it must be shown or assumed that monetary transactions follow the same rules as those of arithmetic, an abstract mathematical discipline. For example, if I purchase a Sunday newspaper for $2.50 and hand the seller a $5 bill, I anticipate that I will receive $2.50 in change (5.00 – 2.50 = 2.50) and will proclaim that the seller has made a mistake if any other amount is returned. Similarly, I will be satisfied if he gives me two quarters and two dollars in that order or two dollars and two quarters in that order (1.00 + 1.00 + 0.25 + 0.25 = 0.25 + 0.25 + 1.00 + 1.00). By manipulating the actual change in a manner corresponding to the manipulation of abstract arithmetic, buyer and seller both believe that they have engaged in a correct transaction. This is based on the assumption or demonstration that the laws of arithmetic apply to such transactions. Such assumptions are not automatic. For example, if I choose to buy a 50-cent pack of gum along with my newspaper and the salesperson returns $1.97 to me, I do not conclude that the laws of arithmetic are in error but instead realize that there is a 6% sales tax on taxable items in the community in which I am making the purchase. Are all equivalents of the purchase encompassed in this application of mathematics? If the salesperson from whom I buy the newspaper hurls 250 pennies at me or supplies me with the equivalent of $2.50 in Serbian groats, even though I am bound to agree that the arithmetic was correct, the transaction was nonetheless unsatisfactory.

This illustration suggests two major problems that commonly arise in the application of mathematics to real-world situations. The assumptions that underlie the mathematical concepts used may not, in fact, apply to the real world. Two and two makes four only under the very special situation in which the quantity in question is "conserved" when the items in question are added together. When quantities are conserved, enormously powerful predictions can be made on the basis of manipulating them arithmetically, but enormous confusion can result if quantities that are not conserved are treated as if they were. One of the great advantages of the developmental rigor in mathematics was that it made it much clearer what assumptions had to be met in order for a mathematical principle to be applied to a particular situation in the real world. The second kind of difficulty that arises in applied mathematics concerns the confusion of the problem that can be solved through mathematical means with the overall concerns that went to the problem. Clearly, making change does not consist entirely of providing the correct dollar amount to the purchaser.

In this book, I try to show that many of the phenomena of psychoanalysis are usefully modeled using nonlinear dynamics and that, in fact, these are far better models than linear models. I argue that although analysts have not been aware of it, that like the protagonist of Moliere's *Le Bourgeois Gentilhomme* who was delighted to discover he was speaking "prose," we have been speaking linear dynamics without realizing it and that this underlying mathematics has shaped our theoretical and practical discourse. I also try to show that nonlinear models are useful—they help us do analysis better.

Metaphor and Analogy

People who are familiar with mathematical ideas will commonly note that a subject they are studying appears to lend itself to the conceptualization suggested by those ideas and that the language of mathematics seems a promising way to talk about the subject at hand. Sometimes this is the first step in the development of a genuine application of mathematics to a discipline. At other times, it remains an incompletely developed analogy or metaphor that may nonetheless be useful in the discipline's progress. As Wilfred Bion notes in *Learning from Experience* (which incidentally uses mathematical concepts), this process is subject to all manner of difficulty, as, for example, when the abstractions from the system study are treated as things in themselves or seemingly meaningful statements are used to disguise troubling ideas. Matters are further complicated in our culture because of the enormous prestige of mathematical and scientific ideas so that investigators are forever tempted to consciously or unconsciously increase the scientific status of their conceptualizations through reference to mathematics.

When mathematical ideas are used as analogies or metaphors without being fully developed into an application, the wise investigator and skeptical reader will remain constantly focused on the adequacy of the metaphor-analogy to do its assigned job. Where metaphor is involved, constant attention to the metaphoric nature of the discourse is essential lest the metaphor become confused with the actuality of the situation, as happened in the American study of ego psychology where functional entities such as superego were reified and treated as if they were concrete realities. This process continued to a point where, rather than promoting understanding of human psychological function, discussions of these putative entities slowed the development of psychoanalytic thought (Gill and Holzman, 1976).

Especially in the study of nonlinear dynamics, a confusion of tongues is likely to emerge in the following fashion. It is a long-standing practice in mathematics to use ordinary words to refer to abstract mathematical concepts. The choice of these words commonly involves a considerable degree of whimsy, as well as emotional valence. For example, multiples of the square root of –1 are commonly referred to as imaginary numbers, presumably because of the difficulty of imagining such entities. In pure mathematics, these names seldom lead to problems because mathematicians understand very well that they are simply being used as names for formal concepts and that their more everyday associations have nothing to do with the mathematical work done with these concepts. (To the student's question, how can you possibly multiply two things that are imaginary and get something that is real? The mathematician would simply respond that the student's seemingly metaphysical question is based on a misunderstanding of how the mathematician is using the words *imaginary* and *real.*)

In the area of nonlinear dynamics, researchers have chosen to use highly evocative words to describe some of the fundamental concepts of the field. Words like *chaos, catastrophe,* and *complexity* were chosen precisely because they are suggestive of an aspect of the phenomena that are studied under these rubrics that easily slide between their technical meaning and their common usage. This is, of course, particularly likely to happen when investigators who are anxious to use the new mathematical concepts that become available but reluctant or unable to follow mathematical text rely on popularized accounts of mathematics as a basis for the development of their ideas. Nonlinear dynamics has been both fortunate and unfortunate in having repeatedly been the object of enthusiastic popularizations that, along with promoting much interest in the potential applications of the discipline, have also contributed to a freedom in the use of technical terms that confuses discourse.

So why not ban the use of nonlinear dynamic concepts unless they are used in the technical mathematical fashion? The answer is threefold: such approximate use may be an initial step in a process of a fuller mathematical development; even without a full mathematical treatment, nonlinear dynamics sometimes points to phenomena that are common to nonlinear systems and invites recognition of these phenomena in ways they would not have been seen but for the imprecise use of nonlinear dynamics; and, finally, a knowledge of nonlinear dynamics alerts one to an implicit linear worldview that interferes with engaging phenomena that do not fit within it. The nonlinear position thus becomes a worldview rather than a technical method. It is this worldview to which I hope to introduce you in this book.

The heart of this book is a description of the evolution of my thinking about nonlinear dynamics and psychoanalysis. In what follows, I hope you will see how this adventure is well worth taking.

A Dream

Three of my sons and I are sitting in the living room of the cottage in Woods Hole along with my father, who is wearing a hoodie. We are talking, and I notice my father, looking out from under the hoodie, appears to be a man of perhaps forty, whose eyes are full of delight, whom I realize to be full of ambitions and dreams like myself and my sons. (I dreamt this on what would have been my father's 111th birthday, July 13, 2014, two weeks shy of my seventieth birthday.)

The Word "Mathematization"

Like all human interactions, psychoanalysis may be described as a sequence of events occurring over time. The most obvious of these events are the words spoken by the analyst and patient. But any number of other features of the situation, such as the analyst's and patient's physiological responses during the session, could, in theory, also be studied. A group of investigators have devoted themselves to the careful study of the micro-process of psychoanalysis. Collecting data through principally audio recordings, these investigators have explored their data for regularities. A major dimension of these researches has been the explorations of ways to reduce the data so that it can be systematically studied. In this context, *reduction* means selecting elements of the data that are significant and, for the time being, ignoring other elements of the data whose study is likely to prove less fruitful.

When an economist studies how families make a living, she might examine just the total household income and discover meaningful aspects of the economics of families from this feature, even though such an approach eliminates many features of the situation from study. The economist is said to have reduced the problem though this focus. Psychologist Wilma Bucci has developed a measure of emotional salience, "referential activity," which uses the vocabulary of speakers as the data for analysis. Because it can be applied to quite short speech segments, the referential activity of both the analyst and patient can be measured across analytic sessions. Mathematicians have long used a method known as *time series analysis* to study how this method allows researchers to extract regular patterns from seemingly disorganized data to an extent that is impossible from simple inspection of the data itself, or even from its graphical representation. Consider, for example, the determinant of an analyst's speech at a particular moment. These determinants will almost certainly include not only a response to what the patient has just said but also responses to what both the analyst and the patient have said multiple steps back in the conversation. In clinical practice, the analyst uses his theory of how analytic process evolves to pick out pertinent background for the understanding of these responses, but time series analysis provides a means for systematically investigating such questions.

Many people contributed to the work reflected in this volume: Sara van den Berg, for information about witches' progeny, Drs. J. Bongiorno, Bertram Cohler, M. M. Gill, K. M. Lipkin, Ms. Susan Heinemann, Donnel Stern, Arnold Goldberg, my wife, Jeanne Galatzer-Levy, sons, Isaac, Benjamin, and David, and daughter-in-law Sara Zoeterman, provided ideas and critiques. Bridget Eckstein and Scott Jung provided expert editorial assistance.

Chapter 1

A First Step—Qualitative Change from Quantitative Change

Catastrophe Theory Psychoanalysis

The relationship of quality to quantity is a problem in psychoanalysis. We know from everyday life that changes in the amount of an experience can lead to qualitative shifts in the experience. Musical themes repeated three or four times as in a Mozart symphony or a folk song are pleasurable, but when they are repeated many more times, they may become tiresome, or, sometimes, the very process of repetition becomes fascinating and hypnotic, as in the work of Philip Glass or the performance of gamelan orchestras. Extremely brief stimuli may fail to reach consciousness yet still influence psychological life (Snodgrass, Bernat, and Shevrin, 2004). Noxious stimuli, when they reach certain intensity, can qualitatively shift in their effects, becoming traumatic. In each instance, a quantitative shift results in a qualitative change.

Until recently, no adequate conceptual tools were available to address how quantitative change results in changed qualities. In fact, just as Freud did in the *Project for a Scientific Psychology* and Chapter 7 of *The Interpretation of Dreams,* we tend to think of quantity and quality as distinct and separate dimensions of reality. This sharp categorical distinction continues despite the realization that qualitative differences reflect underlying quantitative variation. Intellectually, we know that the sensations called yellow and purple reflect differing wavelengths. But experientially, we know even better that they are qualitatively different colors. We know that water and ice are the same substance but qualitatively different as a result of a quantitative variation, in temperature. Starting in the 1960s, a new branch of mathematics, *catastrophe theory*, emerged that studies how qualitative change can result from quantitative variation. This chapter examines catastrophe theory in relation to psychoanalysis.

The problem of the relation of qualitative change to quantitative change lies at the intellectual heart of several psychoanalytic controversies, but the general problem of the relationship of quantity to quality went unrecognized. It did not come into clinical focus because it is abstract.

As you will see throughout this book, very abstract ideas can clarify and enrich many areas of psychoanalytic investigations. But a combination of factors has led most contemporary psychoanalysts to be skeptical of high-order abstractions. Our day-to-day work focuses on personal meanings and narratives. Indeed, psychoanalysis is most effective when it speaks to the details of an analysand's life. High-order abstractions have little if any direct place in the consulting room. Worse, they commonly confuse clinical discussions. Publications that use terms like *transference*, *ego*, or *projective identification* in descriptions of clinical events commonly leave readers confused. If you try to figure out what in particular happened when the patient "had a negative oedipal transference" or "internalized the analytic attitude," you will realize how the abstractions that pervaded psychoanalytic writing in the mid-twentieth century obscured at least as much as they revealed.

Abstract discourse reached a pinnacle in the work of a group of European analysts who immigrated to the United States to escape Nazism. Led by Heinz Hartman, Ernst Kris, Rudolph Lowenstein, and David Rapaport, these analysts attempted to make psychoanalysis scientific by clarifying the theoretical constructs first developed by Freud as "metapsychology" (Galatzer-Levy, 1997b). In the 1980s, the once enthusiastic students of this group, Merton Gill, Philip Holzman, George Klein, and Roy Schafer, launched a brilliant attack on the ego psychology edifice that showed how it added little to the understanding of people, masked areas of real ignorance, and interfered with the study of how people make meaning.

The combination of its apparent distance from clinical work and the enormous loss of reputation of abstract psychoanalytic thought that resulted from the demolition of American ego psychology left most American psychoanalysts with little taste for abstract conceptualizations.

The revolt against abstraction does not mean careful study of abstractions is useless for psychoanalysts. As you will see in this and later chapters, abstract ideas do not go away. Rather, they become hidden as unarticulated principles often treated as common sense. These unarticulated principles often shape clinical work and psychoanalytic thinking generally. Being unarticulated, they are immune from examination, questioning, and development. Thus, we must return focus to these questions, often going back to Freud to see how implicit yet powerful assumptions enter psychoanalytic discourse.

The model of scientific discourse within which Freud developed his metapsychology excluded quality from its domain (Klein, 1970; Gill, 1976; Galatzer-Levy, 1976). Freud's ideas about what constitutes "scientific" study derived from the school of Helmholtz (Galatzer-Levy, 1976), which was founded in an oath to describe biological phenomena in terms of forces of "equal dignity" to those of physics. Qualitative investigations, like Goethe's studies on color, had no place in a Helmholtzian view of studying life or psychology. The idea that quantity and quality reside in separate domains has been a central theme in Western philosophy since Aristotle (Ross, 1928), but it came into sharp focus only when researchers started to study "information" near the end of and following the Second World War.

At that time, it became apparent that information has a quantitative dimension because questions like "How much information can be transmitted over a particular telephone line?" became of great practical importance and led to the development of an entire discipline, *communication theory* (Arbib, 1972). Yet it was also clear that information has a qualitative dimension. The content of the transmitted message remains important. While twenty pages of Moby Dick contains less information than twenty pages of the Yellow Pages as judged by quantitative measures, from a qualitative point of view it is clear that the information in Moby Dick is both more valuable and, in some important way that is hard to specify, more extensive. Attempts to quantify information never resulted in a clear picture of how quantitative change could result in qualitative change because the relationship of "information" as defined in terms useful for discussing its transmission and "information" as meaning could not be worked out.

This common separation of quality and quantity has led to implicit assumptions about the intellectual work to be done when the two appear in concert. Psychoanalysts tend to accept a general idea that phenomena in which qualitative change appears to result from quantitative variation are in some ways unreal and must be explained away or ignored. For example, how should we think about it if, following an interpretation, seemingly qualitatively new analytic material, like a memory of childhood, emerges. Analysts are likely to think of the new material as having been there all along and that the quantitative shift in some way led to its uncovering. We are even more likely to think it is a "good" interpretation because new things emerged, leaving it implicit that they emerged from the unconscious, where they were in some sense always present.

Psychoanalytic Approaches to Qualitative and Quantitative Change

Three concepts—epigenetic sequences, trauma, and "internal catastrophe" in psychosis—illustrate how quantitative change is implicitly thought to result in qualitatively new phenomena.

Epigenesis, the unfolding of development, transforms time into changing psychological qualities. Freud (1905c), A. Freud (1965), Erikson (1950), and Mahler *et al.* (1975), among many others, proposed various epigenetic sequences of psychological development. But they ignored how the passage of time might result in these qualitative changes. Latency followed the oedipal phase, which, in turn, followed the anal phase. Starting with Abraham (1924), analysts have charted developmental sequences but seldom asked how it is that individuals follow these sequences. The negative of this question, the description of how these sequences may be interfered with, is, of course, well studied. It is one of the peculiarities of psychoanalysis as a general psychology that its clinical origins make us much better versed in how things go wrong than how they proceed normally.

An implicit solution to the question of how the passage of time results in regular sequences of development is that observed psychological changes are the visible result of underlying biological changes. These biological changes are of course beyond the scope of psychological investigation. But this solution merely puts the problem back to a different level without resolving it.[1] Qualitatively new phenomena emerge as the individual develops and the main determinant of these changes is the passage of time. A qualitative change results from quantitative variation.

Trauma is another example of qualitative change arising from quantitative change. Although the idea of trauma seems to be readily understood, defining it psychoanalytically has proven more difficult. Greenacre (1967) defined it as an experience whose intensity is such that new defenses are precipitated. The economic view of trauma as an "overwhelming" of the ego apparatus (A. Freud, 1967) also specifies a relationship between quality and quantity. Such terms as *overwhelm*, *too much*, or *breaking point* denote a qualitative change linked to quantitative variation. These references to quantity are the one invariant in definitions of trauma and correspond well to the subjective experiences commonly called traumatic.

A third example of qualitative change is the "internal catastrophe" (Freud, 1911), marking the onset of psychosis. Both the initial catastrophe and the (psychotic) restitution may be regarded as qualitative changes in psychic functioning. These changes are classically described quantitatively as massive shifts in cathexis, i.e. the quality of psychological operations remains unchanged but there is a large scale shift in the extent to which various psychological processes are engaged. Much of the debate on the nature of these changes (Holzman, 1976) and, in particular, whether they are continuous or discontinuous with neurotic pathology (Arlow and Brenner, 1969) implicitly involves the relation of quantitative variation to qualitative change. For example, despite the strong phenomenological evidence for qualitative change in schizophrenia (Grinker and Holzman, 1973; Meehl, 1962), there is a reluctance to view the underlying phenomena of psychosis as qualitatively different from those observed in healthy and neurotic people. In part, this reluctance is based on the intellectual difficulties in specifying qualitative change and especially in relating it to quantitative variation. We are reluctant to accept empirical findings that seem at odds with the idea that apparently qualitative changes associated with quantitative changes must arise in some other way than from a significant change in quality arising from quantitative change.

Freud struggled with the problem of quality in the "Project" (1895a) and remained dissatisfied with his own solution. Basically, he saw qualities as determining how a switch was set or a how a device separating possible directions of a fluid's flow was directed. Qualities in this sense regulate the direction in which quantities will go but do not, by themselves, provide motive power to the system. Freud seldom referred to qualities in an abstract sense in his published writings. His reference to them in *The Interpretation of Dreams* (Freud, 1900) is predominantly to explain the function of consciousness. It is a reworking in psychological terminology of the ideas of the "Project."

Later analysts have dealt with the relation of qualitative to quantitative change in many ways. The most common solution is simply to ignore the problem. For example, the use of the terms *overwhelm* or *too much* in the discussion of trauma and the integrity of the self (Kohut, 1971) appears to continue quantitative discourse but includes a reference both to quantity and resulting qualitative change.

A second solution is to imply that the phenomena under discussion result from some deeper cause, which lies outside the universe of discourse under discussion. For example, psychological development over time (a quantitative change) results from biological embryology so that qualitative psychological changes have biological counterparts that are outside the scope of psychological study.

A third solution is to deny the existence of qualitative change. Freud's theory of shifting cathexis implies that an apparently qualitative change reflects only quantitative shifts in the psychic energy. Such a view is inadequate as a description of the development of, for example, psychic structure (Rapaport, 1960). Modern conflict theory explains apparently qualitative change through shifting intensities of unconscious fantasies (Brenner, 1979). Concepts such as primitive ego nuclei (Hartmann, 1939, 1950) attempt to solve the dilemma of positing a preexisting structure so that qualitatively new phenomena need not be introduced.

One might argue that if *quantitative* variation cannot result in qualitative change, then whenever qualitative change does occur, one should look for a *qualitative* change as its cause. For example, a fantasy might be determined by new information. Although it is seldom formulated in this way, narrative and hermeneutic approaches rely heavily on the idea that adequate psychoanalytic explanations involve coherent stories, which are evaluated primarily in terms of how well their qualitative elements fit together.

The problem that the relation of qualitative to quantitative change pervades psychoanalysis often goes unrecognized. Analysts have made assumptions about how quantity and quality relate and have shaped theories based on these assumptions, but we have not found ways to talk explicitly about these assumptions. Instead, we treat them as so obvious as to be unworthy of comment.

Precisely the same difficulty arises in other sciences. Just as in psychoanalysis, the problem is often put aside with verbal sleight of hand. In fact, until the route toward a general solution appeared, scientists in other disciplines treated the relationship of quantity to quality pretty much as analysts do by making strong but implicit assumptions about that relationship. Many physical phenomena involve qualitative change resulting from quantitative variations. Think of water freezing or boiling, glass breaking, or rockets leaving the earth's atmosphere. In these instances and many others, small shifts in a quantity initiate dramatic qualitative physical changes. Until recently, conceptual and mathematical difficulties in studying of such phenomena interfered with even noticing such things occurred.

A brief venture into how this problem occurred in the physical sciences will give us a better understanding of the nature of the problem as it appears elsewhere, including in psychoanalysis.

Studying Change—The Triumph of Differential Equations

The success of classical physics and most modern physical sciences rests on the use of mathematical formulations called differential equations. Differential equations describe how variables change with regard to one another. For example, they describe how a charged particle moves in an electric field, how planets move under the gravitational forces applied to them, or how a magnetic field is generated by an electric current. They also describe the rates at which chemical reactions occur, the transmission of impulses along nerve axons, the movement of weather systems, and the growth of populations. They are part of the core curriculum of all engineering programs because the design of everything, from antiaircraft carriers to the circuitry of smartphones, depends on them. They form the mathematical basis of most of our knowledge of the physical world.

Isaac Newton invented differential equations to explore how objects moved under the force of gravity. He showed how very simple laws could predict celestial phenomena with great accuracy. It soon became apparent that the idea could be generalized to the study of a wide range of physical phenomena. The idea of differential equations and their application to the physical world transformed physics and the Western worldview forever.

Newton posited that the acceleration of an object was proportional to the force applied to it and inversely proportional to the object's mass. Written as an equation, this becomes

$$F = ma$$

where F is the force, m is the mass, and a is the acceleration (all in appropriate units). Acceleration is the rate of change of velocity, and velocity in turn is the rate of change of position. So we now have a law relating force, mass, and the rate of change of a rate of change. Newton realized that we can use this equation to find out the position of an object at any moment—that is, if we know the object's acceleration, which we have calculated using Newton's law, we can find its position and velocity provided only that we know its initial position and velocity.

Finding a function that describes the location of a particle given its acceleration (and initial position and velocity) is called "solving" a differential equation. More generally, solving a differential equation means that, starting with a differential equation that describes the rate of change of some variables with respect to other variables, we find a mathematical function (i.e. a rule) that connects the underlying variables in question. This function is called the solution of the differential equation.

Let us look at a very simple differential equation from physics. Long before Newton, Galileo showed that the acceleration of a body acted on by gravity near the earth is a constant that is independent of the weight of the object. So we have an equation for the acceleration:

$$a = G$$

where G is the gravitational constant in question. This is a differential equation—the rate of change of velocity is constant for a falling body. The solution of this equation has several features corresponding to our intuition of the physical situation. The solution can be specified in terms of common simple functions: There is only one solution, and small variations in the initial conditions result in small changes in the solution. According to this equation, slightly different starting points will yield similar paths of motion.

Many natural phenomena can be described by differential equations having explicit, unique, and stable solutions. To name a few: the motion of a pendulum, the vibration of a violin string, the rates of chemical reactions, the shape of magnetic and electrical fields. The triumph (and failure) of classical physics lies in the study of these equations. Much attention was devoted to these equations. Techniques were developed for their solution as well as theorems demonstrating general conditions under which solutions existed and were unique. The general theory of differential equations is among the triumphs of mathematics.

However, problems emerged. As often happens, when a method approaches its limits, major problems were seen as technical difficulties. For example, some of the differential equations of physics predicted infinite values for some variables. This could not be right because physical systems cannot take on infinite values. Such "singularities" were treated, as the name suggests, as unusual occurrences. If we think of solutions to differential equations as being qualitatively different from one another as meaning that the shape of the graph of the solution was fundamentally changed, then the solutions of many differential equations changed in character as a result of changes in the constants of the equation. For example, with the parameter set at one value, the form of the graph might be a closed curve like an ellipse, while at another value it might be an open curve like a parabola.

Poincaré (1886), the great French mathematician and Freud's contemporary, whose work we will meet again, showed that for differential equations of the type that were most important to physics involving a function of one variable (e.g. time), only four basic types of such singularities are possible. Singularities of the type described by Poincaré occur in nature and are no mere artifact of mathematical formalism. Imagine a rocket being launched from earth at an angle from vertical. The path it will follow depends on its force. At one extreme, the force will be too weak to move the rocket, and it will just sit there. Increasing the force, it will follow a parabolic path, rising into the air and falling again to the ground. With still more force, it will be launched into an orbit that circles the earth; and finally, with still more force, it will "escape" and continue on into space.

The types of singularity described by Poincaré in 1886 are orderly. Even though they represent qualitative changes in the solution of differential equations, those changes are easily recognizable as smooth transitions from neighboring types of solutions. It is easy to intuit that escaping the earth's gravity will at some point result from a slight change in trajectory that sends the rocket on its way into orbit instead of falling back to earth and that a further nudge will send it off into space. The theory of these changes is one of the most beautiful in modern mathematics (Hurewicz, 1958). Differential equations that result in this sort of orderly transition are referred to as "linear."[2]

But far more complicated shifts involving qualitative change that results from quantitative change are common and easily observed. Ice melts into a liquid, waves "break" (quantitative change in depth results in qualitative change in wave form), a drop of ink falling into a glass of water breaks apart into droplets. Such phenomena were not discussed in physics courses until the 1990s. The theoretician's lack of success with these problems resulted in inattention to the phenomena themselves.

Although most people have a practical sense of what it means for things to be "qualitatively different," sharply specifying what it means to say that two objects, ideas, or images are qualitatively different is difficult. Mathematicians confronted with this problem came up with precise ideas that apply well to the objects they study. For simplicity, we will begin with curves in space. Think of a piece of string whose ends may or may not be joined. Curves are regarded as qualitatively the same if they can be continuously deformed into one another without cutting or joining points together. If the curves were to be made of infinitely elastic rubber, two curves are qualitatively the same if and only if they can be deformed into each other. The branch of mathematics that studies this sort of situation is called topology. Curves that can be deformed into one another in this way are called *topologically equivalent*. The idea of topological equivalence can obviously be extended to objects of three or more dimensions. The sphere and the cube are topologically equivalent. Imagine each is made of rubber; each could be deformed into the other by simply stretching without either cutting or pasting. On the other hand, a donut is not topologically equivalent to either. No matter how you stretch it, without cutting or pasting, the hole remains, making it different from the cut or stretched sphere.

Topological equivalence is included in our intuitive notion of qualitative likeness. If things are topologically different, we tend to think of them as qualitatively different. But it is a broad concept for psychological discourse. For example, from a topological point of view, a donut and a coffee cup are equivalent (one hole), but most of us would not consider them qualitatively similar. So if two things are qualitatively alike, they are certainly topologically equivalent; but things can be qualitatively different even though they are topologically equivalent.

Catastrophe theory shows that quantitative changes can produce topologically distinct results and, hence, qualitative change. However, under this very broad definition, quantitative change can result in qualitative change, and so this line of thinking is worthy of pursuit. Freud (1900) approvingly cites Aristotle who adopts what appears to be a topological view:

> … the best interpreter of dreams was the man who could best grasp similarities; for dream-pictures, like pictures on water, are pulled out of shape by movement, and the most successful interpreter is the man who can detect the truth from the misshapen picture (p. 97, fn. 2).

Psychoanalysis will need to construct an idea or ideas parallel to topological equivalence that are appropriate to psychological discourse in order to use topological ideas well in investigating psychological phenomena. We are used to this sort of work. A very similar task is familiar to psychoanalysts who observe that dreams or symptoms whose manifest content varies may have the same or closely related latent content. We regard dreams or symptoms that share the latent content as, in a significant sense, equivalent.

Until the end of the nineteenth century, differential equations were studied primarily to yield numerical value, for example, to predict the precise location of a heavenly body in the sky or to design weapons. These solutions could be represented graphically and, from the very beginning in Newton's work, these graphic representations yielded striking results like the demonstration that planets move in elliptical orbits under gravitational forces. Starting at the end of the nineteenth century, a group of mathematicians recognized that the form taken by the solution of a differential equation should be a primary object of study, that these *qualitative* features of differential equations were at least as important as quantitative calculations. Whether a planet forever circles the sun in an ellipse or flies off into space is at least as interesting as locating it at a particular point at a particular time.

Differential equations can be used to study any type of reasonably smooth change. The same basic type of equations apply whether one is studying the motion of planets, the growth of cities, the transmission of excitement in a nerve cell, or the form of water waves. The general concept of differential equations can be applied to almost anything involving change.

As the study of differential equations focused increasingly on the topology of the forms that represented solutions, mathematicians realized that they did not have to limit their study of differential equations to ordinary familiar Euclidean spaces, such as the plane or ordinary three-dimensional space. They explored differential equations on a broad class of spaces called differential manifolds, which are essentially all the spaces in which it makes sense to speak of the change in one variable with respect to another. They found that, even in this very general class of spaces, certain properties of differential equations continued to hold.

Singularities—changes in the quality of the solution of differential equations—occur in all of this broad class of spaces. But, surprisingly, the nature and number of singularities depends solely on the dimension of the space. This result limits the number of topologically distinct phenomena that can arise in any situation. No knowledge of the detailed structure of the space is needed. For example, a two-dimensional space need not extend infinitely in all its dimension as a plane does. The space in question might, for example, be the surface of a donut rather than a plane. Yet the rules about possible singularities would remain the same. All that is really needed for these very general findings to hold true is that the concept of a rate of change of one variable with respect to another makes sense in the space.

By the beginning of the twentieth century, a fairly clear picture had emerged of the topological forms generated by differential equations, although characterizing the changes that occurred around singularities, values where the solutions of the equations changed abruptly or gave infinite values, turned out to be far more difficult. Before the middle of the twentieth century, these points made little sense to mathematicians and, especially when they occurred in the equations of physical systems, were generally treated as "pathological," meaning that in some way the differential equation that described the system was not functioning as it should.

While mathematicians had developed a comprehensive and powerful theory of change that took place smoothly, abrupt or qualitative change was beyond their methods. Perhaps because those methods had proven so amazingly powerful in the physical sciences, huge energies were devoted to trying to extend and refine them to cover situations where the equations seemed to predict nonsensical results. Thinking of the situations where equations predicted abrupt change as pathological had an interesting effect. It kept mathematicians from considering that the equations might be pointing to a group of phenomena that differed sharply from the smoothly transitioning world predicted by those equations.

By the middle of the twentieth century, largely as a result of investigating the very general properties of differential equations, an ever clearer picture of the nature of singularities began to emerge, and whole new fields of mathematics, catastrophe theory and chaos theory, developed to study them.

One of the early triumphs in the field was René Thom's (1974) exposition of catastrophe theory, a comprehensive description of the types of singularities that could occur in a certain important class of differential equations.

Catastrophe Theory

Thom, who began his work as an abstract mathematical investigator, soon realized that his ideas were very suggestive for the study of embryology. The central concepts of Thom's work are *catastrophe point* and *morphology of a process*.

It is useful to think of an entire process as a single object, including its temporal dimension. To get a feel for this, imagine the frames of a motion picture separated and stacked in a pile. What would have been the time dimension of the movie if shown normally is now represented by the height of the frame in the newly created deck. One could specify a point in the process as a whole by specifying the location of the frame in the deck and the location of the matter of interest on the frame. Similarly, any morphological process can be viewed as an entire unit. A point in a process is specified by the location in space and the time at which it occurs. If at points near a chosen point the process changes little so that it goes on in a smooth way near that point, this point is called *regular.* Otherwise, it is called a *catastrophe point.* In every neighborhood of catastrophe point, things change abruptly. Catastrophe points are where things change abruptly.

Thom calls the set of catastrophe points, along with the specification of what happens at each point, the *morphology* of the process. Catastrophe points may be divided into two classes:

- *Ordinary catastrophe* points lie isolated along an edge on either side of which lie ordinary points. Things change abruptly at ordinary catastrophe points, but around them, change is smooth.
- In contrast, *essential catastrophe points* have other catastrophe points arbitrarily close to them in all directions. In the region around such points, phenomena become chaotic.

When Thom developed catastrophe theory, he put aside essential catastrophe points as presenting intractable problems. As we will see later, by doing so he was able to address an already difficult problem well, but he also missed out on what would become the most interesting developments in nonlinear mathematics.

In Thom's terms, catastrophe theory studies the morphology of processes. The *dynamic* of a process is the set of forces underlying the process. Like a psychoanalyst, Thom moves from the level of observable phenomena to their underlying causes, "From a macroscopic examination of the morphology of a process, and a local and global study of its singularities [catastrophe points], we can try to reconstruct the dynamic that generates it" (Thom, 1974, p. 7). Thom points out that the purely geometrical theory is "independent of the substrate of form and the nature of the forces that create them." That is, just as in other areas of applied mathematics, important properties of systems are pretty much independent of the particulars of their makeup. The equations of fluid dynamics, for example, tell us a lot, whether we are studying water moving through a pipe or cars going down a highway. Major features of systems are determined by their shared equations.

It is time to pause for a moment to reassure the psychoanalytic reader that we are not off on some mathematical misadventure that will take us far from psychoanalytic concerns. One of the major tasks Freud set for himself was to develop a general theory of mental functioning. Although he had done so earlier in the unpublished project and to a lesser extent in *On Aphasia*, Chapter 7 of *The Interpretation of Dreams* is a major attempt in the direction of a general theory. Contemporary readers of this chapter often become hung up on what appears to be neurological theorizing. At the same moment that Freud says that he is moving to a purely psychological theory, the diagrams he includes in the chapter are so suggestive of brain structures that readers almost always mistakenly think he is still in the realm of neurological investigation. Freud appreciated the idea that abstracting central features of a situation can lead to useful general theorizing about them without requiring that the substrate of those features be specified except that they conform to certain rules.

In the case of catastrophe theory, Thom showed that only seven types of catastrophes occur at ordinary catastrophe points in four-dimensional Euclidean space (Zeeman, 1975). To appreciate what this means, consider that any process that can be described in terms of four quantities has, at most, seven different ways in which abrupt changes can occur without it becoming nearly chaotic and that this holds regardless of the particulars of the process. Thom's finding holds whether the particular situation involves the weather, electric motors, individual human activities, or economics.

An important instance of a four-dimensional Euclidean space has as its points a position in ordinary three-dimensional space associated with a fourth dimension, time. A vast number of phenomena strongly resemble the catastrophes of four-dimensional Euclidean space. It is often possible by simply inspecting the catastrophe, e.g. by looking at a graphic representation of it or listening to a sufficiently detailed description, to discover which of these seven types is in effect. Since four dimensions (three spatial dimensions and time) describe all physical phenomena, Thom's result states that all phenomena in which discrete sharp changes occur (i.e. that involve only regular catastrophes) may be described by one of seven catastrophes. This means that if we have enough information to identify the type of catastrophe point involved, we should be able to make qualitative predictions about the nature of the process.

A Clinical Illustration

Consider an ambivalent patient who alternately expresses intense love and intense hate toward the analyst. Let us assume that the patient always has both feelings in some sense, but when one feeling is expressed, the other is barred from awareness. Which feeling is manifestly expressed depends significantly on the relative amount of the feelings.

Corresponding to each pair of quantities of love and hate, there will be at least one manifest behavior. We can represent this graphically. The combination of love and hate are represented as points on a plane with axes being intensity of hatred and intensity of love. Corresponding to each of these points is a behavior (or behaviors) as represented by a surface above the plane (see Figure 1.1).

Clinical experience teaches that certain phenomena are expected. When either love or hate is clearly dominant, the behavior simply manifests this feeling. Where the amounts of love and hate are similar,

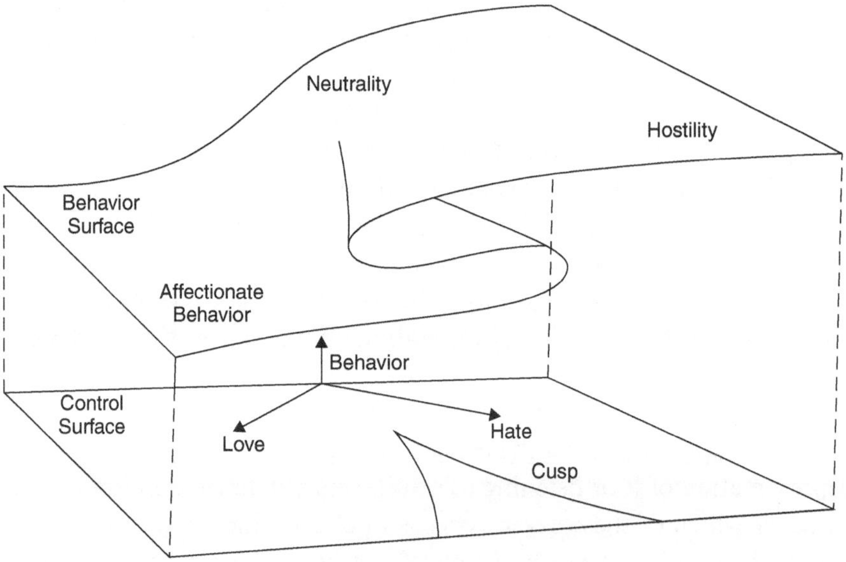

Figure 1.1 A Cusp Catastrophe: Manifest Behavior as a Function of Love and Hate.

ambivalence (i.e. rapid movement between loving and hating behaviors) is manifest. If both are of low intensity, neutral behavior results. If the emotions are both intense and relatively equal in intensity, a number of familiar phenomena occur. The behavior is bimodal, with sudden shifts from one form to another. The transition from overt hostility to affection occurs at a different point from the reverse. There is a tendency to continue the mode of behavior already present. Finally, there is a marked effect on the final state of manifest behavior depending on the starting point. A reasonable model of ambivalence would include all of these features.

Let us consider a model that relates underlying feelings of love and hate to hostile and affectionate behaviors in order to see how a common clinical situation can be explored using catastrophe theory. For purposes of this illustration, defenses against the expression of emotions and other complicating factors are omitted from our considerations. Figure 1.1 represents a model of ambivalence as a three-dimensional figure based on one of Thom's seven catastrophes, the "cusp catastrophe." The base of the figure represents the intensity of the underlying emotions, love and hate, which are treated as independent (i.e. one can vary without the other varying) of one another. Using the language of catastrophe theory, they are called control variables and they are represented on a control surface. The term *control* comes from the idea that if we were modeling a piece of machinery, these variables would be determined by how we set the controls on the machine. The third dimension represented in the figure is behavior. Think of behavior as ranging continuously from hostile to affectionate, with affection represented as lower on the vertical axis and hostility as higher on that axis. The folded sheet, the behavioral surface, represents the behaviors associated with the various intensities of love and hate. Notice first that for some values of love and hate, more than one behavior is possible with a given intensity of these variables. The degree of love and hate do not always uniquely determine what the behavior will be. The region in the love-hate plane where more than one behavior can occur is shown as a cusp in the love-hate plane. When the love-hate variables change, the point on the behavioral surface changes. In this model, we assume that motion on the behavioral surface is continuous—that is, it traces a path on that surface. Jumps from one sheet to another that do not follow such a path do not occur.

The lower sheet of the behavior surface represents overtly affectionate behavior, and the upper sheet, overtly hostile behavior. An intermediate sheet formed by the fold provides a pathway by which movement can occur between the hostile and affectionate sheets. It is the unstable state where both behaviors are manifest. Outside of the area of the cusp-shaped area under the fold, the behavior is simple in the sense that it represents a level along the hostility-affection axis appropriate to the level of underlying love and hate. Note that another path from affectionate behavior to hostile behavior is implied by the diagram. This path lies through an area where the intensity of both love and hate are quite low. Thus, the model predicts two kinds of transition from affection to hostility. One occurs when, after a period of not very strong feeling, love or hate is intensified, and the appropriate behavior results. The other occurs in the area of the cusp and involves a rapid transition through a brief unstable state from affection to hostile or hostile to affectionate behavior.

Let's look at what happens in the region of the cusp. Here, manifest behavior is determined by the person's past history. It is not fully determined by the intensity of underlying love and hate. If a person starting on the lower (affectionate) surface develops increasing hatred, his behavior moves along the lower sheet of the behavioral surface until it reaches the right-hand side of the cusp, the behavior remaining affectionate. On reaching the right side of the cusp, a sudden shift occurs onto the intermediate sheet, and the behavior becomes mixed. But this is a very unstable state. Even slight shifts in position of the love-hate surface move the behavior off the intermediate sheet and onto the affectionate or hostile sheet. If the jump continues to the hostile sheet, even if there is an increase in the quantity of love toward the object, the behavior remains on the upper sheet until the left-hand side of the cusp is again reached. Notice further that if the intensity of love and hate both become very great, the intermediate sheet becomes more stable in the sense that variations in love and hate are less likely to move the individual off this intermediate sheet.

Note that the model not only satisfies the requirements we laid out at the beginning for a model of ambivalence, but it also predicts something that we had not included but that is clinically often the case, i.e. that when ambivalence is extremely intense, there are times when the individual seems simultaneously to express both intense affection and intense hostility toward the object of these emotions—for example, clinging to and hitting that object at the same time. It predicts that stable transition from hostile to affectionate behavior will occur only when the intensity of feelings of both love and hate is at a reasonably low level. Most important, it tells us that manifest behavior, even in the absence of defensive operations, does not necessarily reflect the intensity of underlying feeling but that there is a stability consisting in a strong tendency to maintain whichever behavior the individual is engaged in *despite* shifts in underlying intensities.

Thom referred to the general mathematical process illustrated by this example as a *cusp catastrophe*. Cusp catastrophes are characterized by (1) sudden changes from one form of behavior to another (bimodality); (2) transitions from the top sheet to the bottom sheet do not occur at the same points as transitions from the bottom sheet to the top sheet (hysteresis—the property that the state of a system depends not only on the current forces working on it but also its history); (3) a middle zone, where bimodal behavior occurs, is unstable but becomes more stable with higher overall intensity; and (4) initially small differences in the system can result in large final differences.

A word is in order about hysteresis. From classical physics and its applications in everyday life, we tend to think that the motion of a system depends only on the forces currently acting on it. However, in many physical systems, this is not the case; the past history of the system makes a significant difference in how it responds to forces applied to it. This can be observed, for example, in electric motors. For psychoanalysts, this suggests that some of the phenomena we attribute to memory, in the sense of some sort of mental representation of past events, may be remembered in a very different sense than is built into the system.

We have thus seen that an important psychological phenomenon can be described as one of Thom's seven elementary catastrophes. This illustration also shows how such formulations might be useful in theorizing. If we are discussing a phenomenon in which hysteresis occurs, we might suspect a cusp catastrophe and look for the other three phenomena associated with a cusp catastrophe. The categorization of a catastrophe suggests the associated phenomena for which it is appropriate to search. Since the publication of the original version of this chapter, a variety of psychological functions have been modeled using catastrophe theory. Sadly, psychoanalysis was robbed of an extraordinary investigator, Jerome Sashin, who doubtlessly would have contributed far more to these catastrophe theory models in psychoanalysis, and many other aspects of psychoanalysis, were it not for his premature death (Sashin, 1985; Sashin and Callahan, 1990).

Catastrophe Theory and Psychoanalysis

Psychoanalysts commonly find it challenging to see how ideas like catastrophe theory are relevant to the "experience near" world with which we work. As a community, we have become suspicious of abstract theorizing. But, more important, it is not obvious how abstract mathematical formulations can inform psychoanalytic work and understanding. As I hope the previous example illustrates, a catastrophe theory–based description of a clinical phenomenon provides us with at least two new tools. First, by providing a model, it points to aspects of the situation that may otherwise be overlooked, like the intermediate behavioral sheet described for ambivalence. Second, and more difficult to appreciate, it suggests that some of the aspects of clinical situations that were thought to require elaborate explanations may need no such explanation. In the ambivalence example, notice that the absence of behavioral expression of certain feelings does not require explanation in terms of defensive operations but is built in, as it were, to the nature of the situation.

The power of mathematical thinking lies in the variety of different phenomena that can subsume under one theory, provided that conditions apply that make that theory applicable. To employ topological ideas, as we do here, concepts of distance and rate of change are needed for "psychological" space. However, we do not need a quantitative measure of this distance; the theory works for any space where "distance" has meaning. Similarly, we do not need an explicit means of calculating "rates of change"; only the knowledge that a concept of rate of change could be applied is needed to know that the ideas of catastrophe may be applied to a system.

The methods of catastrophe theory provide a systematic method for describing the qualitative changes that arise from quantitative change under the special circumstances to which it applies. Catastrophe theory was the first step in exploring how qualitative change can arise from quantitative change, not as an artifact of insufficiently deep appreciation of the phenomenon but as an intrinsic part of it. It showed that concepts of quantitative variation need not be removed from theory building because qualitative change is also involved. Catastrophe theory provides mathematical tools appropriate to psychoanalysis, which studies both quantitative and qualitative change. It was the first step in what became the flood of new ideas in nonlinear mathematics, many of which are potentially useful to psychoanalysts.

Catastrophe theory itself has not lived up to its initial promise either in psychoanalysis or in general, despite some very promising beginnings in the work of Sashin and Ruelle (1991). The principal reason is that the entire theory is a special case of a much broader group of ideas called *nonlinear dynamical systems theory* (which we will explore throughout this book). Remember that catastrophe theory applies only in the vicinity of ordinary catastrophe points, but a much larger group of phenomena can be encompassed in broader theories. The other problem was that a small group of catastrophe theorists, headed by Christopher Zeeman (1977), made exaggerated claims for catastrophe theory, particularly as applied to the social sciences, which ultimately brought the theory itself into significant disrepute (Saunders, 1980).

Catastrophe theory was a first step in the direction of the nonlinear study of complex systems, in particular psychoanalysis. It points to the kind of ideas and the methods that will develop into a nonlinear view of psychoanalysis.

Notes

1 Sometimes the shift from the psychological to the physiological makes the time dimension seemingly disappear from the problem, e.g. puberty results in elevated sex hormone levels which contribute to the physical and psychological changes of this period. But here again, a quantitative factor is transformed into a qualitative change, though time is replaced with change in hormonal level, the underlying qualitative-quantitative problem remains.

2 The terms *linear* and *nonlinear* have become so much a part of common speech and they are often used in such vague ways that it is easy to forget that they originate with a specific mathematical meaning. Remember

that the equation of a line $mx + b = 0$ differs from that of more complex geometric forms like a parabola, whose equation is $ax^2 + b = 0$, in that the variable term is not multiplied by anything but a constant. Every equation that involves multiple variables by themselves or other variables is *nonlinear*. A differential equation is linear if the derivatives in it are multiplied only by constants. All other differential equations are nonlinear. The common uses of these terms tend to suggest something simpler than the actual distinction yet contain an element of truth, i.e. the linear equations describe a much simpler and more orderly world than nonlinear equations.

Chapter 2

Characterizing Our Ignorance[1]

Sometimes analysts feel confident that we know a fact.

Consider two scenarios:

1 The mother of a child dies in a car crash. A child who had been vigorous and happy loses interest in almost everything and develops stomach pains. We feel confident of a causal relationship between the accident and the child's mood.
2 In contrast, we meet a child with few interests and similar somatic complaints whose history includes no clear moment when the symptoms emerged. If we resist filling in the story based on the psychoanalytic theory to which we happen to subscribe, we are forced to admit our ignorance. Even when careful analytic work enables us to develop a coherent explanatory narrative, we must admit that however therapeutically useful the narrative is, its relationship to historical realities remains unclear (Spence, 1982; Schafer, 1992). This uncertainty should persist even when our own and others' rhetorical style, in or out of the analytic session, leads to definitive sounding statements. We remain, to varying degrees, ignorant.

Much of the progress of science consists in recognizing what we do not know, what we cannot know, and the nature of our ignorance. This chapter is about how this idea applies to psychoanalysis, in particular, the vexing question of differentiating actual deficits in development from apparent deficits that are a product of unconsciously motivated activity.

Major developments in science are based in the recognition of various kinds of ignorance. The development of empiricism rests on the realization that some aspects of reality cannot be known through sheer cogitation, (e.g. Hume, 1739). Apparent imprecisions in empirical investigation were first seen as correctable human failings but later recognized as aspects of the empirical method itself (Fisher, 1951)—that is, measurements of any type, no matter how well done, will by their nature fall over a range of values. Nevertheless, the term *experimental error* is used to this day for that branch of statistics that studies these phenomena, a tribute to the hope that these "errors" are correctable (Topping, 1955).

Some phenomena, e.g. genetics, entropy, and quantum mechanics, appear inherently statistical. This suggests inevitable limits of our knowledge. Some investigators suggest that when phenomena appear to be statistical, deeper knowledge of the same phenomenon can restore our potential to predict and understand in a non-probabilistic way (Bohm, 1957).

Though philosophers had long discussed the limits of human knowledge, the usefulness of thinking about what it is possible to know shifted with the development of the special theory of relativity (Einstein, 1931) and the related emergence of positivistic philosophy. Working physicists now agreed that the idea of an absolute reality whose nature we seek to discover was no longer viable. It was replaced with a reality whose nature lies in the processes of observation. Einstein posited that there was no absolute position or velocity of an object but only its position and velocity relative to a particular observer. Furthermore, there is no universal time but only time as measured by particular clocks. Combining these seemingly obvious ideas with the concept that the speed of light is the same for all observers, Einstein came to a theory, special relativity, that is not only foundational to modern physics but, more important, has led to surprising and accurately measurable predictions. In special relativity, "ignorance," or rather recognition of the absence of knowledge of a supposed external reality, permits prediction and a worldview in which nature can be known precisely.

Quantum mechanics, as exemplified by the Heisenberg (1930) uncertainty principle, takes away even this comfort and demonstrates that real experiments, by their very nature, may have unpredictable outcomes. Ignorance of the physical world is an inevitable result of the process of observation. Our inevitable ignorance extends even to mathematics where Gödel (1931a, b) demonstrated that even some true mathematical statements cannot be proven. Cohen (1966) showed that these "undecidable propositions" include matters of substantial mathematical interest, i.e. they include propositions whose truth matters and are not merely mathematical oddities. An additional class of problems is forever insoluble because it can be proven that the computations necessary are too complex ever to be performed (Stockmeyer and Chandra, 1979).

Mathematicians once believed that, though perhaps devilishly difficult to solve, the equations that govern the motion of physical bodies could be solved and lead to predications about physical events. The study of nonlinear dynamics showed that these equations could never be solved in the hoped for sense. The "classical physicists" of the late nineteenth century pictured a physical world that could be captured in solvable equations (McCormmach, 1991). By 1940, all of that had changed, and although physicists were capable of predicting many phenomena, the clockwork universe was forever gone, replaced by a world in which important aspects of reality can never be grasped with the clarity of a clockwork mechanism.

This bleak picture has another side. As the fact of our ignorance is demonstrated, the nature of our ignorance is elucidated. The recognition of various types of ignorance led to insights about that ignorance. The recognition that the world could not be known through cogitation alone led to the development of empirical methods; the study of the inevitable impression of measurements yielded understanding to the statistical distribution governing errors of observation; recognition that some phenomena are governed by probabilities led to the elucidation of the laws of probabilistic phenomena; with universal frames of reference abandoned, the special theory of relativity specified interrelation of observations from differing inertial frames; starting with the realization that the position and momentum of a particle could not be known simultaneously. Heisenberg discovered the relation of the imprecisions in measured position and momentum; and the unprovable true statements of mathematics were partially characterized, as were the practically uncomputable problems. These discoveries initiated research into what we could not know. Each of these contributions added to a new sort of knowledge, which I will call the *characterization of ignorance*. Such knowledge has two virtues: It is itself a surprising piece of information about the world, and it saves us from futile efforts to discover what is unknowable or meaningless.

Most psychoanalysts believe that ignorance reflects failed observation and that by improving observation one can come ever closer to truth. This leads to a fruitful, meticulous attention to correctable sources of misperception. Since the mid-1940s, analysts have recognized that simple failures to systematically record analyses subject analytical data to gross distortions (Galatzer-Levy *et al.*, 2000). Countertransference distortion in observation and theory (Stolorow and Atwood, 1979) is closely scrutinized as potentially misleading the analysts. Analysts have been preoccupied with basic methodological issues to an extent that is unique among scientists and have actively engaged the question of the scientific status of our work. Errors arising from these sources, however, are not the object of this chapter. It is, however, pertinent to the idea of the characterization of ignorance that the recognition and delineation of countertransference phenomena, which were originally seen as interferences in analysis, led to powerful ways of knowing about patients (e.g. Racker, 1957; Tower, 1956).

Freud treated ignorance as an indication that further investigation was needed. Many of his writings, such as *The Interpretation of Dreams* and *Jokes and Their Relation to the Unconscious*, begin with a statement that some interesting phenomena call for explanation and proceed to approach the general problem by breaking it down into smaller, more easily solved problems, whose solutions come together as a solution of the original problem. Freud assumes that problems have solutions and that the major source of ignorance is an incomplete investigation resulting from having not yet applied available methods adequately or not yet having found a method to approach a particular problem. Especially in his writing before 1917, Freud is almost always stimulated by a problem and rarely asserts that a problem cannot be answered.

Freud (1920a, b) believed that the ignorance demonstrated by the analyst's inability to predict reflects a potentially rectifiable lack of knowledge of quantities whose interactions are manifest in human behavior. Waelder (1963) studied the principle that Freud called "over determination," which Waelder properly renamed "multiple determination," and observed that some failures of prediction were inevitable in psychoanalysis no matter how good the observations. But he also observed that such ineptitude at prediction occurs only in unusual circumstances. In the previous chapter, I suggest that the failure of prediction does not result from the absence of knowledge of underlying quantities but rather from the inherent erratic quality of behavior in the vicinity of sudden shifts and changes. This unpredictability results from the very structure of the phenomena under study and is extensively studied by using the methods of nonlinear mathematics.

When psychological phenomena are usefully modeled using nonlinear methods, we are not only inevitably ignorant (in the sense of being unable to predict behavior), but we also have an intimate knowledge of our ignorance. For example, as discussed in the previous chapter, though we are unable to predict the moment-to-moment manifest behavior of a highly ambivalent person, we can state that it is subject to sudden shifts between two states in response to minimal stimuli. If the phenomenon can be shown to be appropriately modeled by catastrophe theory, it can be demonstrated that only seven types of catastrophe can be operative. As a result, our practical focus shifts from a search for more detailed knowledge of quantity to an examination of phenomena to discover which sort of catastrophe is in effect. More generally, if we recognize that some form of nonlinear model might explain a phenomenon being studied rather than simply collecting ever more data, our attention should shift to identifying what sort of nonlinear process might be occurring and then collecting data to help differentiate among possibilities (Guastello and Gregson, 2011). This is a relatively benign kind of ignorance. It leaves us with a surprising but still knowable world.

A more disturbing sort of ignorance results from the analyst's inevitable effect on the patient. Such effects have long been familiar in that the analyst provides a preconscious focus for transference and thereby functions in a way that is analogous to day residues in dream formation. The nature of the patient's unconsciousness is elucidated by the recognition that transference manifestations are the result of the day residue and the transference from the unconscious. If the analyst can identify both the day residue and the transference manifestation, he is able to determine the remaining term—the patient's unconscious fantasy. The model is roughly that of a beam of light shining through an object—knowing the nature of the initial light and the light that emerges, we are able to determine things about the nature of the object through which the light passed.

We know this model does not adequately describe psychoanalysis; analysis affects the patient, and it is therapeutic. Even though basic structures may remain relatively unaltered or at least retain their form, the fact of therapeutic change indicates that analytic procedures alter the observed substrate. Even this is not altogether unsatisfactory. Processes that alter what is observed may at least tell us what was there originally (as chemical analysis often does). The most distressing and most likely effect, however, is that the observed is altered by the process of observation in a way that is only partially knowable. This would be analogous to the Heisenberg uncertainty principle in which it is recognized that the process of observation itself changes the observed so that its pre-observational state can never be precisely known. In psychoanalysis, the situation is further complicated because analysts themselves are changed by the experience of analyzing.

The severity of ignorance is somewhat relieved if we attempt to characterize it. We quickly observe what is essentially tautological but also a matter of clinical experience—stable configurations are relatively unaffected by a variety of things the analyst does, and unstable or absent configurations are greatly affected.[2] The analyst's capacity to affect psychic configurations is a measure of the stability of that configuration. As an illustration, consider again a beam of light passing through an object. If this object is extremely stable in its chemical and physical structure, the passage of the beam of light will not affect it in any significant way. In contrast, if this is not the case, say if the chemicals in the object are photosensitive like photograph film, the very method of observation will alter the structure, e.g. by bleaching or melting. Further, the nature of these alterations will be determined by properties of the light itself (wave length and intensity).

The alteration and creation of psychic configuration through observation may be illustrated by depressive affect for which many people lack adequate language. If in the course of treatment the analyst provides words, or helps the analysand find words, for previously unverbalized and unverbalizable experiences, entirely new processes are initiated by this step alone (Fonagy *et al.*, 2002), and the nature of the depressive experience is transformed simply by putting it into words. However, the analyst's action is necessary for the observation to take place (Anthony, 1975). The process of putting ideas, fantasy, and emotion into words is generally recognized as shaping the experience itself (e.g. Whorf, 1956; Wittgenstein, 1968).

"Inexact interpretation" may also produce new configurations as "the patient seizes upon the inexact interpretation and converts it into a displacement substitute" (Glover, 1931, p. 356). These may be like religious conversion experiences. For example, a borderline patient came across a book on sadism and "recognized" that he was a sadist. He then took on many of the characteristics described in the book.

Observing that a new process is initiated is in itself a datum of the greatest importance. The degree to which the analyst's activity shapes what emerges becomes not merely a warning to avoid the delusional notion that what is thereby discovered existed prior to its discovery, but it also provides us with the information of the instability (or absence) of preexisting structure.

Patients for whom the analytic material is relatively uninfluenced by the analyst's activity have highly stable psychological configurations. Their analysis, modeled on the analyst as day residue, will be slightly influenced by the nature of the analyst's activity. The difference between compliance and instability may be illustrated by highly stable character defenses. The obsessional patient who complies with the analyst's demand that he be more affective will carefully mimic affective experience in an obsessional way. The analyst quickly realizes that nothing basic has changed and further appreciates the stability of the character defenses.

In contrast, groups of patients' analyses are profoundly influenced by the analyst's activity. It is customary to see the differences in the findings of these analyses as a reflection of the inadequacy of the analyst's theory and technique. The "true" underlying configurations are then debated as if they were independent of the analytic process. The assumption that there is a true underlying configuration is often mistaken. From the point of view of this chapter, we may assume instead that these variations are indications of the instability or absence of these configurations prior to analysis. Consider the two major theories that attempt to explain middle-range pathology, i.e. borderline and narcissistic conditions (Kernberg, 1975; Kohut, 1971, 1977). They are radically divergent in their characterizations of the psychodynamics of these conditions. Both authors provide convincing clinical evidence for the validity of their theories, and both authors have large communities of analysts who practice on the basis of those theories. If we grant that both sets of clinical observations are valid, the most important datum about the patients becomes that their analyses can be supported by radically different formulation. The fact that the stable configurations that are ultimately demonstrated depend strongly on the analyst's technique suggests that the configurations are products of the analysis. They did not antedate the analysis. We can conclude that there was a relative absence of stable configurations before the analyses.[3]

Pine (1974) has come to a similar conclusion from his observation that it is difficult to specify the nature of borderline pathology. In his clinical exploration of borderline conditions in childhood, he says,

> Much of the general use of the concept "borderline" is somewhat fuzzy, it seems to me, because the phenomena are fuzzy. … A geologist may describe the shape of a stone with precision; but not so a meteorologist a cloud. Some of the children who have been described as borderline have the quality of changing shape, a fluidity, which is far less characteristic of the neurotic child. The apparent imprecision in description may itself be a reflection of the imprecision, i.e., the absence of clear structure in some of these children (p. 350).

(Incidentally, this is a beautiful example of using the fact of one's ignorance to gain insight into the situation being studied.)

The viewpoint of this chapter implies that psychic structure has a spectrum of instability, the details of which are knowable through the study of our ignorance. It is to be hoped that we will not feel obliged to pay undue attention to the search for nonexistent, preexisting configurations in our patients but rather will wonder whether our ignorance reflects the absence or instability of what we are attempting to know. Like other sciences, psychoanalysis can benefit by both recognizing and eliminating areas of ignorance. However, the very unknowability of a structure indicates the most important fact about it—its instability.

Notes

1 An earlier version of this chapter appeared in the *Annual of Psychoanalysis*, 8:77–82, 1980.

2 Configurations refer to a set of elements and the relations among these elements. The elements may be "psychic structures," "actions," "functions," "thoughts," "fantasies," etc. In particular, this discussion does not depend on a reified notion of psychic structure, nor, for that matter, is it incompatible with such a notion.

3 Two alternative hypotheses are (1) that despite their apparent overlap, Kernberg and Kohut are talking about different patient populations, and (2) that the therapeutic effects observed derive from something other than the analysts' conscious interventions. The first hypothesis seems unlikely based on the authors' clinical descriptions and the latter based on both authors having demonstrated thorough descriptions of clinical process how specific interpretations affected the analytic process.

Chapter 3

Chaotic Possibilities

Toward a New Model of Development[1]

Most psychoanalytic models of development and change assume an orderly, sequential, and predetermined unfolding of psychological functions and structures. Interferences with this orderly unfolding challenge the individual and may lead to pathology. These models derive from a worldview associated with the descriptions of change through linear differential equations, which predict a smooth, orderly world. The study of complex systems and their associated nonlinear dynamics predicts a very different kind of world: a world with abrupt changes, discontinuities, idiosyncratic developmental lines, and disproportions between causes and effects.

The worldview of nonlinear dynamics suggests new possibilities for the psychoanalytic model of change and development and invites confrontation with the adequacy of many widely accepted models. These new possibilities include discontinuous, sudden, and qualitative shifts not only in manifest behavior but also in in-depth psychological functioning.

Concepts of development rank second only to clinical experience in shaping analytic theory and practice. Despite its diversity, most analytic thought about development follows a pattern Freud borrowed from late nineteenth century embryology in which preset steps smoothly unfold to yield a mature organism. Pathology can often be described as the result of derailments in normal developmental sequences. Most analytic debates about development focus on which of several sequential models is most useful in conceptualizing normal and disturbed development.

Developmental ideas, acknowledged or not, pervade analytic theory and practice (Fonagy and Target, 2003). Many analysts work as though paths of development are well-established facts[2] and could be used with confidence in thinking about clinical work, although this attitude is less common today than it was for much of the history of psychoanalysis. With the appearance of competing developmental theories and the general lessening of theoretical–technical rigidity, this attitude has shifted. In their clinical work, many contemporary analysts try to remain flexible, examining how well various developmental models apply to particular patients. Even so, we continue to listen to what patients say, using specific developmental theories and general concepts of development. Some of these concepts have become so much part of analytic thinking that they remain unquestioned. By introducing ideas of nonlinear dynamics into the study of development in psychoanalysis, I hope to enlarge the range of pictures available to clinicians and raise awareness of implicit conceptualization that informs clinical understanding.

The basic psychoanalytic model, the assumption of developmental sequences, may be questioned. The study of nonlinear dynamics suggests alternatives to the sequential model. This chapter first explores conceptualizations of development commonly used in psychoanalysis. Then some ideas from nonlinear dynamics relevant to thinking about development are described. While describing each of these ideas, I give examples of how the concept is relevant to a psychoanalytic understanding of development. Throughout this chapter, brief clinical examples are given, *not* as evidence of the theory and certainly not to provide a full analytic understanding of the material but rather to point the analytic reader toward the type of clinical issues illuminated by nonlinear dynamics.

The Idea of Development in Psychoanalysis

Freud's discovery that neurosis originates in early childhood experience, combined with his long-standing interest in embryology, led him to explore psychological development. Analysts clarified developmental models. However, starting with Freud, they recognized that the many factors operating on and within the child, combined with the difficulty of assessing these factors, severely limited the application of developmental concepts to individuals. Clinicians commonly use developmental models as heuristic guides to understanding analysands. Many analysts are convinced that development almost always follows specified outlines—psychopathology and therapeutic progress can be described by reference to the individual's developmental status. Contemporary clinicians are less likely than earlier analysts to try to force the stories of individual lives to the template of developmental theory. Still, despite variations in its use, the underlying model of normal development and its variations was unquestioned until recently.

Freud's vision of the relationship between development, psychopathology, and treatment is founded in the idea that psychopathology results from development gone awry. Specific failures of development result in specific pathology, in the same way that specific embryonic damage results (or at least was believed to result) in specific lesions in the mature organism (Sulloway, 1979). To truly cure, treatment must undo the effects of failed development, preferably creating a situation closely approximating undisturbed development. Freud (1905a, 1908, 1909a, b, 1914a, b, 1916–17, 1923b, 1926, 1940), Abraham (1924), and Reich (1949, 1975) pioneered descriptions of the impact of psychosexual developmental problems, building a magnificently inclusive description of personal distress and character based on developmental variations.

Later, psychoanalytic theorists elaborated these ideas. They often focused on aspects of development not included by other theorists. Some argued that the early analysts were mistaken in their descriptions of development. Yet the underlying strategy remained similar to Freud's—normal sequences of development, their variations, and the consequence of these variations for later psychological life were described. Klein (1923, 1928, 1935, 1937, 1945, 1957, 1969), Winnicott (1945–58, 1953, 1958, 1960a, 1962, 1963a, b, 1965), Mahler (1952, 1958, 1968, 1971, 1972; Mahler *et al.*, 1975), Kohut (1966, 1971, 1977), Gedo and Goldberg (1973), and Lichtenberg (1975, 1979, 1983), to mention but a few, followed this strategy.

Among major psychoanalytic thinkers, Anna Freud (1965) uniquely suggested that the fact of development, rather than its particulars, deserves a central place in analytic thinking. The concept of developmental lines arose from the observation that the concordant development of id, ego, and superego, so beautifully outlined by Abraham, fit poorly with observations of children. Anna Freud also argued that the interaction of developmental lines is as important as the individual lines themselves. Clinical experience taught her that correlating children's development with age-typical norms failed to provide clear pictures of normal and disturbed childhoods. Instead, she underlined that the failure of developmental progress is the central feature of childhood psychopathology. When development progresses, she said, even if it deviates from a norm, the child has engaged the major psychological task of childhood. When development does not progress, the child is disturbed, even though symptoms and other indicia of pathology are absent. Anna Freud concurred with earlier theorists that psychological development moved toward a final goal and referred to in the "drive to the completion of development."

Anna Freud's student Erik Erikson (1958, 1963, 1964, 1968, 1978, 1982, 1984) enlarged the study of development in another direction. Freud's depiction of development was unappealing in that development is described as essentially complete (but for some modification at puberty) with the resolution of the Oedipus complex. Jung (1933, 1954) challenged this idea and was the first to describe development as ordinarily lifelong. Within Freudian psychoanalysis, Peter Blos Sr. (1941, 1962, 1967, 1968) and Anna Freud (1958), among others, suggested that adolescence was a period of further development. But even these writers, consistent with their picture of development as moving toward completion, held that psychological and physical development shared an endpoint in late adolescence. Erikson posited that development continues across the life course. Two currently popular psychoanalytic ideas center on life-course development. One describes a lifelong process of separation-individuation (Panel, 1973a, b; Schafer, 1973, 1976a, b; Henderson, 1980; Rangell, 1989). Another describes the self and its relation to others as transformed across life course (Cohler and Galatzer-Levy, 1990; Galatzer-Levy and Cohler, 1993).

In 1924, Abraham was able to summarize the then-current knowledge of development in a neat chart. Reviewing later psychoanalytic concepts of development, we note that, except for Anna Freud's model, they all can be encompassed in variations on Abraham's (1924) developmental chart. Analysts as diverse as Erikson (1963) and Gedo and Goldberg (1973) summarize their conceptualizations using such charts. In all these models, development is described as occurring in an orderly series of steps roughly tied to the person's age. Satisfactory progress in each step is necessary for the full engagement in the next step. Psychoanalytic developmental theories share this feature with a wide range of developmental theories from other traditions (Case, 1992).

Many psychoanalytic controversies center on which of these models, so similar in the sense of positing an orderly sequential unfolding of psychological function, is most satisfactory. Klein vs. Anna Freud, Kohut vs. ego-psychology, and ego-psychology vs. id-psychology are each controversies about which of these sequential tables the analyst should use. A central question of analytic technique might be formulated as follows: Given a developmental model, how is the patient to be moved from a less adaptive, more immature position on its chart, to a more adaptive, more mature position?

Clinical experiences as well as teaching, writing about, and explaining human development show how useful the idea of orderly sequential development can be. These models organize and make sense of vast and disparate data; they clarify communication; and they are among our most powerful tools for understanding the psychological world. Only the concepts of conflict, unconscious psychological process, and the self come close to being as useful in describing psychological life. The sequential developmental paradigm is so powerful that it appears natural and inescapable to many of us.

However, the seeming naturalness of conceptualizing development as an orderly sequence may derive from its familiarity. This familiarity results in part because the psychoanalytic developmental paradigm rests on earlier and pervasive ideas about development. Reviewing how these ideas entered psychoanalysis helps clarify why they appear so natural. Freud directly borrowed the idea that psychological development is sequential from his study of embryology (Sulloway, 1979).

For Freud, the pertinent general findings were as follows:

1 Embryological development is ordered and complex. How the embryo builds to its final organization may not be obvious, but each step in the developmental sequence is part of an orderly process.
2 Wilhelm Roux showed that specific lesions of the embryo consistently produce specific later developmental changes and pathology. Because of the complexity of embryonic development, the impact of a particular lesion can only be understood as it affects the overall embryonic development.

3 Using Haeckel's principle that ontogeny recapitulates phylogeny, and equating social with biological evolution, Freud posited that less socially and psychologically evolved communities would manifest similar features to the immature members of more evolved societies.

Only the last of these three major ideas has dropped from current psychoanalytic thinking. In addition to the embarrassment it caused by implying that whole societies are infantile and inferior, it was also empirically found to be false, as was Haeckel's original notion (Gould, 1977) about the relationship of ontogeny and phylogeny. However, the other two should have been dropped. As it turns out, the experimental data from which Roux made his generalization was not as strong as his writings suggested (Needham, 1959) and the link between lesion and outcome is not as strong as Freud believed. In addition, the apparent rigid unfolding of development found in early embryologic studies is now understood to be far less clear and far more contingent on the embryo's environment than was believed until recently (Dusheck, 2002).

In addition to its great utility, Freud's basic model has survived partly because it has had no significant competitor and partly because, as a result of their own analyses, most analysts are convinced about the impact of early experience on later development in the manner Freud suggested. Successful personal analyses almost always produce a convincing and ever clearer story of the analysand's development. These stories are therapeutically useful (Bakhtin, 1981; Schafer, 1992; Bruner, 2011). To be therapeutically effective, they must conform to the requirements of the genre to which they belong, in this case, psychoanalytic explanation, which includes the notion of developmental sequences. In other words, the powerful personal experiences emerging of their personal analysis that convince many analysts of the correctness of psychoanalytic developmental theory are often convincing precisely because they conform to the analyst's preexisting vision of a good developmental story. Thus, most analysts have an intense and convincing experience that seems to support the sequential view of development. This experience-based conviction is easily confused with the much more comprehensive notions of sequential development on which Freud and later psychoanalytic investigators' work rests.

Problems with the Standard Psychoanalytic Model of Development

Because the assumption that development occurs in an orderly sequence is so powerful, it has neither been widely questioned nor has data supporting its broad assumptions been widely doubted. Almost from the beginning, Freud recognized that limitations in our knowledge of individual lives and the complexity of the processes of development made prediction impractical in psychoanalysis. In a brilliant paper, which presages some of the ideas of nonlinear dynamics, Waelder (1963) built on Freud's concept of over determination to try to explain why prediction is not possible in a complex system like the mind.

The hermeneutic trend in psychoanalysis, as represented, for example, in the work of Schafer (1992), is one source of questions about the claims of developmental theories. Schafer takes the view that, in analysis and in other constructions of personal meaning, people's stories of their own development—their *beliefs* about the impact of past events—shape psychological life. For example, in the novel and movie *Cold Comfort Farm* (Gibbons, 1932; Schlesinger, 1996), the story generated by a grandmother's currently recalled belief that she had seen something nasty in a woodshed shapes her own and her family's lives. The belief in the developmental impact of this event, not the event's direct psychological impact, has a profound effect. The story is comic because the grandmother's vision of development is close to our own. The grandmother and her family make the same mistake we do, believing that bad events inevitably affect and explain subsequent development. The novel and movie share a punch line and carry the same relief, namely, that it is the belief rather than the event that shapes us. Thus, we are freer than we had thought. Schafer's cogent idea that it is the currently told story of past events rather than the causal effects of past actualities that shapes psychological life is a major strike against Freud's developmentalism.

A second problem with the sequential developmental viewpoint in psychoanalysis is that, for specifically psychoanalytic concepts, data about the sequences of development is poor. Its primary source is the psychoanalytic reconstruction of past occurrences, and these reconstructions are largely based on the assumption of meaningful developmental sequences. For example, the careful descriptions of individual cases at the end of *Psychological Birth of the Human Infant* (Mahler *et al.*, 1975) assume the developmental sequence they purport to evidence. None of the children described in detail proceeds through development in the manner predicted by the theory. Mahler and her co-workers explain the deviations, but this leaves the data in an unsatisfactory state as a support for her underlying assumptions. Unlike the biological research that led Freud to his epigenetic model, we have no equivalent of tens of thousands of slides of embryos regularly repeating developmental sequences, nor do we have clear demonstration that specific developmental lesions regularly produce specific adult pathology. In fact, we have considerable data to the contrary.

Empirical studies of early development showed that expected continuities often did not occur. Kagan's (1978) path-breaking studies of infants raised in states that appeared to be of severe deprivation only to emerge by age eight as apparently healthy children led him to question the idea of continuity as the dominant theme of development and to empirically demonstrate, in a variety of contexts, that developmental discontinuities and variant paths to similar endpoints are common in human development (Kagan, 2000). Building on Kagan's observations and integrating them with psychoanalytic conceptualization, Emde (1995; Emde and Spicer, 2000) showed that developmental creativity—in essence, surprising turns in development—is a central feature of normal development, especially in the face of adversity.

The prospective study of psychopathology has given substantial support to the idea that discontinuity is common in development. Cicchetti (1996; Luthar *et al.*, 2000; Cicchetti and Rogosh, 2002) demonstrated that the absence of ordinary discontinuities can lead to pathology and that "resilience" may arise from taking a fortunate path in discontinuous developmental processes. Sameroff (1995; Sameroff and Fiese, 2000a, b) shows that the limitations of predictions based on individual and environmental factors result from the inherently complex structures of interaction between the child and infant and its environment. These complex structures are, by their nature, nonlinear and exhibit significant discontinuities. Psychoanalysts are not alone in this difficulty. Reviewing the literature on psychological developmental studies of all types, Lewis (1997) observes that, while much data has been gathered to explore how presumed developmental sequences vary in populations, data supporting the existence of such sequences are rare.

The fundamental developmental model in psychoanalysis is not in a satisfactory state. It is retained because the model offers a solution to key questions about mental function by providing a picture of how it emerges. It appears to solve the glaring puzzle of how something so complex as the human psyche can exist. But its foundation in observation is weak, and, as I show later, it is inconsistent with what we know about the emergence of order in complex systems generally.

Order and Its Genesis

When we encounter complex orderly systems, including psychological systems, an obvious question is how they came to be. Researchers in the seventeenth century argued for the homuncular theory of development, which posits that each germ cell contains a physical model of the mature organism with a plan for the organism's development. The theory's advocates recognized that it was problematic. (For example, the model would have to contain mini-models of all future generations.) However, these theorists were unable to think of another mechanism to transmit information about how to build an animal. In fact, lacking a general concept of information, they could not clearly formulate the problem but struggled with it in inchoate form.

Richard Wolff, an eighteenth-century biologist, proposed a radically different model: epigenesis. The model postulated that development consisted in the progressive time-specific differentiation of cell types to produce mature organisms. Epigenetic models provide a way to talk about how complex organisms emerge from apparently simple beginnings. The mechanism of epigenesis remained mysterious, but the principle at least partially describes the recurring finding that new structure appears to emerge from nowhere. In today's language, we would say that, in some sense, precursor cells carry the program for the organism's development, and embryology's task is to describe that program and how it is implemented.

Only recently have plausible explanations of this process become available. The explanation of how the information moves from its encryption in DNA to the elaborate organisms we see is the current major theme of developmental biology. The basic model has also evolved so that it is now clear that epigenesis, whatever its mechanisms, is contingent on the environment in which the organism is developing.

The logic of the epigenetic position seems unassailable. You cannot get something for nothing. There must be a mechanism that explains the complex structures that we observe, and the only conceivable mechanism is that those structures are coded in the physical material transmitted from cell to cell. In similar fashion, it would appear unassailable that some program for psychological development needs to be transmitted and results in personal development.

For us, epigenetic models have very much the same status that homuncular models had for those who believed in them. Because believers in homuncular theories could see no other way than the germ cell containing a small model of the mature organism by which information about mature structure could be transmitted, they were wedded to the theory. So, too, finding it impossible to conceptualize other than variations on epigenetic models by which complex order can emerge from undifferentiated beginnings, we remain committed to epigenetic models.

Another Model for Developmental Processes

Four decades ago, a new picture of the nature of processes in general began to emerge. In his amazing book *Structural Stability and Morphogenesis: An Outline of a General Theory of Models*, Rene Thom (1975) made two observations—one mathematical and one psychological. Understanding the central mathematical idea is relatively easy. Differential equations describe how things change. Most of the laws of the physical sciences can be expressed as differential equations. Until the middle of the twentieth century, mathematicians focused their study on a group of equations called linear differential equations. The reason for this focus was essentially practical. A lot could be said about linear differential equations, while nonlinear differential equations were very much harder to tackle. With some important exceptions, the approach to nonlinear differential equations was to approximate them by linear ones, even though it was well understood that this effort was fundamentally flawed.

Linear differential equations, when used to describe the world, predict a smooth, orderly universe on every level. Their mathematics correspond to a world that makes sense to our modern intuition—an orderly, sequential world in which effects are roughly proportionate to causes. Linear differential equations were so startlingly effective in the physical sciences that mathematician Eugene Wigner wrote a paper titled "The unreasonable effectiveness of mathematics" (1960) underlining how astonishing it is that the predictions made through mathematical computations so accurately predict events in the real world.

Thom's mathematical result was the description of the fundamental configuration of certain types of nonlinear differential equations in their own right, not as approximations of linear differential equations. He found that these equations did not describe a smooth, orderly world but rather a world that was fundamentally jumpy and disorderly—although jumpy and disorderly in an orderly way. To emphasize the qualitatively different, jumpy, disorderly world described by the equations he studied, Thom humorously called the abrupt changes "catastrophes" and named his theory "catastrophe theory."

Thom's psychological discussion was also spectacular. He asserted that the "unreasonable effectiveness of mathematics" in the physical sciences does not result from a mysterious coordination of the human mind and nature but from systematic, unconscious inattention to intractable problems, simply not noticing phenomena that could not be explored mathematically. For example, the beautiful classical theory of "water waves" simply omits surf, even though every student of water waves has seen it (Stoker, 1957). The omission was not rationalized. No one said surf was unimportant or uninteresting. It was not even stated that the problem of surf was intractable and so would be put aside. When it could not be incorporated in the theory, surf became effectively invisible. Thom believes we do not perceive data for which we have no theoretical approach, and, if we do not entirely ignore it, we quickly put it aside and pursue it no further. When information becomes somewhat theoretically tractable, it becomes interesting, and relevant phenomena are observed.

Thom's observations apply particularly well to a discipline like psychoanalysis in which the analyst's efforts to make sense of patients' associations inevitably involve preconscious selections of the portion of the data to which the analyst attends. When data fit within a preexisting theory, the analyst likely observes them, but when they lie outside that theory, the analyst does not even note them. For example, Quinodoz (1999) describes the apparently paradoxical anxiety dreams that follow periods of successful working through. In the absence of an adequate theory to explain the dynamics of these dreams, they were largely understood as indicators of incomplete working through or new anxiety-arousing material emerging in the analysis. However, armed with a theory that allowed him to understand this type of dream as a capstone of the working-through process, Quinodoz was able to observe them repeatedly in analyses. Data which would otherwise have remained invisible became visible when the observer had a theory that could encompass them.

Thom's catastrophe theory was soon followed by further developments under names like "chaos theory," "the theory of fractals," and "nonlinear dynamical systems theory." What these points of view share is a new picture of the world that includes discontinuity, manifest disorder and jaggedness, and attention to systems that are complex (at least in comparison to the systems studied in the classical physical sciences). This new model has been applied to an ever-widening range of disciplines, including history (Gaddis, 2002), the study of marriage (Gottman *et al.*, 2002), and brain function (Haken, 2002). The major finding was that, far from being truly chaotic and disorganized, the world as studied by chaos theory is organized but organized profoundly differently from the way we are accustomed to thinking of organization. Furthermore, these new forms of organization are intrinsic properties of complex systems.

A word about intuition, many of the findings of chaos and complexity theory seem counterintuitive. But intuitions are largely prejudices developed over time. For people in technologically advanced societies, these prejudices commonly result from living in a world carefully engineered to behave in an orderly way. For example, the "intuition" that a car's acceleration is smoothly proportional to the amount of gasoline fed to the engine arises partly because automobiles are carefully engineered so that acceleration is proportional to the depression of the gas pedal. In fact, the amount of gas fed to the engine is not proportional to how far the gas pedal is depressed. Recognizing that our intuition arises in a world carefully engineered to behave linearly makes the question of whether an idea is or is not intuitive less impressive.

On a more psychological level, coherent personal and group narratives contribute to people's sense of organization, effectiveness, and meaning. This sense of well-being is only loosely tied to the narrative being a veridical description of the past. The shift from the medieval worldview, in which everything has meaning because everything reflects the deity's intentions, to the modern view that the physical world obeys impersonal natural laws was largely resisted because of the decreased sense of meaning inherent in the modern view (Lewis, 1964). Similarly, theories suggesting that the world often does not operate linearly, in a way consistent with current ideas of coherent narrative, are distressing and only reluctantly accepted.

Consequences of Nonlinear Dynamics for Concepts of Development

What major changes in the worldview result from the chaos theory? First, we learn of a whole world of possible new structures. The great beauty of this world is now familiar in terms of fractal designs (see, for example, Mandelbrot, 1982; Barnsley, 1988; Devaney and Keen, 1989; or websites such as Sprott, 2002). Fractals are patterns of enormous complexity generated by simple rules. They usually contain elements that, on magnification, have structures qualitatively similar to but distinct from the fractal of which they form a part. Fractals are pertinent to psychoanalysis because their existence shows that structures of enormous complexity can be generated by simple rules. In an earlier chapter, I demonstrate how the apparent complexity of obsessional symptoms can be described as built up from self-similar patterns over very different time scales. The monthlong oscillations of the obsessional's functioning, being composed of oscillations in attitudes, manifest time frames of about an hour, which in turn emerge from alternating attitudes lasting several minutes, which are themselves composed of speech patterns, which, over time frames of seconds, exhibit the same type of alternating positions.

Another group of structures that is important in the study of dynamical systems is "strange attractors." An attractor is a pattern of motion toward which a system tends over time. For example, if a heavenly body comes sufficiently close to the sun, it will either be pulled into it, pass it by after deviating in its path of motion toward the sun, or come to orbit the sun. Each of these patterns is an attractor for the motion of the body. The motion of the body need not actually follow the pattern of the attractor, but rather the motion tends toward the attractor. Descriptions of attractors often do not represent the motion directly. For example, if two similar pendulum clocks are hung on a wall together, their pendulums, after a time, will become synchronized. This synchrony is an attractor for the system of the two clocks.

Intuition—problems of which I discussed earlier—suggests that systems will, over time, settle into stable patterns of relatively simple motion, such as oscillation between a small number of states. The study of nonlinear dynamics demonstrates that this is often not so. There are perfectly well-defined patterns of motion that lead to sudden jumps between seemingly stable configurations. Such systems never settle into a simple pattern of motion but instead, abruptly and without obvious reason, shift from one pattern to a qualitatively different configuration. When a system has attractors in which abrupt qualitative changes in motion occur, it is said to have strange attractors. (It should be noted that the term *motion* is used in the broad sense of change in the system and is not limited to change in position with time.) Strange attractors almost always result when the equations governing the system are nonlinear.

Familiar examples of such changes include phase changes in substances. At ordinary pressures, water changes from ice to liquid at 0°C and from liquid to gas (steam) at 100°C. The change is abrupt: At one temperature, water is in one form, at another, in the other. Given time to come to equilibrium, the temperature completely determines the water's state. There are no intermediate states. From many points of view, ice, liquid water, and steam are qualitatively different substances, with markedly different physical properties.

The apparently qualitative shifts associated with strange attractors have broad implications for our picture of development. First, they lead us to recognize that dramatic shifts may reflect real and deep changes in configuration, not merely superficially changed manifestations. For example, the shift in psychological function that commonly occurs between ages five and seven (Shapiro and Perry, 1976)—the shift into "latency"—is described from the point of view of classical theory as the manifest result of the strengthening of the superego that comes with the first resolution of the Oedipus complex and the simultaneous weakening of erotic drives. Although the resulting manifest behavior changes, the child's underlying dynamics remain unchanged. Only the quantity of the various elements shifts. The concept of strange attractors suggests that, instead of being simply a shift in the surface of behavior, the shift may have resulted in an entirely new pattern of psychodynamics being in force and that the underlying pattern, as well as the superficial behavior, has altered.

Taken further, the study of strange attractors suggests that systems may move between entirely different regimens in highly unpredictable ways, which may either be entirely intrinsic to the system or result from minuscule perturbations of it. One of the best-studied strange attractors is the Lorenz attractor, which is characterized by extended episodes of nearly periodic behavior, which suddenly and unpredictably shift to an entirely different periodic behavior, only to return after a time to the original periodic behavior. In the case of the Lorenz attractor, these shifts are intrinsic to the system and do not result from any perturbation at all. In toddler development, it is common to see movements back and forth between clinging behavior and vigorous assertions of autonomy. Several analytic theories characterize the shifts as resulting from conflicting, mutually incompatible motives, whose relative ascendance determines how the child behaves at a particular moment.

The theory of strange attractors suggests that a better description of this situation is that the child's behavior reflects an underlying Lorenz-like attractor, with the intrinsic feature of two very different regimens and shifts between them that are intrinsic to the attractor itself. Consideration of this possibility spares us from looking for motives for shifts when intrinsic characteristics of the system lead to those shifts. It also focuses our attention on the nature of the system itself and its careful description.

The world of linear equations may be roughly characterized by rules like big changes have big results, small changes have small ones; simple causes yield simple results, and complex causes have complex results. The world of nonlinear dynamics has very different rules. Small causes *can* give very large changes; simple causes *can* yield very complex results. A popular example of small changes causing big results is a classic finding of chaos theory—the butterfly effect—that under appropriate circumstances, a flap of a butterfly's wing in

Sumatra can determine whether Chicago will have a snowstorm five days later (Stewart, 2002).

Assumptions about the relationship between the intensity of cause and effect can lead analysts to misinterpret clinical data about development. A clinical example illustrates this point. Ms. R, whose mother died during her second year, was raised by a father whose severe compulsions were interrupted by moments of extreme violence against her other caretaker, a sister five years older. As the sister moved into her teens, she became psychotically phobic and demanded Ms. R's constant attention. In late adolescence, Ms. R developed progressively severe obsessional symptoms and anxiety states, including frequent panic attacks. Despite her horrendous background and continued symptoms, Ms. R did well academically and married a man who was tender, respectful and warm. In the ninth month of her pregnancy with her first child, Ms. R attended a movie. Suddenly, a near-hallucinatory image of her sister and father lying in coffins appeared on the screen. At that moment, her symptoms disappeared, not to return again for six years. Then her symptoms recurred with great intensity, leading her to enter an analysis, which, despite lasting almost half a century, appeared to have little effect beyond holding her together at a low level of function. As she described it in a subsequent analysis with me, her analyst, a widely respected clinician, treated her sudden remission as "unreal," and tried to show her that her life had not miraculously changed in a moment and that her belief that it had changed her life resulted from an identification with her father's magical thinking and was false.

Because the analyst is deceased, we have only the patient's statement about his attitude. However, the attitude she attributes to him is consistent with views he expressed repeatedly as a teacher. The analyst's assumptions in this regard were consistent with commonly held ideas about the proportionality of change to cause and the idea that dramatic manifest transformations are unlikely to reflect change in depth. Except that the analyst persisted in his position despite the treatment lasting so long and going so badly, most psychoanalysts would probably adopt some version of his position. In a subsequent analysis, I considered the possibility that something had really changed and that a qualitative shift in function had resulted from quantitative changes in the forces acting within her. This not only fit better with the patient's experience and her rich description of it, but it also opened what turned out to be the therapeutically useful idea that real change was possible despite the patient's advanced age of eighty-five. The appreciation of discontinuity, as well as continuity, and the capacity to recognize that change need not be proportionate to cause opened new analytic possibilities based on a concept of development arising from nonlinear dynamics.

To understand why nonlinear dynamics is the appropriate framework for understanding systems like the mind, we need to look briefly at the history of the mathematical understanding of the natural world. Until the middle of the twentieth century, research and mathematical models were limited to those systems in which simple rules resulted in simple solutions. From Newton's demonstration that a simple law of gravitation could exist, through innumerable successes in describing physical systems over the last four centuries, scientists repeatedly showed that simple systems could be generated by even simpler laws. Much of the success of this program resulted from focusing on real systems that could be well approximated by simple models. For example, the solar system can be described well by ignoring the interactions between the planets themselves (that is, solving the problem as though only each planet's interaction with the sun mattered) and then improving the resulting solution by treating the interactions between the planets as perturbations of the resulting regular motions, which can be of only three types (Hurewicz, 1958). However, if we introduce just one more step in our discussion, asking to solve the equations that result if we try to predict the motion of three bodies under gravitation (a problem Newton already proposed), the situation becomes mathematically intractable. Over the last forty years, it has become apparent that highly regular systems, such as Newton studied, are at one end of a spectrum that ranges from great regularity to pervasive irregularity.

The part of that spectrum that is beyond regularity was first noted to be of great practical importance by Weiner (1961), who showed that systems that include feedback are inevitably characterized by complex nonlinear evolution. For a system to learn from the environment's responses to its action, feedback is essential. This is because adaptation requires change in the system. When an adaptive system is perturbed, it must not simply return to its pre-perturbation state.

Rather, adaptive systems must enter new states as a result of experience. Thus, any system that can "learn" is inherently unstable. The capacity to learn carries with it the risk of disorder.

Between absolute order and sheer chaos, there is an area of complexly evolving systems. If complexity and interestingness—the capacity to adapt to changing circumstances—are desired, systems must be on the edge of chaos, a topic to which we will return in a later chapter. Because of the mathematical structure of the capacity to learn, such systems are at risk of two inherent dangers—stagnation, moving into a stable imperturbable configuration, and disorder, where all meaningful regularity is lost.

In fact, we have an example of interesting, complex systems in neural networks. Neural networks are the best models we have of real nervous-system function. They benefit and suffer from the feature that, while they are adaptive in the areas where they function well, they are not predictable nor are they reliable in the way that machines are reliable. Short of running the neural network itself, it is difficult or impossible to predict its detailed behavior. The results of neural networks are often surprising, and small shifts to their input can produce dramatic changes in the output. Neural networks can be "creative" in the sense of developing patterns not anticipated by their designers.

New learning occurs in adaptive systems on the edge of chaos, between the twin dangers of stagnation and disorganization. This suggests that during periods of development, we would expect not to see an orderly unfolding of preprogrammed structures but, instead, periods of relative disorganization. Insofar as there is any underlying program, it would be expected to be an arrangement designed to create a situation at the edge of chaos. During periods of development, people seek out stimuli and explore the world, while at the same time avoiding stimuli of traumatic (i.e. disorganizing) intensity. In certain circumstances, the balance would be expected to be problematic. A great deal of psychopathology can be conceptualized as resulting either from an incapacity to protect against overstimulation or a too-successful effort to avoid such stimulation with the result that little or no new experience occurs. The periods of seeming regression that often accompany the beginning of new developmental phases are examples of such disorganization.

In terms of developmental theory, the most interesting feature of the very complex systems is their underlying simplicity. In the nineteenth century, an argument commonly used in favor of divine creation concerned finding a watch in a desert. Were this to happen, the argument went, we would assume that there was a watchmaker. The complexity of biological organisms, thus, was taken to prove God's existence. Darwin showed the fault in this argument. He demonstrated that the complexity of living organisms could result from natural selection involving no design. Natural selection is an intrinsically simple process requiring only an environment that favors one inheritable form over another. It involves no intention to create squid, bacteria, elms, and people. When complex form results from a process containing no model or blueprint of that form, we speak of "emergence" and call the resulting form "emergent."

Nonlinear dynamics suggests that development can occur by other means than epigenetic unfolding of predetermined developmental lines. In a nonlinear system, configurations need not be specified in advance. The rules generating highly complex systems may be very simple and their relationship to the final structure obscure and unpredictable. If the system needs to adapt or to solve some problem through its ultimate structure, then the end result of the evolution of the nonlinear system is limited to a range of possible solutions. However, the means by which the system reached that state and the details of the ultimate state need not be specified in advance. For example, Thelen and Smith (1994) show that, although young children's walking gait solves the problem of upright locomotion within the parameters imposed by bodily structures, children learn to walk in diverse ways, none of which should be construed as a built-in plan for learning to walk. More broadly, human development may be conceptualized as resulting from certain relatively simple rules of neural network function (Spitzer, 1999) operating within the context of biological needs and individual experiences.

Many predictions based on dynamic system models differ from those based on epigenetic unfolding. These models predict that desirable development may follow many unpredictable routes to satisfactory and often similar outcomes. In this model, new desirable structures may emerge (in the sense described above)—that is, without a preexisting prescription. Atypical development is not necessarily "off track" (in the sense of being undesirable) but should be considered as a possible unexpected developmental route. Because nonlinear development is often surgent, periods where little change occurs do not necessarily represent failed development, nor should very rapid development be automatically equated with superficial or incomplete development. Finally, since development does not have an intrinsic end—that is, it is not the result of an inborn blueprint aimed at a final state—the outcome of development is only properly assessed by its practical consequences, not some pre-formed image of normalcy.

The nonlinear, non-epigenetic model of development suggests a shift of analytic attention away from steps along a developmental line to the processes active in development itself. The presupposition that a normal developmental line must connect early states to mature ones should be abandoned. Research exploring developmental lines must be re-examined with an eye to the question of whether the assumption of the line's existence led to distorted interpretation, the data by which, for example, very different processes were artificially lumped together and described as representing variations on a single process. For example, the shift from relative reliance on caretakers to relative independence that occurs during the toddler period has, at various times, been seen as a derivative of the anal phase, a manifestation of separation-individuation, or a change in the nature of attachment, to name but a few. The beginning and end of the process are fairly clear and easily observed, but the presumptive underlying process is far from clear. While interpretation can shoehorn almost all observations into any one of these models, the fit is often strained. In nonlinear systems models, unlike epigenetic models, the fact that processes share initial and endpoints does not indicate that the paths joining these points are the same. Instead, it leaves us free, in each case, to explore the path taken by the individual and suggests that often multiple paths will occur between various developmental points.

The analyst confronted with a patient who frantically clings to potential caregivers for support needs to no longer ask which developmental line is interrupted, because multiple pathways can lead to the phenomena of relative independence. Similarly, the question of how the patient may be helped to resume development along the path that was earlier interrupted becomes inappropriate, and the quandaries it raises—for example, how the adult analytic patient can be provided with the experiences that promote infants' development—may be put aside. Recognizing that multiple developmental pathways can have essentially similar ends and that the freedom to experience and develop is the core contributor to needed development, the analyst will no longer focus on how to get the patient back on a prescribed developmental path but rather on creating an environment that permits optimal disorganization in which the patient may find novel means for moving forward.

Environmental influences can be more easily integrated into a nonlinear systems model than they can into epigenetic models. In epigenetic models, environmental influences ordinarily complement the unfolding internal program by providing needed supplies for the preprogrammed intrinsic process (Winnicott, 1960b, 1965; Green, 1975). In the epigenetic model, pathology results when the environment either fails to provide needed supplies or distorts the epigenetic process by exposing the child to experiences that turn it away from normal development. In contrast, nonlinear models predict that input from the environment, while essential for development and shaping it, need not complement some preexisting plan. It needs to provide only a sufficiently rich experience that the system can become organized under its influence and a sufficiently calm environment that the developing individual is not thrown into chaos. Experiences will shape resulting development, but how they influence its development is not predictable. In particular, experiences that are generally regarded as untoward may, in this model, lead to desirable developments, not because the damaging consequences are overcome but because the experience is initially integrated into the neural network in a fashion that leads to improved functioning.

Phenomena like "resilience," in which individuals do well despite being exposed to situations that would be presumed to damage development, do not require a special mechanism to explain them. Rather, the phenomena reflect the same underlying mechanism that leads to desirable outcomes. The relative absence of experience leads to stagnation in neural networks so that the model would predict that environmental deprivation, such as occurs, for example, in maternal depression, would be likely to have particularly negative effects on the developing child. It may be that traumatic events actually operate to decrease the input to higher cortical functioning. Sufficiently intense danger results in an interference with the use of cortical processing in favor of more rapid emergency emotional system processing (LeDoux, 1996). Thus, in trauma, the cortical network may be deprived of experience despite the intensity of the external event. Because, once operating in this mode, information reminiscent of the traumatic event sets off processes that continue to block cortical processing of the information, trauma may result in substantially reduced cortical input and operate like deprivation in development.

Even extremely dreadful events, if integrated into the personality, may have stable and valuable developmental consequences. A historical example may be used to illustrate this point. Sixteen-year-old Sojourner Truth, a slave in Upstate New York in the 1830s, passively idealized her owner who had promised to keep Sojourner's family intact. When he sold family members, Sojourner had an apocalyptic experience. Lasting a brief time, it involved an initial sense of profound disappointment, a sudden realization of the presence of God in her life, and a commitment to struggle for the abolition of slavery. This experience appeared to have effected a lasting transformation in her personality that permitted her to act consistently, vigorously, and effectively over six decades to achieve her goals as a major leader, first of the abolitionist and then the feminist movements (Gilbert, 1993; Mabee, 1993; Painter, 1996). A complex, apparently structural change emerged in minutes. The skeptical reader is likely to say that this change must have rested on earlier positive experiences, and, indeed, Sojourner's very bleak childhood seems to have included the loving care of her mother. But the reader should also consider the possibility, based on a nonlinear dynamics model, that the characterological shift described was as dramatic and stable as Sojourner claimed it was.

A nonlinear dynamic system model applies particularly well to systems involving two or more individuals whose developments interact. The idea that developmental processes affect not only the child but also the caretaker was first introduced by Benedek (1959), who suggested that as children pass through various developmental stages their parents re-engage and rework the psychological issues of that period. Subsequent studies, especially of early development, have shown that the caretaker-infant influence is typically bidirectional and is often best described as some sort of synchronization of parent-child function (see, for example, Stern, 1985; Wolff, 1987).

Analysts and infant researchers have been challenged to find ways to describe these complex interactions, which involve a kind of mutual entrainment of schedules and actions. Coupled oscillators (two oscillators, each with its own properties, which have been joined together into a single system by connecting them) have long interested mathematicians and students of dynamical systems. The coupled oscillator system provides a model of the child-caretaker (or analyst-analysand) system. A simple example of coupled oscillators is two pendulums joined by an elastic band. In Chapter 5 on "good vibrations," I describe the coupled system analyst-analysand.

Some of the more interesting features of coupled oscillators include the way in which they come to form regular patterns of motion, the fact that these patterns often involve complex motions, and that neither oscillator may come to a stable state but instead may move between various states. For example, the oscillators may come to alternate high amplitudes of oscillation. The joining of two oscillators results in the emergence of patterns, not only for the system as a whole but for each of the oscillators that would be impossible without this coupling.

Many of the properties of dynamic systems depend on their dimension—that is, the numbers of variables that can change independently of one another (for example, a train running along a track operates in one dimension because its position is determined by one parameter; the shoulder joint is a two-dimensional system because its state is described by two parameters). Phenomena that are impossible in a system of a lower dimension become possible in systems of higher dimensions. The joining together of two individuals into a single unit for the purposes of development effectively creates a higher-dimensional structure in which changes, impossible in the lower-dimensional configuration, become possible. The joining together of child and caretaker effectively produces such a higher-dimensional system, which then allows development in ways that neither person alone could achieve. This may be one reason that the caretaker's psychological investment in a particular child and the development of attunement between child and caretaker is so important. Instead of simply providing responsiveness to the child's independently generated developmental needs, we can think of the relationship as resulting in a new system whose dynamic properties are more than the sum of the properties of the infant and caretaker separately. (Clearly, these ideas apply to the analytic dyad also, but this is a topic for a later chapter.)

Clinical Implication

What can go wrong with a complex system? It can stagnate or become disorganization. These correspond to the two major forms of psychopathology. They are also the basis of a central psychological dialectic. Fear of disorganization commonly leads to defensive organization that is stable but maladaptive, but functional configurations are insufficiently stable and make finding personal meaning, comfort, and satisfying relations with others hard.

Analytic theories of development tend to focus on the various problems people confront and the various solutions they find to those problems. The focus is seldom on the *process* of solution. For example, analysts note that anal phase anxieties are often resolved with obsessive-compulsive defenses. But the process by which this solution is discovered is, at best, hinted at rather than clarified. It is within this context of describing problems and solutions that the various developmental charts were drawn. These charts are misleading. First, they suggest orderly sequential psychological steps in normal development and imply that the goal of analysis should be forward movement along those steps. Second, they suggest that the problems and solutions are most important rather than the processes by which problems engaged and solutions developed.

I suggest that the core feature of normal developmental situations (and, by extension, a central aspect of the analytic setup) lies in the ability to construct a way to solve problems, a means to find a context in which the psychological work that leads from less to more satisfactory solutions can take place. Good problem solution is characterized by the re-establishment of function within the area of complexity—that is, within the area where more complicated development remains possible and neither stasis nor disorganization occurs. This is the area characterized in studies of complex systems as "on the edge of chaos." While it is, of course, important that particular psychological problems be solved, it is even more important that the solution leave room for further development. The person who is terrified by the potential meanings of an idea may avoid the idea by rigid insistence on normative meanings or by evacuating the meaning of the sentence that incorporates the idea. But both approaches destroy the possibility of meaningful further development of the idea.

Take, for example, a person who is discomforted by the idea that it is wise to anticipate future problems and attend to them earlier rather than later, an idea summarized in the proverb, "A stitch in time saves nine." One way to avoid the problem might be to insist on literalness, "There is no such thing as a stitching time, and furthermore you cannot quantify the effects of stitches in this manner, so I need not bother myself with this silly saying." Another might be to engage in clang associations that so widen the meanings of the metaphor as to eliminate that meaning: "The rich bitch witch weaves the future, and every one of her stitches ties down the baby." (In other words, I don't have to plan anything; it's pointless, limiting, and destructive anyway and reminds me of my mother.) As Bion (1959) taught, both of these approaches to language more than adequately defend against awareness of the meaning of the metaphor but do so at the price of destroying the most powerful developmental tool we have: language.

Good development certainly need not be according to some elaborate preordained plan referred to as normal. In fact, any preordained plan will unlikely stand up well to the vicissitudes of life, which inevitably contains surprises for which it is impossible to plan. It is development *per se* that is central to both health and cure.

We may think of development as associated with two factors: one being the adaptational challenge the person faces; the other, the capacity to maintain work within the area of complexity. Problematic or failed development results when the individual lacks the freedom to explore configurations of function in a sufficiently disorganized way that allows new possibilities to emerge.

Mr. M had been an extraordinarily good boy, well-liked by parents, teachers, and friends, all of whom he pleased with his warm consideration. He had a set of elaborate rituals that he needed to perform before sleeping and after using the toilet. These involved keeping "everything in order." As he passed through adolescence and young adulthood, his superficially pleasant manner continued to make him popular with others, but he had an increasing sense of angry frustration because he was not really living a life. Efforts at intimacy were either aborted by inhibitions or ended after he joylessly engaged in a "normal" sexual act. He sought analysis because his life had become an endless series of meaningless performances. Though specific anxieties soon became clear in the analysis, the overarching theme of the analysis was the way that Mr. M responded to any new emotional situation by attempting to find a "normal" response and attempting to use it. No unsolved problems were permitted, and so no truly new solutions had emerged since he adopted the "good boy" posture in latency. Mr. M could not allow himself near the "edge of chaos" and so was doomed to forever repeat his traditional limited solutions to all manner of psychological challenges.

Just as a nonlinear model of development predicts that in many situations long periods of manifest inactivity will occur followed by dramatic developmental change, so, too, it predicts that developmental processes will often not operate by the slow accretion of change but that the process will, in many instances, be characterized by shifts that are preliminary to an abrupt and qualitative change in function. This means that both in development and the analytic situation (Palombo, 1999), abrupt change should not be treated as in any sense unreal but should be recognized as a common way in which change occurs in complex systems.

Analysts who organize their thinking in a linear fashion tend to listen for evidence of continuity in the narratives of analysands' lives. They attempt to show how earlier, if previously unconscious, aspects of character became manifest or were uncovered in apparently abrupt processes, which, when understood in sufficient depth, were not abrupt at all. This attitude minimizes the significance of the manifest, apparently abrupt, change. It puts aside the question of why and how the change occurred abruptly and even suggests that the appearance of abruptness is an illusion arising from a defense against recognizing the unconscious determinants of the change.

Ignoring the manifest discontinuity, or putting it aside as an epiphenomenon, reflects not only an appreciation of unconscious processes whose actions are not available to awareness but also the adoption of a linear worldview that assumes continuity and proportionality of cause and effect. This assumption implies that abrupt changes are never real and therefore require explanations in terms of how and why the analysand has misperceived them as being real.

If we put aside assumptions appropriate to linear systems, we open the question of whether these abrupt but lasting changes in manifest function represent significant reorganization of the personality (i.e. structural change). With the inclusion of this additional possibility, the focus of investigation widens from the search for latent continuities to questions such as whether, in appropriate circumstances, people's minds can become significantly disorganized and then successfully reorganized, or whether, in a particular circumstance, a dramatic but quite real shift in underlying function has occurred.

If we reduce the status of the various epigenetic sequences to mere descriptions of ways people have commonly dealt with the biological and social situations that confront them, and understanding the history that we hear and reconstruct in the psychoanalytic situation as largely shaped by the use to which that history is being placed in the present rather than accurately reflecting past events, we open the possibility of exploring nonlinear processes in normal development and psychoanalysis.[3] Nonlinear models have the advantage that they better fit the data of development and suggest an approach to therapeutics that avoids the implicit expectation that the process will result in the approximation of a putatively normal development sequence. Phenomena like qualitative shifts in functioning and non-pathological variation in development and mature function fit within a nonlinear theory. It suggests an approach to therapeutics in which the major work of the analyst is to provide an environment in which development can be resumed in safety rather than an attempt to achieve any particular developmental aim.

Notes

1 An earlier version of this chapter was published in the *International Journal of Psychoanalysis*, 85:419–442, 2004. Reprinted by permission of John Wiley & Sons, Inc.

2 Interestingly, Freud's first extended discussion of development, his description of psychosexual development in the *Three Essays on the Theory of Sexuality*, contrasts dramatically with other major writings of the first period of psychoanalysis—*Studies in Hysteria, The Interpretation of Dreams, The Psychopathology of Everyday Life*, and *Jokes and Their Relation to the Unconscious*—in that while all of the other books contain exhaustive descriptions of data relevant to their subjects, the *Three Essays* are remarkably devoid of data about child development.

3 Schafer (1992) convincingly demonstrates the curative effects of developing coherent narratives in psychoanalysis. The genres of life narrative that are personally acceptable and that feel authentic are based on the analysands' expectation of a satisfactory narrative, which, when it comes to their own lives, feels like it must be linear. The therapeutic usefulness of a linear narrative should, however, not be confused with evidence that development occurred in the way the narrative indicates. It will be interesting to see, as nonlinear thinking becomes increasingly accepted as part of the general culture, whether increasingly nonlinear narratives will have the same organizing and therapeutic effects that linear narratives have today.

Chapter 4

An Example of Nonlinear Developmental Thinking[1]

Occasionally, I read a paper that is so good that it both moves me deeply and at the same time changes my thinking. I was fortunate in being asked to comment on such a paper in the *Journal of the American Psychoanalytic Association*. It was, among other things, a brilliant illustration of how nonlinear developmental thinking can transform analytic work. In this brilliant clinical paper, Avgi Saketopoulou (2014) provides a stunning integration of theory, empirical studies, and clinical work. She summarizes the clinical portion of the paper,

> ... patients' body dysphoria is often left unaddressed even by analysts who seek to work within their analysands' gendered experience. Through a detailed, in-depth account of work with a five-year-old trans girl (female-identified, male-bodied), the developmental implications of the natal body's not becoming sufficiently mentalized in the course of treatment are tracked and explored. Attention to unconscious fantasy and its transformations shows the importance of helping transgender patients whose bodies are a source of suffering to be able to psychically represent their pain as a critical step in the process of a psychologically healthy transition.

At the beginning of analysis, the child cannot bear any reference to her male body and is thrown into states of enormous distress by any reference to it or even suggestion of such a reference. No progress is possible in dealing with a body that does not fit with the child's gender because that body cannot be the subject of thought. The paper marks a major step in the sea of change in psychoanalytic outlook and practice from a time when analysts acted as part of the oppressive dominant community by pathologizing sexual and gender variation to a time when analysts have largely recognized that these variations represent life ways that are deserving of respect and support, while at the same time maintaining a commitment to an understanding of their multiple significance for people.

In late nineteenth-century Europe and the United States, the possibility of separating sexual activity from reproduction combined with the relaxation of anti-sexual moral attitudes and the recognition that sexual frustration contributes significantly to psychological distress converged to create an intellectual and medical environment that invited the exploration of the complexities of gender and sex. In the mid-nineteenth century, Krafft-Ebing (Krafft-Ebing, Rebman *et al.*, 1939) conceptualized the variations that he found as forms of pathology, thereby moving discourse about sexuality away from morality and law and toward medicine. He began a catalog of the range of human sexuality and gender. Sigmund Freud and Havelock Ellis continued this exploration, noting that the variation in manifest behavior that was thought of as immoral or pathological reflected processes that were part of ordinary human psychology. Psychoanalytic thinking appears to have significantly regressed, in the sense of moving toward more prescriptive attitudes toward sexuality, starting in the 1920s with Wilhelm Reich's (1924) and Karl Abraham's (1924) descriptions of rigid developmental lines for normal sexuality. Worse, they equated overall psychological normality with normal development of sexuality along these normative lines, an attitude that became particularly problematic with regard to the psychology of women and same-sex desire, about which psychoanalysts like Deutsch (1945) and Bergler (1956) created a vision of mental health that had the impact of old-fashioned moralism with the added force of medical and scientific authority. It was not until the 1970s that feminist, gay, and later the queer critique of psychoanalytic thinking, combined with increased descriptive data about sex and gender, moved analysts towards a progressively less-knowing, evermore exploratory, and curious attitude about these matters. Psychoanalytic theories of sexual development and its relationship to general psychological development grew ever more rich and complex.

As Saketopoulou correctly asserts, in the very recent past, an individual born with a male anatomy who believed herself to be female would automatically be assumed to be suffering from significant psychopathology by virtue of this belief, and while many analysts might have recognized their inability to relieve this supposed psychopathology, they would have been likely to attribute any difficulties from which such patients suffered as the product of psychodynamics that shared an origin with the patient's gender beliefs. By putting aside such preconceptions, something that can be done only by recognizing the intellectual, institutional, and personal psychological pulls to retain them, Saketopoulou was able to remain open to locating the problems she faced in terms that reflected that patient's concerns. She avoided a temptation to normalize the child. Instead of adopting a therapeutic aim of moving toward predefined normalcy, she adopted therapeutic goals involving an increased capacity to face and address what the analysand regarded as problems of living. She was more interested in helping the patient find a process that worked for her than in moving to some respecified endpoint.[2] Within this context of relative liberation from preconceptions about a child who knows herself to be a girl while having a male anatomy, Saketopoulou is able to engage the awful dilemmas that her young patient faces.

Saketopoulou invites us to free ourselves from a point of view that can only distract from understanding transsexual patients. She wisely comments that "the search for etiological underpinnings treats the transsexual experience as a unitary phenomenon rather than as the end point of heterogeneous developmental pathways and complex compromise formations. … Gender aggregates polyvalently not lending itself to being theorized generally." This is an important statement because, as with many other situations, especially those involving gender and sexuality, the conviction that common endpoints in development result from common developmental processes leads to useless thinking. Mutually reinforcing discourses about homogeneous etiology and homogeneous outcomes leads to confusion and a failure to explore the heterogeneity of both.

The notion that shared outcomes reflect shared developmental paths was clearly demonstrated to be wrong by Thelen (Thelen and Smith, 1994) with regard to walking—children learn to walk through extremely varied developmental routes, even though the endpoint, the actual way in which they walk, is very similar between children. The confusion in psychoanalytic thinking can be traced back to Freud's idea about developmental pathology. Freud, for example, equates obsessive-compulsive character features with problems in anal phase development. Whatever the merit of this idea, it interfered with explorations of both the varied phenomenology of obsessive-compulsive symptoms and their varied etiologies. Freud's view that equates the endpoint of development with the pathway that led to it originated in his early education in the embryology of his day (Sulloway, 1979), experiments that seemed to show that specific lesions in the embryo led to specific lessons in the adult organism. As it turned out, the original biological finding was mistaken and occurred with only some lesions, but when the specificity did occur, it was impressive enough to be passed on as a general principle of development, not the occasional finding that it was.

Having put aside the preconception that developmental outcomes always result from specific developmental pathways, Saketopoulou makes the theoretically and pragmatically sound argument that one should "treat their [transsexual persons'] gender not as a symptom, but as a viable subjective reality." As Freud showed in the series of works starting with *The Interpretation of Dreams* in 1900 and ending with the *Jokes and Their Relationship to the Unconscious* in 1905 (Freud, 1905b), from the point of view of psychodynamics, essentially no difference occurs between symptoms and a variety of "normal" psychological configurations. To label something as a symptom means to regard it as intrinsically undesirable and a potential object for eradication through treatment. The labeling of transsexual states as symptoms places the analyst in the undesirable position of passing judgment for the patient about what is wrong and/or distressing while at the same time inviting the analyst to engage in what is usually an impossible task of altering the person's gender. The situation obviously parallels the widely explored issues of same-sex desire, in which efforts at therapy for that desire have now almost universally been recognized as both wrong-headed, in the sense that same-sex desire is not in itself a symptom, and practically undesirable, in the sense that these efforts generally failed and in the process caused great distress.

Saketopoulou then asks, if transsexuality is not in itself a symptom, why then is her young patient Jenny, like many transsexual people, so distressed? She suggests that, "[t]he ensuing emotional difficulties often result from the traumatic and unmentalized impact of being trans rather than their originary cause as is often assumed." She observes, "When gender is tenaciously conflated with bodily morphology, such individuals often feel unseen and unknown," thus suggesting a plausible interpersonal developmental contribution to the distress commonly observed in trans individuals. "Feeling unseen and unknown" is, of course, a product of the perception of the trans person and arises from the confluence of actual attitudes of those in the environment and, at any given moment, preexisting expectations of the individual. For the transsexual person, the expectation of remaining unseen and unknown is plausible. The transsexual's very existence threatens foundational worldviews of many people. The example of Chiland's, "so goodbye to the difference between the sexes and between the generations ... the sexual compass of psychoanalysis" horrifyingly illustrates the threat that transsexuals pose when clear gender difference is regarded as foundational to a worldview.

Although she does not develop the idea in this paper, Saketopoulou's rejection of binary gender gains strong support from thinking about gender from the points of view of complex systems and nonlinear dynamical systems theory. Harris (2005) has shown how the idea of gender can be conceptualized in terms of "attractors." If we imagine representing aspects of gender in a multidimensional space whose dimensions correspond to aspects of what we ordinarily think of as gender, such as gendered anatomical features, gendered social roles conventional in a given community, the sex of objects of desire, etc., we could think of gender development as pathways through this gender space and could conceptualize individuals at any given time as located at some place within that space. Some of these pathways are particularly common because a variety of forces tend to keep the individual on (or nearly on) them. The two most common of these, femininity and masculinity, represent broad pathways with ill-defined and context-dependent boundaries, along which most individuals travel.

Multiple factors tend to strengthen certain gender attractors. For example, internalized representations of the privileged position of the heterosexual man in our society result in intense resistance in individuals who think of themselves as heterosexual men to thinking or acting in ways that do not fit with this attractor. These resistances further stabilize the attractor because they actively discourage any move away from it. However, gender attractors may overlap, and movement from one attractor to another is at times possible if some factor displaces the individual from one gender attractor to another. Gender attractors that are, for whatever reason, particularly stable will be more common and more easily recognized. However, it should be noticed that a powerful stabilizing factor for a gender attractor within a community is the recognition of that attractor by the community so that, for example, the recognition of what is now labeled transsexuality in Europe and the United States has tended to stabilize that attractor and led to certain forms of it becoming more visible and stable than they were even a short time ago.

When individuals live under an attractor that is associated with great pain or when a gender attractor is sufficiently unstable that an individual cannot feel secure that he or she is on a specific attractor, the resulting anxiety leads to defensive operations. I suspect both of these factors affected Jenny. On one hand, the presence of male genitals made her a defective girl and caused anxiety for that reason; at the same time, the presence of those genitals brought into question her belief that she was a girl at all and so made her anxious by destabilizing her view of herself. Defenses designed to maintain the stability of the attractor, e.g. to maintain Jenny's self-description as a girl, commonly include elements that interfere with the attractor's evolution and the exploration of alternative attractors and explorations of any possibility that might call her femininity in to question. To ask the question, "How is it that I am a girl with boy's genitals?" much less to explore possible answers to that question threatened to radically destabilize the child's organizing view of herself. To ask the question, "How can I be an admirable girl with boy's genitals?" is to risk the possibility that she cannot be successful as a girl. Thus, to ask either of these questions and to explore possible answers would endanger any sense of psychological well-being so that she had to rigorously protect herself from anything that might even raise these questions. When the question cannot be raised, finding a satisfactory answer is, of course, impossible. Jenny's terror became self-perpetuating. Only when Jenny, with the help of her analyst, was able to consider the possibility that she can be a girl with a penis is she able to enter into a process of liberating mourning for the perfect girl she should have been.

Saketopoulou brings to her work visions of development that provides her and her patient with the opportunity to explore developmental possibilities that could not even be considered if one assumed the existence of straightforward developmental lines. Thus, she notes that the population of transsexual children ultimately bifurcates into a group of "persisters"—people who experience their natal genitalia as so inconsistent with their self-experience that they continue to believe that surgical and hormonal intervention is necessary—and "divergers"—individuals who do not experience such a need or who find that the disadvantages of these procedures outweigh their benefits. She notes that there is no way to differentiate these two groups in childhood.

This sort of developmental bifurcation has been well studied in the field of nonlinear dynamics. Imagine a developmental path as a highway that at some point divides, one branch going toward divergent development and the other toward persistent development. Until shortly before the highway actually divides, very little can be predicted about the direction in which the cars will go from their position on the roadway, except that they will continue along one or another of the legs of the bifurcation. As the cars approach the bifurcation, it becomes less likely that they will move from a lane leading to one side of the bifurcation to another, but the search for early determinants of the way the vehicle will go by observing that vehicle at several miles from the bifurcation will be, in large measure, futile. As systems increase in complexity, the difficulty of prediction becomes ever greater so that for a system like gender the bifurcation between persisters and divergers is almost impossible to predict except in unusual circumstances. The fact that it would make life easier for all concerned to be able to predict the child's adult wishes and thereby either avoid unneeded and problematic hormonal and surgical intervention or to intervene earlier and spare the youngster the distress associated with having the "wrong" body does not alter the fact that such prediction is not possible and is very likely never to be possible.

In "Mourning and Melancholia," Freud (1917) describes the fractionating process in which aspects of the object are recognized, intensely cathected, and then either further integrated in the self or put aside often after a process of further fractionation. When this occurs, one might frame the process either as the individual creating a new type of boundary or interdigitation of boundaries between self and object or alternatively as in some sense, recognizing that the nature of the boundary was all along different from what it appeared. The process of mourning is thus a process of reintegration through reimagining the object, its relationship to the self, and the nature of associated boundaries. It is only possible when the pain of recognizing that pre-existing boundaries can no longer be maintained becomes tolerable.

Because Jenny's analyst was able to live with the realization that the boundaries usually drawn between masculinity and femininity could be maintained for Jenny only at incredible cost and could communicate to the child that exploring these boundaries need not be the source of overwhelming distress, Jenny was freed to do the work of mourning and to begin exploring visions of herself with an appreciation of the creative possibilities that come from such work.

Notes

1 An earlier version of this chapter appeared as "Exploring a Complex Systems Map of Gender: Commentary on Saketopoulou," *Journal of the American Psychoanalytic Association*, 62(5): 815–21, October 2014. Reprinted by permission of SAGE Publications, Ltd.

2 Attempts to study the effectiveness of psychoanalysis are often frustrating because they focus on supposed endpoints of the process, such as symptom relief, or progress along one of the developmental lines, which may not be relevant, meaningful outcomes as the emergence of a process for problem solving in the course of analysis (Galatzer-Levy *et al.*, 2000; Sandler and Dreher, 1996).

Chapter 5

Good Vibrations

Analytic Process as Coupled Oscillations

In this chapter, I offer a model of how psychoanalysis works. My goal is not a universal theory of psychoanalytic action. The action of analysis probably varies widely between analyses. Instead, I describe one mode of psychoanalytic action that may be far more common than currently recognized.

Often, patients describe their ideas about how analysis works in more or less disguised form. The following vignette illustrates an analysand theory of analytic cure that is close to my ideas that come from a nonlinear dynamics viewpoint. This fragment is not intended as evidence for the theory. Its purpose is to invite readers to contemplate ideas from a clinically familiar position. Therefore, I include no data or discussion exploring alternative understandings as would be appropriate were the vignette being put forward as evidence for the general theory.

Nearing the end of a successful analysis, a young man dreamed: *I was climbing a hill today when I spotted a pack of wild Croatians salting the meat of yesterday's killing. They looked at me as if they wanted to burn my clothing, so I fled to the nearest Beergarden and informed the manager of the Croatians' proximity to their fine establishment. I thought I was getting through to him until he told me to sit down and wait for the waitress to serve me. "Damn it, man!" I cried, "Don't you understand the pressing nature of this issue?! There are feral sub-humans nourishing themselves for the pillage of your Beergarden!" He giggled and I sighed, and then we giggled and sighed together until my fears slowly melted away.*

This analysand began analysis enormously distressed, contemplating suicide, after breaking up with a girlfriend. The breakup pained him less than the recognition that, like other painful events in his life, the experience threw him into a frenzy. He drank heavily, was promiscuous with women and men, and ruminated on life's meaning. He fantasied about ripping off his clothes, burning them, and running naked through the streets. He found the analytic setup hard and its schedule arbitrary. Sometimes, he felt like he said everything in the first minutes of a session; other sessions should have lasted for hours; I should have been available at 3 a.m. but should not have forced him to get up for sessions at 10 a.m. Though I thought I understood and cared about him, for several years he believed I did not understand how urgent his situation was. I am prone to giggle.

The analysis mostly proceeded along conventional lines. The patient's use of action and hypomanic defenses to avoid pain was quickly identified and worked through repeatedly. An idealizing transference emerged, but the patient suffered because he "could not get enough" of the analyst. He longed to be admired by the analyst but feared he was not admirable. As these transferences were worked through and made increasing sense in terms of the analysand's development, he grew frankly competitive with the analyst and felt the weight of having so much of his life tied to analysis. We came to a point where he was symptomatically improved, and his outside life included a deeply pleasurable professional involvement and a satisfying intimate relationship. We agreed to terminate several months before the dream, which came about six weeks before the end of the analysis.

The dream includes a theory of therapeutics. It refers to terrifying primitive fantasies that were central to his distress. Fantasies of primitive oral aggression that are ignored by caretakers who were too inhibited and/or afraid to help the analysand with his often projected aggression had been repeatedly identified and interpreted. Erotic and exhibitionistic wishes repeatedly emerged and were clarified. But, in the dream, the cure does *not* come from confronting and working through those fantasies. It comes from our giggling and sighing together. Confronted with terrifying ideas, the analysand enters treatment because he has no alternative. The analyst all but ignores these fantasies, forcing the patient instead to enter an obscure shared affective state that never addresses those fantasies. Together, analyst and analysand come to a peaceful rhythmic state that somehow makes the terrifying ideas "melt away."

While the analysis was ongoing, I did not think of myself as behaving like my image in the dream; I tried to address what was urgent to the analysand, to explore his inner life, and to interpret his dreams and fantasies—that is, I proceeded more or less in the ordinary tradition of North American psychoanalysis. The analysand and I developed considerable insight into his dynamics. Yet the overall cast of the analysis moved in the way described in the dream, repeatedly going from states of agitation, fear, and a sense that I would not help him to calm as at times we seemed to be in sync.

The Nonlinear Dynamics of Psychoanalytic Cure

The idea that interpretation cures by making the unconscious conscious began to be questioned in the 1930s (Strachey, 1934). A series of theoretical, clinical, and empirical investigations led analysts to believe that other factors are central to therapeutic action (Gabbard and Westen, 2003; Smith, 2007). A vast literature suggests something other than interpretation as the therapeutic ingredient in psychoanalysis or that psychoanalysis is not unimodal but includes several different techniques appropriate to various patients (Gedo, 1979; Becal and Carlton, 2011).

Nonlinear dynamic systems theory contributes additional possibilities. It demonstrates how enormously complex, yet ordered, structure can emerge through simple rules. About fifty years ago, mathematicians demonstrated that, inordinately, in some sense literally infinitely, complex structures can emerge through simple rules. Fascinatingly beautiful fractal graphics (e.g. the Mandelbrot set) are, remarkably, often generated by simple rules, reducible to a few lines of computer code (see http://sprott.physics.wisc.edu/fractals.htm/). Particular instances of order appearing without a defining template were among the great scientific discoveries. Adam Smith (1776) and Charles Darwin (1859) showed that complex order could emerge from simple rules. Smith demonstrated that coherent economies emerge from individual efforts to maximize wealth in a market; Darwin showed that heritability and selection for fitness result in distinct species. Edelman (1987) proposed a model of how consciousness can emerge from neuronal selection. This central finding of vast complexity generated by simple rules, an example of what is called *emergence* (discussed in more detail later in this book), is counterintuitive. We tend to believe that complex systems result either from some being's intentions or from following a preexisting description of the system. Assumptions that complex systems must result from complex rules shape research programs that attempt to uncover those complex rules. The concept of emergence suggests a search of simple underlying rules instead. It suggests that the simple rule, "He giggled and I sighed, and then we giggled and sighed together until my fears slowly melted away," could be seen as an example of a simple rule with complex outcome and process.

Psychopathology can be described from a nonlinear dynamics viewpoint. Though the details vary, we observe two central sorts of disturbance. In one, the person repeats the same basic scenario regardless of context. In these forms of pathology, creative solutions become impossible. In the other form of pathology, disorganization reigns, nothing fits together, things fall apart. One person may suffer from both forms of pathology.

Nonlinear dynamics has a term for situations where actions tend to a particular configuration. The configuration toward which they tend is called an *attractor.*

Systems of all types can be described in terms of attractors. Consider a pendulum. When its motion is disturbed, it tends to return to regular, periodic behavior. The pendulum's motion can be plotted as the displacement angle over time. If friction is present, the pendulum eventually comes to rest so the attractor is reduced to a single point. "Attractor" in nonlinear dynamics does not refer to some force compelling action but rather to a pattern of motion toward which the system tends.

For centuries, the study of motion was limited to linear systems where changes in outcomes are proportional to changes in inputs. A beautiful finding of classical mathematics is that linear systems have a small number of possible attractors (Hurewicz, 1958). The study of nonlinear systems shows that the attractors could be far more complex. "Strange attractors," a feature of many nonlinear systems, predict motion, which, though entirely determined, are themselves richly complex. (Here, "motion" refers to any change over time, not only physical change in position but also motions like the evolution of strings of thoughts or the movement of the stock market.)

Restating the two types of pathology in terms of attractors, the first kind of pathology (repeating the same fundamental thing) is a disturbance in which available attractors are too simple and too stable to allow good adjustment for varied situations. By "good adjustment," I mean not only adjustments that are not bad but also adjustments that allow for the exploration of new possibilities and thus more refined or otherwise more adequate adjustments. In the second kind of pathology (characterized by lack of order), there is no reasonably stable attractor toward which the individual tends. No meaningful pattern emerges, or patterns that do emerge do so so transiently as to be of little use. Psychological health involves engaging attractors that are neither too rigid nor too disorganized. These attractors are sufficiently complex that rich creative possibilities exist in them.

Is there some relationship between attractors that are too stable, attractors that are adequately complex, and attractors that are chaotic in the sense that meaningful prediction is impossible? Students of nonlinear dynamics discovered a characteristic of systems that can become chaotic. First, consider a stable system in which changes in conditions are proportional to changes in outcomes. Imagine throwing a rock with nothing in the way. The distance the rock travels is proportional to how fast you throw it. The system is stable; it behaves predictably. But in some situations, small changes make big differences. The rock thrown at a pane of glass bounces off until, thrown just a little harder, the glass breaks. If it is thrown a little less hard than this critical value, we can predict that the glass will not break; if it is thrown a little harder, we can predict that the glass will break. A change in the force that crosses this critical boundary produces qualitatively different results. Imagine systems in which changes in initial conditions (the force with which the rock is thrown) result in ever more distinct outcomes. Such systems are of increasing complexity. Imagine throwing a rock at several panes of glass, located behind one another, and trying to predict how far the rock will go. With each new pane of glass we impose, the prediction becomes more difficult. Imagine a system in which no matter how small the change, something new happens—this is a chaotic system.

Chaos does not mean total disorder but a condition where changes in the system, however small, result in major changes in the system's evolution.[1] The sensitivity of chaotic systems to initial conditions varies. Fairly good predictions can be made for a considerable time, even though arbitrarily small initial differences lead to significantly different outcomes in the long run. Likewise, non-chaotic systems may grow increasingly complex as some property, often some quantitative elements, moves the system toward chaos. (Mathematically, the road to chaos can be described by a single number called the "Lyapunov exponent" [Strogatz, 1994].)

Weather is a good example of a chaotic system. In fact, chaos theory developed from attempts at predicting weather. In most instances, naive observers can predict the weather for several hours by observing the current weather ("looks like rain"), and sophisticated meteorologists are able to do so for several days with great difficulty and rapidly diminishing reliability in the details ("a cold front moving in from Canada will bring us rain six days from now"). At the same time, the prediction of seasonal averages of the weather is relatively easy. Writing this in early summer in the northern Midwest of the United States, I can feel confident not only that the weather will be warm for a few months but also that in six months it will be substantially colder. If I guess at the temperature for later today, I will probably do pretty well. But if I try to predict the temperature more exactly either in a few days or for six months from now, my prediction is likely to be off. This sort of prediction is typical of what can be done for a system, like the weather, that operates under strange attractors.

A general principle of nonlinear dynamics is that complexity emerges on the edge of chaos (Langston, 1990). For a system to have rich multiple possibilities involves its being nearly chaotic and at risk of falling into chaos. If one of the goals of analysis is developing a capacity for a richer, more complex way of dealing with psychological events, this principle implies that hoped-for analytic change risks disorganization. An inevitable compromise exists between stability, the need for novelty, and the risk of chaos. The sense that new ideas are dangerous and that development often risks trauma is a central dilemma, not only for analysands but also for all people who are changing. Ideally, one explores novelty as freely as possible without risking disorganization, yet the two are inevitably linked.

Incapacities to change or to achieve a reasonable degree of stability can be described as being too near or too far from the edge of chaos. Life too far from the edge of chaos is an endless repetition as the world is again and again interpreted and reacted to in the same manner. Life too near is fragmentation and disorganization and is generally so unbearable and maladaptive that individuals rarely remain in these disorganized states for long. Massive emergency rigid reorganizations, like those described by Dr. Schreber (1988), quickly replace the near chaotic state.

Defenses are mobilized against actual or feared disorganization. They are governors regulating the degree of disorganization associated with novelty. They are double-edged—the cost of protection is often the limitation of creativity and new learning. Many forms of psychopathology are usefully conceptualized as resulting from too extensive use of defenses; treatment loosens them. Some psychopathology involves inadequate defenses; treatment involves developing more adequate defenses. Defenses are means of attempting to achieve optimal complexity. Analysis is intended to bring the person into an area neither of undue stability nor of disorganization but "on the edge of chaos" where novelty and creativity are possible. This state does *not* involve a putative "normal" endpoint of development but an ongoing capacity for change.

How Does Analysis Facilitate Development?

Some observations about analysis: First, with exceptions, analysands see their analysts "a lot"—several times weekly and for a long time, usually years. The analysis takes on its own life. Analysts have elaborated numerous contradictory theories about therapeutic action. Currently, ideas about the analyst-analysand relationship and the analytic setup seem to better account for analytic action than ideas about particular mental content (Gabbard and Westen, 2003). For example, it matters more that analyst and patient work together to find meaning than that they search for that meaning in oedipal fantasies, vicissitudes of the paranoid position, or deconstruction of social expectations. If the analysis goes well, analyst and analysand often feel surprised by developments (Reik, 1948). Finally, psychoanalysis, a subspecies of human interaction, shares salient features with interactions like friendship, love, and parent-child relationships so that, when it goes well, both parties are deeply affected.

Humans have evolved to be biologically highly social, deeply sensitive to each other, recognizing human aspects in others, and shaped by our interactions (e.g. Cozolino, 2014). Neuroimaging studies of empathy using subjects who saw someone for whom they cared exposed to pain found that their brain centers involving affective response to pain lit up in much the same way as in the person in pain, but the centers involved in the perception of pain lit up only in the person actually exposed to it (Singer *et al.*, 2006). Empathy is biologically based and may be hard-wired in the normal brain (Baron-Cohen, 1995).

Similarly, neuroimaging studies show that humans recognize faces and respond specifically to them on a biological basis (Kanwisher *et al.*, 1997). In some sense, we recognize people as like us and similar to us from birth. If you stick out your tongue at a baby less than an hour old, she responds by sticking out her tongue (Meltzoff and Moore, 1977), a remarkable feat given that the baby has had no chance to learn that she is like you, much less that she has a tongue corresponding to the slight change in her perception that results when you stick out your tongue. Humans are hard-wired to interact.

The problem of how people interact and so profoundly affect one another is related to another problem. How is it that various parts of the brain interact to produce unified action and experience? How is it that the sound in a room, including a speaker's voice, stimulating the hairs in the cochlea, the light hitting retinal receptors, and the listener's past experiences, leads to a unified perception of a lecturer rather than a buzz of disconnected sounds, lights, and memory fragments? This is remarkable because the neurons doing the computations that lead to unified perception are slow computational elements, and the required computation is vast. This question is called the "binding problem."

Rudolfo Llinás (2001) proposed a model in which binding is achieved by the temporal organization of brain function through the operation of underlying brain rhythms. Shared rhythm, whether arising as the result of following some central coordinator or appearing spontaneously in a system, allows a system to develop into a new whole, often with properties greater than the sum of its parts. The beauty of a Mozart symphony does not result from individual sounds but rather the multilayered temporal organization of those sounds. This organization is made possible by specifying the temporal relationship of the sounds to a well-defined underlying rhythm. Experience is not the sum of sensations but the temporal organization of sensation in relation to preexisting patterns, which make them comprehensible. Meaning and significance result from the temporal coordination of various aspects of brain function.

Such coordination continues beyond individual skulls and individuals' actions so brain functions of couples and groups become temporally coordinated. The importance of temporal coordination has been repeatedly demonstrated in infant development, e.g. the development of the sleep cycle (Sander, 1969, 1989; Sander *et al.*, 1970) and turn-taking of even preverbal conversations (Condon and Sander, 1974a, b). Similar temporal patterns may be the most convincing evidence of being accurately understood, as when a mother's affectively attuned grunts patterned after her infant's efforts to reach for an object (Stern, 1985) communicates that the mother understands what the baby is intending to do.

When actions are repeated or nearly repeated, it becomes easier both to coordinate actions between two parties and to detect the presence of coordination. We speak of oscillation in a system when the system moves repeatedly within some limited range. An oscillator is a system that exhibits oscillation in this broad sense, be it the stock market, the heart, a violin string, the population of fish and algae in a pond, or the topic of discussion in analytic sessions. This general concept of "oscillator" challenges the psychoanalytic reader unaccustomed to mathematical abstraction and who tends to associate specific images with terms used to represent abstraction. "Oscillator" implies nothing mechanical, simple, or even material. (Abstractions are powerful tools, but they can lead to discomfort and even inaccuracy if they ignore important particulars of a situation, and hence psychoanalysts often find them discomforting [Bion, 1977].)

A useful way of representing an oscillator is to picture the various states of the oscillator as points in a space. For example, a pendulum is described by using two variables by its angle from the vertical and the rate of change of that angle; an analytic patient's association might be described by three variables in terms of the subject matter, the intensity of affect, and the richness of language used. The space of possible points for a system is called *phase space*, and movement of the system through phase space is the *trajectory.* The most interesting and important features of systems concern the shape of the trajectories, the paths through phase space (Abraham and Shaw, 1992). The mathematics of oscillators is among both the most beautiful and the most practical aspects of mathematics.

Oscillators are said to be coupled if they are connected in some way. Like the theory of oscillators in general, the theory of coupled oscillators is powerful because many details of the coupling can be ignored in mathematically modeling them. The resonant vibrations of harmonic piano strings, the coupling of two weighted springs by a rubber band, the coupling of two neurons through connections in a neural network, and the back and forth movement of dancers, all are usefully conceptualized as coupled oscillators. Recognizing their common properties as coupled oscillators enriches the understanding of all of them, although this focus potentially calls attention away from significant particulars of the particular situations.

Some of the properties of the system created by coupling two oscillators are contingent on the properties of the coupling mechanism. It has become apparent, for example, that the coupling of mental states between individuals operates in surprising ways. If two pendulums are connected by a spring, the evolution of the system will depend in part on the stiffness of the spring. Minds are in part connected by mirror neurons. Mirror neurons fire not only as the result of direct experience but also in response to similar emotionally salient experiences in others (Kohler *et al.*, 2004; Rizzolatti and Craighero, 2004). Failure of this normal mechanism of coupling is implicated in developmental psychopathology of children who are not appropriately influenced by interactions with others (Oberman *et al.*, 2006). More psychologically, mind-mind coupling is facilitated by the emergence of a "theory of mind," i.e. the belief that other people have mental states that are like one's own and that their actions can be comprehended in terms of intentions (Gallese, 2003; Tomasello *et al.*, 2005; Trevarthen, 1980). The means by which minds become linked have specific characteristics that affect the nature of the relationship between the two oscillators in the system, just as the connecting of two simple oscillators by a stiff spring leads to different motions than if they are connected by a limp spring. In the case of interpersonal interactions, it is likely that the mind-brain of each party connects to the mind-brain of the other through multiple channels. In this chapter, we will conceptualize these multiple links as constituting one overall connection. However, it is now known that multiple linkage, such as almost certainly occurs in interpersonal interactions, can profoundly change the nature and speed of linkage. The theory of coupled oscillators will likely further develop along the lines based on the remarkable phenomena that result from multiple connections between systems (Watts, 1999; Newman, 2013).

Collections of coupled oscillators may be conceptualized as a single oscillator whose phase space includes the dimensions of each of the separate oscillators. (For example, if we imagine two pendulums connected by a rubber band, the entire system may be described as moving through a four-dimensional phase space, two of whose dimensions are the position and momentum of the first pendulum, and two of whose dimensions are the position and momentum of the second.)

Brain function involves the coupling of numerous oscillators. Neurons are oscillators, moving between polarization to depolarization. They are coupled with other neurons so that neural systems are systems of coupled oscillators. These neural systems interact both as such and often through shortcuts that shape their information processing. The result is unified brain function (Basar, 1998). The degree of interconnections of neurons varies. For some purposes, it is useful to conceptualize a group of neurons as acting together as a module (Callebau and Rasskin-Gutman, 2005). While such divisions of brain function are useful for certain purposes, all the brain's neurons are ultimately interconnected so it is also useful to think of unified brain states. For some purposes, recognizing the brain as an integrated whole is essential (Freeman, 2000). Similarly, a different picture of psychological function emerges if we draw the boundaries of the system to include the mind-brains of two participants in a relationship.[2] I propose that it is useful to conceptualize the interpersonal interaction called psychoanalysis in these terms.

The study of coupled oscillators began in the seventeenth century. Christian Huygens had labored to develop pendulum clocks accurate enough to allow ships' captains to track time in a way adequate to measure longitude. One day, while ill in bed, he observed that the pendulums of two clocks he had built and fastened to the wall were in synchrony. Since the pendulums had the same period, it was hardly surprising that, once in synchrony, they remained so. But Huygens discovered that if he deliberately desynchronized the pendulums, after about half an hour the synchrony re-emerged and continued. He found that if the clocks were completely physically separated, or if the pendulums swung perpendicular to one another, they did not synchronize (Huygens, 1665[1893], vol.5, p. 243; Strogatz, 2003). Huygens's clocks were the first instance of a physical phenomenon where order emerged from apparent disorder. From these beginnings, mathematicians have explored the properties of coupled oscillators, which are characterized by the intrinsic motion of each oscillator and the nature of their coupling.

Huygens's clocks have a feature so obvious as to easily escape notice. The very idea of the clocks being in synchrony requires two clocks. Just as there is no sound of one hand clapping, there is no synchrony without at least two elements. The addition of other elements, additional dimensions to a situation, makes configuration possible that could not occur in simpler systems. (Dimension here simply means the minimum number of variables needed to describe a system.) Whereas the single pendulum of a clock moves in a one-dimensional space, the position of two pendulums taken together is two-dimensional. In this two-dimensional space, the concept of synchrony has meaning, though in each dimension separately it does not.

Dimension changes everything (see Stewart, 2001). Consider the question of how to move from a point inside a circle to one outside it. In a two-dimensional system, for example a plane, no matter how much you bend and twist the circle, you must cross the circle to get to the point outside it. But if you consider the two-dimensional surface as embedded in a three-dimensional space, you can jump over the circle and reach the other point without ever crossing the circle. A problem that had no solution in two dimensions has a simple one in three.

Combining increased dimensionality with appropriate coordination between elements of a system can result in new and useful configurations. Consider a leg for a moment. It is a compound pendulum with fulcrums at the hip, knee, and ankle. Used separately, our legs are not good for locomotion. At best, we can hop. But coupled, both neurologically and mechanically through the pelvis, these oscillators provide an excellent means of moving. Depending on how we use them—to walk, run, or jump—our two limbs move us forward, moving in synchrony, counter synchrony, or near synchrony.

Something more results from combining these motions in an appropriately coupled way than a sum of the results of each motion. The smooth walking gait is *qualitatively* different from imposing the separate motions of each leg and arm upon one another. This walking gait is not only quantitatively different from what one limb can do, but it is an entirely new entity. Coupled systems of oscillators are rich in emergent phenomena that can result from them.

Looking at the elements of coupled oscillators separately, we discover that not only the system composed of each of the oscillators has a new form, but each oscillator moves qualitatively differently from its movement when it is uncoupled. New patterns of motion appear that were not in evidence in the separate oscillators. Each oscillator "learns" to do something new, something it could not do independent of the coupled system.

The coupling of oscillators (even if the coupling is very subtle as was the case for Huygens's clocks, which were simply hanging on the same wall) results in a new system with properties that go qualitatively beyond those of each component of the system. The system may allow processes in each component that could not occur in the components separately. The most interesting configurations of such a system emerge when the coupling between them is sufficient for there to be mutual influence but is not so strong that they are locked together. If one element of the system is too massive, it will simply drag the other element along with it; no interesting new configuration emerges, or if it does, it emerges very slowly. The most novel and interesting configurations result from optimal coupling of oscillators that exert mutual influence.

Attachment theory, self psychology, relational psychologies, and Harry Stack Sullivan's interpersonal theory explore how psychological development depends on interpersonal relations. We can reframe all these ideas as discussions of how the complex oscillators called people become linked, the difficulties that arise in this linkage, the problems arising when the linkage is significantly nonoptimal, and possible repairs of suboptimal linkage. The particulars remain important, but they are usefully conceptualized in the framework of coupled oscillator theory just as the general theory of drives provides an outline for descriptions of particular drives in individuals.

The psychoanalytic setup may be thought of as designed to create an environment conducive to reworking patterns of psychological action that have not worked well for the analysand. As such, we expect it to include elements similar to those involved in ordinary development, particularly the development of a good enough linkage between analysand and analyst, one in which they come together to form a new system from which creative new solutions can emerge. Many analysts have recognized that that new system can be conceptualized in terms of coupled oscillators. Among their ideas are Winnicott's concepts of mutual influence, the systems of projective-identification of modern Kleinians, some of the relational points of view, some formulation of the "third," and various alliance concepts. In each formulation, a new entity results from the analytic situation where processes occur in analyst and analysand that could not otherwise happen.

One lesson from Huygens's clocks is that, given sufficient time, connections may be subtle and yet powerful. Huygens's clocks were connected only by the vibrations passed through the wall. The central role of sufficient time and maintenance of the process in analysis is consistent with the idea that the novelty that emerges in the analytic process results from coupling of systems over enough time that new structures may emerge. It took almost 300 years to discover the mechanism of coupling in Huygens's pendulums. It will take much study to elucidate the mechanisms of coupling of human interactions. These are almost certainly multiple in nature and complex in their interaction with one another.

Since coupling oscillators can produce the emergence of effective structures, it is no surprise that means evolved that ensure such coupling. The most obvious is the attachment system (Bowlby, 1969, 1973), pulling young mammals and their caretakers into interactions that result in the mother-infant dyad, able, as Benedek (1959) observed, to alter the development of *both* infants and mother. This tendency to engage with others continues across life, so new structures emerge influencing both individuals. These couplings can result in obvious synchronization, anti-synchronization, or more complex structures. Describing these structures is a major theme of nonlinear dynamics. As analysts become more familiar with these configurations, we will likely be able to recognize them in analytic process.[3]

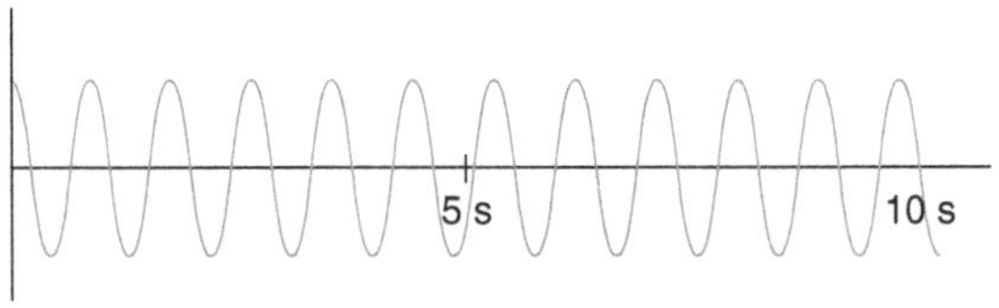

Figure 5.1 The Paths of an Isolated Pendulum, Plotted as Displacement from a Neutral Position Over Time.

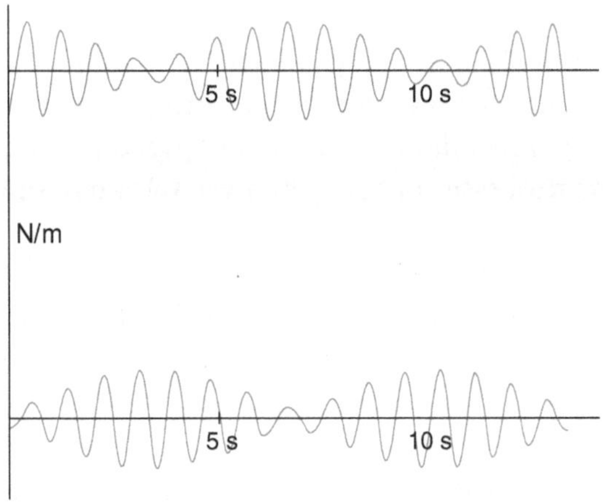

Figure 5.2 One Configuration of the Paths of Two Linked Pendulums.

Even coupling two simple oscillators can lead to surprising results, types of motion impossible for each oscillator separately. Consider two pendulums in a frictionless environment. If the pendulums are displaced from a neutral position, they will swing, and displacement plotted against time will be a sine curve (Figure 5.1).

What happens if we connect the two pendulums by an elastic band? Depending on the relative masses of the pendulums and the tightness of the band, the result is a more complex motion than could ever appear in an isolated oscillator (Figures 5.2 and 5.3).

If we look at one of the oscillators in a system like Figures 5.2 or 5.3 alone, the result is the appearance of an oscillator whose movement is more complex than could be achieved by an isolated oscillator (Figure 5.4).[4]

In the analytic situation, two oscillators, the mind-brains of analysand and analyst, are coupled by producing a new oscillator, the

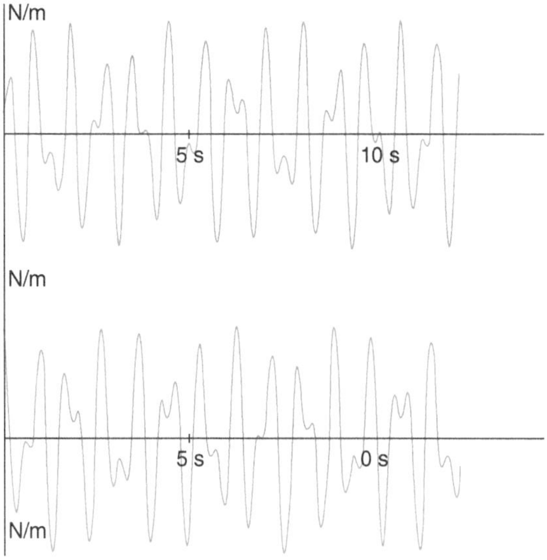

Figure 5.3 Another Configuration of the Paths of Two Linked Pendulums in which the Linkage is Weaker than for the Pendulums Shown in Figure 5.2.

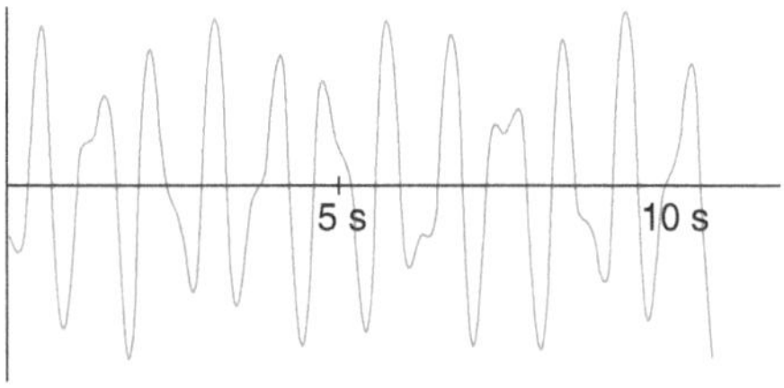

Figure 5.4 The Motion of a Single Pendulum, which is Linked to Another Pendulum in the Same Manner as in Figure 5.3.

analytic dyad. This new oscillator is of a higher dimension than either of the oscillators separately so that new solutions to previously unsolvable problems may emerge. There may be phenomena within the new system that for a time look as though the direction of influence is one way, as when the analyst's suggestion causes an analysand to adopt new attitudes or behaviors. Such direct influence is not the most interesting aspect of analysis. If it occurs, it cannot involve solutions that are novel to the system. Furthermore, it cannot be long-lasting since coupled oscillators are mutually influencing and the inertia of the analyst's personality is rarely so great as to remain uninfluenced by the analysand over time. Analysis is most effective when analysand and analyst join in depth over adequate time so new configurations emerge in their interaction and, in turn, in each individual. This results from a satisfactory analytic setup.

Much of the apparent work of analysis involves creating a setup in which mutual influence can occur. In this model, interpretation and insight *per se* would play a much smaller role in analysis than they do in older formulations. They are no longer the centerpiece of the analytic process. They might constitute a playground where analyst and analysand join or markers of resonance in the analytic situation. Interpretations may create or reinforce affective links between the analyst and analysand.

Here is a clinical example. A fifteen-year-old boy repeatedly listened to interpretations and often agreed with them. He then free associated without apparent reference to the interpretation. After the analyst pointed this out several times, he said, "Yes, I admit and go on." The analyst repeated: "Admit and go on." In subsequent sessions, both analysand and analyst noted several instances of this phenomenon, quickly noting it with the phrase, "admit and go on." Over time, the general character trait manifest in this characteristic response to interpretation came to be called "admit and go on." Using this phrase not only rapidly and effectively called attention to an aspect of the patient's personality, but it was associated with the experience of understanding something together and affirmed the sense of committed cooperation between analyst and patient. Their systems linked more effectively.

One way to think about interpretations is by analogy to the phenomenon that Stern (1985) observed in infants that occurs, for example, when the caretaker provides cross-modal indications of understanding the infant's intentions (see p. 183). (The baby strains to reach for an object and the mother makes sounds that fit the infant's effortful movements. In so doing, she indicates her comprehension of the baby's efforts.) A reasonably accurate interpretation communicates an understanding of the analysand's intentions by the analyst and thus both verifies and supports their being in sync. It shows that the analysand has influenced the analyst while at the same time providing a means by which the analyst may influence the analysand.

Like interpretations, analysts' theories are primarily important in supporting the analytic setup. Theories supporting resonance and continued immersion between analyst and analysand would be predicted to be helpful. Those separating analyst and analysand, for example, by suggesting that the analysand is a different sort of being from the analyst or by encouraging indoctrination, would likely interfere with analysis. Empirical studies of analytic therapies appear to confirm this prediction. They repeatedly demonstrate that it is not the correctness of interpretations (either in the sense that interpretations conform to analytic data or in the sense that they accurately represent analytic theory), but factors like the analytic alliance and the "fit" between analyst and analysand that result in significant change (for a review of these studies, see e.g. Galatzer-Levy *et al.*, 2000).

The tendency in the study of analysis to focus on dramatic moments at the expense of the overall analytic configurations can lead to a misunderstanding of analytic process. The Boston Change Study Group, with whose ideas I largely agree, models analytic process on Stern's (1985) developmental studies, showing how caretaker empathy organizes infant experiences and supports development. They emphasize poignant moments when analyst and analysand seem almost perfectly in tune, the "now moments" when they assert therapeutic change occurs (Stern, 2004). As Palombo (1999) has pointed out, looked at from the point of view of nonlinear systems, the idea of "now moments" as independent of the large contexts of which they are a part is probably mistaken. Nonlinear systems commonly include times when dramatic changes take place, when entirely new configurations of action become evident. The abrupt changes and dramatic moments are part of a unified overall process. The abrupt changes are intrinsic in and determined by the apparently smoother part of the process.[5]

Consider water freezing. As the water's temperature decreases, it becomes slightly denser, until suddenly (in terms of the temperature) a phase transition occurs and the water crystallizes. But the process of freezing is best conceptualized in terms of how the properties of the water change with temperature, not by an exclusive focus on the fact of phase transition (Ricci, 1966). Similarly, strange attractors often involve abrupt transitions.

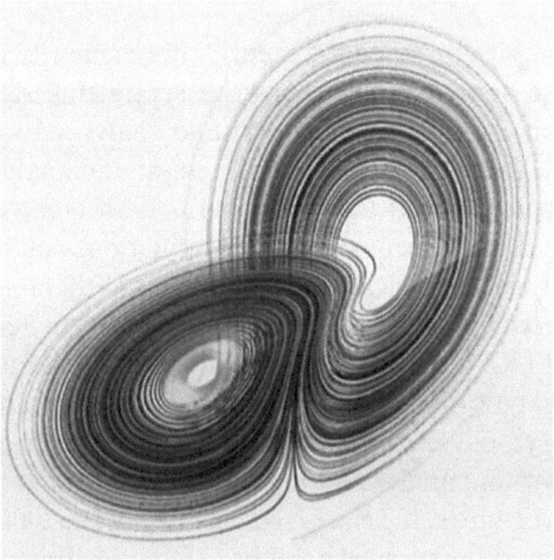

Figure 5.5 The Lorenz Attractor, an Example of a Strange Attractor.

The attractor appears to follow a nearly periodic motion, only to change suddenly and unexpectedly to another almost periodic motion. It jumps back and forth between the two motions in an unpredictable fashion. It is tempting to describe these dramatic changes as the central feature of the attractor, but doing so would be an error—the entire attractor is implied by any fragment of it. So, too, with the analytic setup. While the dramatic moments of attunement associated with visible change will strike us as most important, or the impressive sequences of apparent breakthroughs of insight may seem the most important analytic moments, the entire setup makes change possible. The hours of struggling, jostling, chatting, and speculating are just as central to analytic change as the dramatic apparently transformative moments.

Similarly, although the need for the analyst is most obvious in the traumatized patient or the patient who has been deprived of needed developmental experiences, such needs do not necessarily reflect the depth of the analytic situation. They may make us aware of the need for others in development, but their satisfaction is not necessarily what cures in analysis. I did not respond to my patient's demand for 3 a.m. sessions by coming to see him then, but I had a sincere understanding of his felt need. In fact, to him I seemed unreasonably calm and unperturbed.

The analytic setup may be reasonably thought of as a situation designed to promote optimal coupling of the oscillator-like analyst and patient. Its arrangements are intended to ensure that sufficient time is available for analyst and patient to come into significant relationship of such coupling. Rules like privacy, relative anonymity, neutrality, and abstinence may be seen as arrangements by which the coupled system of analyst-analysand can operate within a realm that becomes neither chaotic nor stagnant, neither dominated by one participant, nor so loosely related that analyst and patient fail to influence one another. Similarly, Winnicott (1965) and Bion's (1977) recommendations that the analyst remain "alive" during the analysis can be seen as part of the effort to move to an optimal state of availability to be part of the emergent analytic system.

The very general model proposed here has many clinical implications. It suggests that much that is important in the analytic process occurs outside the awareness of both analyst and analysand. It also suggests that the content of the analyst-analysand discourse and the insights achieved may be less important than the process of that discourse. It suggests an important role for the analysis of defense understood from a different point of view than is customary. Within the analytic dyad, defenses may be understood as not only keeping potentially distressing material out of contact with other mental content but also keeping that material outside the new oscillating system, analyst-analysand. As a result, defensive operations interfere with the formation and operation of this new system and must be dealt with in some manner if it is to be fully effective.

The ideas described in this chapter are in many ways consistent with the "relational point of view" in psychoanalysis (Mitchell, 1988) and continued efforts to formulate those ideas in terms of nonlinear dynamics (Harris, 2005; Seligman, 2006), though they do not necessarily imply the appropriateness of many of the technical innovations associated with that point of view. What advantage is there in formulating these ideas in terms of nonlinear systems? I believe several occur.

First, at least in their contemporary formulations, many relational ideas seem vague and almost mystical. This seeming mysticism results because we have such poor intuition and little language for talking about emergent phenomena generally and even less language for speaking about emergence in the context of human interactions. A language that describes these ideas clearly can clarify our discourse, and nonlinear dynamics and the theory of coupled oscillators provides such a language. (Like all language, it shapes the way one thinks about the phenomena it describes and suggests approaches to them, thus simultaneously limiting and enriching our understanding.) A second aspect of the theory is that it moves us away from a mind-brain dualism to a discussion of interacting systems. The same principles of interaction apply to interacting minds and brains. A focus on interaction emphasizes that they are the matters of key importance rather than the concrete structures in which they are embedded. Finally, nonlinear systems theory includes methods for quantitatively describing and exploring interactions. It has the potential to provide a framework within which psychoanalytic data can be examined in a way that may actually fulfill the promise of the old metapsychology.

The theory of nonlinear systems described here pays little heed to the matters of mental content that have, until recently, constituted much of our theory and continue to be the bread and butter of our communications to patients. In particular, it appears to have little to do with the narrative point of view, the idea that the goal of analysis is the co-creation of new, more satisfactory (more functional, more authentic, more true) life narrative (Schafer, 1992). However, these ideas looked at from a different angle also fit within the concepts of coupled oscillators. The gradually constructed new narrative, a private creation between analyst and analysand, forms a template for the pattern of interaction in the analysis, a shared pathway along which the analytic couple can move and come to a state of synchronization. Every reasonably successful analytic couple seems to develop a collection of shared narratives, which can often be referenced by a word or two that immediately puts analyst and analysand into a shared, reasonably synchronized area of discourse. The narrative is also a clearly visible product of the developed synchronization of analyst and patient and thus memorializes and represents such synchrony.

It might seem that I am introducing new and difficult ideas that merely put a mathematical veneer on concepts that are developing in simpler language. This might invite imprecise use while giving them the authority of mathematics. However, the apparent absence of high-order theories of psychoanalytic change is an illusion. A group of ideas derived from Freud's mechanistic worldview has been equated with "common sense" (see Galatzer-Levy, 1997b). Freud's implicit worldview derives from the apparent success of linear mathematics in describing the physical world and controlling the physical world and is reinforced by inattention to phenomena that it could not encompass (Thom, 1975). The very term *nonlinear* reflects a linear worldview. Referring to nonlinear systems is like referring to non-elephant biological organisms. It suggests a centrality for linearity that it does not have. Pointing to the nonlinear nature of the psychoanalytic process reveals an implicit assumption central to our thinking about analytic process, i.e. that it is linear.

In what sense do I claim that the analytic situation is usefully described as a system of coupled oscillators? Is it a metaphor? ("The mind is an engine.") A model (like a computer built to emulate mental functioning)? A testable hypothesis? ("Depression always follows object loss.") The claim is none of these. It is a mathematical abstraction. Mathematical abstraction is the realization that the object of study belongs to a class of objects to which a mathematical concept applies. Consider that huge class of things to which arithmetic applies. For every member of this class, the abstract statements of arithmetic apply to the particular situation. Take $2 + 2 = 4$, so adding two potatoes to two potatoes gives four potatoes, and adding 2,000,000 dollars to 2,000,000 dollars yields 4,000,000 dollars. For anything to which arithmetic properly applies, two of those things added to two of those things yields four of them. The remarkable feature of mathematical abstractions is that, once it is known that the abstraction applies, all the mathematical consequences associated with the abstraction apply. Entities that may seem otherwise unrelated—for example, stock prices and fish populations—follow similar courses because they are associated with the same mathematical abstraction. The most satisfactory mathematical abstractions arise when it is clear by the nature of the thing studied that a particular abstraction is appropriate. This is the case for psychological and nervous system functions and coupled oscillators. Interpersonal interactions satisfied the definition of coupled oscillators and so can be abstracted to the mathematics of such oscillators.

However, an abstraction being possible does not entail that it is useful. The motion of a football could be described by using general relativity, but no one would undertake such a discussion to do so because a general relativity discussion of a football has no advantage over the simpler abstraction of classical mechanics. Even though the abstraction of analytic process to nonlinear dynamics is logically valid, the question remains of its usefulness.

Some Applications of the Coupled Oscillator Concept

For the practicing analyst, the coupled oscillatory viewpoint has two groups of implications.

The first group of ideas arises as a logical necessity from the theory and undermines some central heuristics of analytic interpretations. A central hermeneutic step in psychoanalysis is the notion that if two ideas appear in proximity, they must be unconsciously connected (Freud, 1900). This hermeneutic rests on beliefs about the continuity of mental states based in a worldview about causality in linear systems. In a nonlinear system, there is no reason to assume that a simple logical relationship exists between the states through which the system moves. That this hermeneutic is not, as Freud believed, a logical necessity of determinism does not mean it is not usefully explored. It merely means that a failure to find such a connection is not necessarily the result of inadequate investigation or resistance and that other possible connections between ideas in sequence are worth exploring when this hermeneutic fails.

Example: A patient dreamed of the analyst, thinner and younger than he actually was, *vigorously exercising on a treadmill.* Associations concerned a pleasant sexual encounter during the weekend following the previous analytic session. The analysand felt much freer in recent months to enjoy sex as a result of analytic work. The patient's entire life was much better as a result of analysis and the analyst's "vigorous interpretations," which, according to the patient, "pushed me places I never thought I would go." Using the standard hermeneutic, the analyst interpreted the patient's unconscious fantasy of therapeutic action: "Because my healthy-virile young analyst made vigorous interpretations pushing me into new places (i.e. had sex with me), I engaged in particularly pleasurable sexual activities." When variations of this interpretation elicited no new associations, the analyst suggested that the causal link ran in the opposite direction (the fantasy that the patient's sexual performance rejuvenated the analyst but left masturbation as his only outlet). Again, the analysand responded with none of the indicia of a correct interpretation. The standard hermeneutic would lead the analyst to explore alternate interpretations involving causal connections or to drop the matter as not timely. The analyst offered a third interpretation, not based on a hidden causal link, but rather that both the dream and the sexual activity expressed an "optimistic state of mind." Both reporting the dream and the weekend's events and their relation to the analysis were intended to bring the analyst "in sync" with the patient's frame of mind. This produced a rich collection of associations to the analysand's experience that "there are good times and bad times," "times when God is in His heaven and all is right with the world," and times when "life sucks." For her, transitions between these states were mysterious, for, although she could often rationalize the change in terms of events, even these rationalizations seemed implausible to her. The interpretation led to the realization that her moods were contingent on her mother's erratic capacity to join in her experience.

This vignette illustrates two applications of the nonlinear viewpoint. First, since analytic dialogue does not proceed through linear causal chains, other links should be explored. Failure to find linear causative sequences may indicate their true absence. Second, the vignette suggests that, just like physical systems, psychological systems may be best conceptualized as operating under attractors, overall patterns of motion and activity whose large scale properties (rather than stepwise unfolding) are the most fruitful object of attention. The patient's "optimistic" and "pessimistic" state of mind may be thought of as aspects of an attractor with two basins, areas in which the system operates as if under the influence of a single attractor until it jumps to the other basin.[6]

If analysis is a system of coupled oscillators, analysts should attend features associated with coupled oscillators. Changes in analytic listening are of two types: one involves the analyst's focus on coupled oscillation, the other relates to understanding phenomena arising in the process. The emergence of the system of analyst-analysand should result in increasing coordination of the participants' activities. They will not necessarily become more alike, but they will increasingly form a unified whole (like dance partners or the configurations described by Racker [1968], only more numerous).

In analysis, a young man debilitated by obsessive-compulsive symptoms quickly recognized, along with his analyst, that the symptoms were reactions to the analysand's mother's intrusiveness. He proved he was his own master by showing that no one, including himself, could force him to do anything. At first, analysis focused on showing how he simultaneously exercised his will and punished himself for doing so. The focus gradually shifted to interpreting what the patient "really wanted." The analyst commented on transparent erotic and aggressive wishes and associated inhibitions. Sometimes the patient felt blocked from acting on these impulses, sometimes he acted on them, yet he never was aware of wanting to do these things. He felt compliant with the analyst's wishes. The analyst focused on how the patient's knowing nothing of his desires pulled the analyst into stating what the analyst believed were the patient's desires. The analysand experienced these statements as seductive tricks and responded with compliance or rejection. Still, analysand and analyst felt that they knew what was going on and could explore the microprocess of the pattern. One day, when the patient was again fifteen minutes late, having been unable to decide which shirt to wear, the analyst, to his dismay, yelled, "Don't you ever get tired of this shit!" The analysand broke down in uncontrollable sobbing. He hurled a pillow across the room, breaking a small vase. He cursed the analyst, saying the analyst ruined his life. Both men were shaken and retreated. The analyst thought about discussions of negative countertransference (Searles, 1979; Winnicott, 1949); the analysand thought he was a "good patient" expressing "real feelings." Both knew these were rationalizations. Something new had happened, like water coming to a boil. Both felt that, though far more distressing than their usual interactions, there was more promise of mutual influence. Subsequently, the analysis moved between these two qualitatively different kinds of discourse, one of polite rumination and another of intense emotion and action.

Considering this vignette in terms of nonlinear oscillators provides a means of thinking about it and appreciating it better than can be accomplished in other theories. The qualitative change observed, a phase change, is common in nonlinear systems. Though describable as near-simultaneous individual changes, it is better described as a qualitative change in the analyst-analysand system. The transformation reflects a transition in analyst-analysand coupling. Before the explosion, obsessional enactment and interpretation led to little mutual influence. During the explosion (and its repetitions), coupling shifted so analyst and analysand strongly influenced one another. Finally, in nonlinear systems, microscopic changes with small apparent effect can produce sudden, huge qualitative transitions.

Another example is from an analyst accustomed to thinking in nonlinear terms. The analysand, a brilliant corporate executive, sought treatment because his work felt stagnant and repetitious. He recognized this as an intrapsychic problem and wanted an analysis to "attack the difficulty, get it out in the open." In analysis, he spoke only of business situations. Analyst and analysand recognized that these recitals could be defensive, commented on this, and conscientiously tried to "get down to business." But both enjoyed the discussions, and the analyst enjoyed "kibitzing" about business. Both worried that this was not "real analysis," less so the analyst who recognized that a system of coupled oscillators was emerging. It was easy to maintain this position because the analysand improved on many fronts. He became more creative than ever at work. His marriage and relationship to his children improved, though these were hardly discussed in the analysis. Much to his surprise, the patient started painting "on a whim," his first avocation, enjoying it enormously. When, rarely, the analysand referred to dreams or other psychological events, he showed deep and developing insight. A conceptualization involving the unconscious connection of oscillators allowed the analyst to relax and enjoy what in every respect but form seemed a successful analysis. Freud observed:

> Just as the receiver converts back into sound waves the electric oscillations in the telephone line which were set up by sound waves, so the doctor's unconscious is able, from the derivatives of the unconscious which are communicated to him, to reconstruct that unconscious, which has determined the patient's free associations.
>
> (Freud, 1912, p. 116)

I simply suggest that this process is a two-way process.

The system formed by coupling oscillators depends on their relative strength and the nature of their coupling.

Harold, a shy, depressed college junior, felt only slightly interested in academics. He was friendless and occasionally admired girls from afar. Sometimes he drank heavily, only to wake up in the hallway of the apartment building where the girl he was currently interested in lived, without memory of how he got there. Harold and his analyst found the sessions tedious. The stasis and indifference extended outside the analysis. Harold got little relief. The analyst seldom thought of him outside of sessions. Their only mutual influence was to attend appointments. The analyst's conscience forced himself to make inquiries and to try to build an alliance. He learned facts about Harold and Harold agreed to cooperate, but nothing seemed to happen. The analyst wondered about his connection to Harold. Harold dispassionately described a lifelong pattern, which his mother said was present from infancy, of Harold's not interacting in emotional ways except when drunk. He placed himself near adults but was uninfluenced emotionally by them. Harold never molded to his mother's body. Harold felt indifferent to his mother's rapport. The attempt at analysis ended with Harold's college graduation and move to another city. In Harold's analysis, the analyst-analysand affective link was so weak that useful coupling of the oscillators never occurred.

Eliza sought analysis because little interested her. She would take up something then "run out of steam." Her analyst, an enthusiastic and lively candidate, had to resist an urge to be a "cheerleader and advisor" for her patients. Eliza's initial response to analysis was a remarkable transformation. Suddenly, she had interests, lost thirty pounds, and became popular in her social circle. She thought of becoming a therapist and began to dress like her analyst. The analyst recognized a "transference cure" but, with her usual optimism, saw it as a step in the analysis. Being self-observant, she noticed that her report of these ideas in supervision seemed wooden, unlike her usual excitement about analytic insights. As Eliza got better, her analyst's enthusiasm waned and supervision, with her well-liked supervisor, became "a drag," as did working with Eliza. Eliza's identifications seemed "off." She picked clothing appropriate to the analyst's coloring but not to her own. The situation was like that observed between two oscillators, one of which was much more powerful than the other so that initially the weaker oscillator appeared to be driven by the stronger, but over time the weaker oscillator affected the stronger one, producing irregularities in the stronger one and oddities in the entrainment (see Abraham and Shaw, 1992). The analyst was able to become less encouragingly dominating. While the analysand complained that the analyst was less helpful, she came forth with ever clearer material about herself.

Each of these clinical situations might be understood by using various clinical theories. Many of these theories are non-explanatory generalizations of clinical experiences, giving a name to common phenomena. The theory of analysis as coupled oscillators is a unified explanatory theory for phenomena like those described in these vignettes.

Relationship to Other Mathematical and Clinical Models

Since Freud's attempt to apply physics to psychoanalysis, there have been many attempts to mathematize psychoanalysis. Vector analysis was applied to forces in dynamic opposition (French, 1952, 1954, 1958). Information processing (Rosenblatt and Thickstun, 1977a, b) and information theory (Peterfreund and Schwarz, 1971) models solved some epistemological problems of metapsychology but gained little traction among analysts probably because they added little to clinical understanding. Other authors used mathematical concepts metaphorically (Matte-Blanco, 1988). Some of Bion's work is truly mathematical in character (see Bion, 1977). However, few analysts have picked up on this mathematical dimension. Most emphasize Bion's clinically useful descriptions of psychological actions, perhaps because Bion's mathematical comments are terse and require knowledge of advance mathematics.

In contrast to these specific efforts, which seem not to have brought mathematics to psychoanalysis, ideas from general systems theory (von Bertalanffy, 1968) and cybernetics (Wiener, 1961) have informally found their way into psychoanalysis through the general culture. "Boundaries" comes from general systems theory; "feedback," from cybernetics. When these fields were developing in the 1950s, they involved devilishly difficult mathematics that did not yield explicit results because their creators were attempting to explore nonlinear concepts before the mathematics had been developed.

A satisfactory mathematical approach to nonlinear systems began to emerge only in the 1960s, largely in response to the needs of these fields (see, for example, Pontryagin *et al.*, 1962). Starting with Harry Stack Sullivan (Sullivan, 1940, 1964; Mullahy, 1970), continuing through the work of Heinz Kohut (1971) and various relational viewpoints, analysts have suggested ideas originally put forward initially by the Chicago School of Sociology (Bulmer, 1984; Frazier, 1948; Mead, 1934; Park *et al.*, 1925) that personality develops and is supported throughout life in interpersonal contexts (see Galatzer-Levy and Cohler, 1993). Thus, psychoanalytic technique must be understood as interpersonal interactions that repair central aspects of personality. The coupled oscillator concept is consistent with these models but goes further, specifying a means by which interpersonal relations shape the personality. Many of the processes described in detail by Sullivan and his successors might be thought of as entries in a descriptive catalogue of the kinds of links that occur in the analytic and other interpersonal situations. The form of these links significantly affects the coupled oscillator system, so cataloguing them and their impacts is a major direction for development of the coupled oscillator concept.

Conclusion

Coupled oscillators provide novel ways of thinking about how psychoanalysis works. These ideas are not a comprehensive theory of psychoanalytic action, partly because "psychoanalysis" refers to a range of activities. Furthermore, clinical and systematic research shows that other factors account for significant aspects of the therapeutic action. The theory provides another approach to the question and a richer picture of how some well-known modes of therapeutic action operate.

The theory is surely true in a trivial sense—minds/brains are mathematical oscillators and interpersonal interaction couples these oscillators. But are these ideas useful? A range of objections could be raised. The major success of psychoanalysis is in uncovering personal meanings of human actions. Coupled oscillators omit direct reference to this activity. This problem can be remedied through the further description of links. Still, any abstract formulation removes us from discourse on the level of clinical facts and generalizations, which has been so fruitful for psychoanalysis (Gill and Holtzman, 1976).

Finally, only the beginning of this formulation is presented here. In particular, the most interesting instances of coupled oscillators involving various nonlinear oscillators that lead to qualitatively new results remain to be developed. The actual usefulness of these ideas to psychoanalysts depends on a willingness to become familiar with a distinctive way of thinking that holds strong promise for a general theory of therapeutic action.

The next chapter shows how these ideas can inform a classical problem of psychoanalytic technique, the question of the exactness of interpretations.

Notes

1 More precisely, chaos refers to the "aperiodic, long-term behavior of a bounded, deterministic system that exhibits sensitive dependence on initial conditions" (Sprott, 2003, p. 104). Here, "aperiodic" means non-repeating; "bounded" means that the values of all variables remain within a finite range; "sensitive dependence on initial conditions" means that a change, however slight, in the initial state of the system will lead to a large change as the system evolves.

2 Von Bertalanffy (1968) pointed out the power of the choice of the boundaries in understanding systems, but, prior to the development of nonlinear dynamics and complexity theory, it remained impossible to transform this insight into meaningful mathematics that went beyond verbal descriptions.

3 Play involving coupling for its own sake, i.e. driven by the need to develop coupling capacity, is ubiquitous. Although much of this play can be interpreted symbolically as disguised representations of sexual and aggressive fantasies, it might also be looked on as explorations of synchrony and its disruption. The huge number of ball games involving synchronization of actions and attempts at disruption of that synchronization could be seen as experiments and rehearsals of the function of coupled oscillators.

4 The pendulums are examples of linear oscillators. These illustrations involve coupling linear oscillators. This was done for simplicity and clarity. Coupling nonlinear oscillators results in still richer configurations.

5 More recently, they have indicated an appreciation that "now moments" occur within a context of ongoing analytic activity (Boston Change Process Study Group, 2005).

6 That dreams and similar productions reflect something beyond disguised fulfillment was understood in Sartre's (1943) idea of "mood" and Kohut's (1971) idea of "self-state dream" is usefully reframed in terms of attractors.

Chapter 6

Inexact Interpretations and Coupled Oscillators

> My guess was wrong; but it was curious to see how a single well-aimed question gave him a sudden perspicacity, so that he was able to bring me as an answer something of which he had certainly been unaware up to that time. He gave me a pained, even an indignant look, on my bringing a later passage from the poem, "My necklace I have given thee, your lock of hair I take away with me. Look on it carefully, tomorrow you will be gray and you will appear brown again only there." The context shows that the it or her in the third line refers to the lock of hair. In a different context the line could mean "look at her carefully". And add that shortly: "She is rather older than I am."
>
> —S. Freud, *The Psychopathology of Everyday Life*, p. 17

In Freud's view, people are constantly engaged in unconscious mental processes, and the analyst's task is to bring some of these processes into awareness by interpreting patients' associations and other products of unconscious mental activity. Since Freud believed that the unconscious mental processes went on whether they were interpreted or not, he believed that there were "correct" interpretations—interpretations that accurately described these unconscious processes. Analysts are forever making wrong interpretations in the sense that they make interpretations that do not accurately correspond to preexisting fantasies that the analysand has or fail to describe how and why agents (individuals, dyads, aspects of persons' minds, etc.) unconsciously act as they do.

Interpretations are judged by several factors. The accuracy of psychoanalytic interpretations is commonly judged by whether they fit with an accepted theoretical formulation. Although in our era (when most analysts respect multiple viewpoints) it is less common for teachers and supervisors to simply pronounce interpretations as wrong because the interpretations are inconsistent with some theoretical viewpoint, it remains common in discussions of analytic work to criticize an intervention as "unanalytic," "superficial," or "insufficiently deep." Heated arguments about interpretations often center on differences of opinion originating in different theoretical orientations and assertions that an interpretation must be incorrect because it does not fit with one or another theory.

For example, in Kohut's (1971) *Analysis of the Self*, he discusses dreams of decimated cities. Kohut understands these dreams to represent the dreamer's fragmented and deleted self and includes them among what he refers to as "self-state" dreams. As more classically oriented analysts observe, the dreams refer to the destruction of phallic skyscrapers and thus concern castration. Arguments of this type can easily become circular because good theories are supported by their growing from good interpretations, but if an interpretation must be consistent with a given theory in order for it to be good, the result is that theory and interpretation are mutually supportive and there is no way to explore the adequacy of either.

Interpretations are also judged by their completeness—the degree to which they exhaust potentially accurate understandings of a psychoanalytic situation. Since, according to the principle of multiple function, virtually all psychologically significant actions accomplish several things at once, an interpretation that accurately describes part of the process that leads to an action but omits other sources of the action can be seriously misleading.

Finally, interpretations may be judged by their efficacy—the degree to which they accomplish a goal, such as symptom relief or uncovering further directions of exploration.

Interpretations as discussed here refer to statements[1] or propositions, although sometimes interpretations may be communicated in nonverbal form. (The Chicago analyst Lionel Blitzen kept a paper crown next to the couch, which, at appropriate moments, he placed on analysands' heads, thereby communicating, "You have the grand fantasy that you are a king." Whatever we may think of this technique, it remains a way of communicating a proposition.) Many other psychoanalytic interventions exist besides interpretations. Here, I am talking only about interpretations *per se*.

The three criteria—accuracy, completeness, and efficacy—exist in complex relationship. When Freud attempted to operationalize the idea of accuracy of interpretation, he proposed as a primary measure the extent to which it brought forward new material. Issues that are sometimes discussed under the rubric of tact, but that might be understood also in terms of the accuracy with which the analyst understands the analysand's capacity to hear an interpretation (an idea that we are not regarding as part of the interpretation, since it is not stated), may determine how complete the analyst chooses to make an interpretation. Classical metapsychology (Rapaport and Gill, 1959) described the dimensions of a complete interpretation, which might go by the formula "in your (the patient's) perception, my (the analyst's) action stimulated an (unconscious) fantasy whose components included particular (described) motivations, which are, to varying degrees, disguised by (described) defenses and integrated with motives arising in various agencies of the mind, all of which are integrated with (unconscious) memories originating in early childhood to produce the action I am now interpreting." For example, "When I arrived late for your session, you unconsciously felt enraged and helpless, which stimulated fears that I would respond to that enraged helplessness by rejecting you. Unconscious moral disapproval of yourself for having such a state of mind and impulses to hurt and damage me resulted. This complex of thoughts and feelings in the present built on memories that are only partly conscious of experiences with your mother, whom you understood as responding to your upset when she kept you waiting in your crib crying in the morning as an attack on her and an indication of what a defective baby you were. In combination, these factors resulted in your saying 'good morning' to me in a manner that was at the same time the epitome of politeness but with an archness in your voice that communicated your rage and contempt."

In practice, even the most traditionally oriented analysts rarely make such complete interpretations because to do so, as the example suggests, would rarely be useful. Nor do we often make interpretations that are theoretically precise because we almost always lack adequate information to do so. Most of the interpretations that analysts offer are neither complete nor accurate, though they may include some nearly accurate elements. Analysts generally regard the type of accurate and complete interpretation described above as an ideal endpoint of psychoanalytic work and even something one would be able to do near the end of an analysis, whether or not the analyst actually ever provided an interpretation of this type.

Edward Glover (1931) observed that "inexact" interpretations, i.e. interpretations that addressed an issue in a way that both seemed pertinent but at the same time were inaccurate, commonly had a therapeutic effect in the sense that they relieved symptoms. Although Glover was clearly attempting to point to the problems associated with Jungian conceptualizations, his observation is easily generalized to other supposedly inexact interpretations. Today, it is generally agreed that the theoretical correctness of interpretations is only loosely related to their therapeutic effects.

Glover understood the therapeutic effects of inexact interpretations as arising from what we would today think of as the initiation of more adaptive defenses than were being used as part of the symptom being interpreted. The new defense the interpretation suggests still disguises the underlying dynamics of the situation and thereby protects the patient from the anxiety that would result if the patient became aware of those dynamics. In doing so, it interferes with uncovering and working through those underlying dynamics. It may also result in other symptomatic manifestations.

An example from current analytic practice illustrates what Glover had in mind. Mr. C was repeatedly late and occasionally entirely missed his analytic sessions. On occasion, he mentioned that his lateness resulted from "a stop in the restroom." He also occasionally referred to a fascination with his own feces and feeling embarrassed by this fascination. Eventually, his analyst offered the interpretation that Mr. C felt so ashamed of this fascination and so uncomfortable talking about it that he avoided the sessions altogether. Mr. C not only agreed with this interpretation but his attendance became more prompt and more regular. The analyst believed that he had made a successful interpretation. However, both the topic of his fascination and his shame about it disappeared from the sessions.

It was only several years later that Mr. C started talking about children at a playground who were loosely supervised. He wished he could be as free as they were but worried that they might "get in trouble" without adequate oversight. Over a period of several months, these associations led to recollections of how, as a young child, he would defecate in "inappropriate" places when he thought he could get away with it. Eventually, the experience of avoiding the sessions was revisited, and it became clear that the patient had been enacting a fantasy in which he hid the desecration of the analyst's bathroom from the analyst who he believed would punish him for misusing it and "shitting all over your place." Shame was not so central an issue as guilt and the intensity of his own libidinal and aggressive impulses. The inexact interpretation focusing on shame had a therapeutic effect that obscured its inaccuracy and, in this instance, postponed that introduction of the more correct and more useful interpretation. This was the sort of situation Glover hoped to avoid.

In contrast to Glover's depreciation of inexact interpretation, but consistent with a very different view of the function of psychoanalysis as the creation rather than the uncovering of meaning, Winnicott (1986) held that good interpretations are always somewhat off the mark. This allows room for the analysand's creativity and avoids oppressing the analysand with the analyst's authority. From a different point of view, the very idea of an exact interpretation is anathema to those analysts who see the development of more functional life narratives as the goal of analytic work, based in the notion that the use of these narratives in psychological functioning makes them significant, rather than their veracity as judged by other than this pragmatic criteria.

A difficulty arises with regard to this notion, since both analysts and patients, beginning with Freud (1895b), have noted that interpretations that fail to carry conviction and which therefore are seen as not relating to the real issues are consistently ineffective. An interpretation that strikes either analyst or patient as untrue, no matter how useful it might seem, is unlikely to have much effect. Newly developed narratives, in order to function well, must not only provide a useful working story for the patient but also be grounded in continuity with something the patient experiences as fact. Thus, a free-floating, disconnected idea, no matter how functional or accurate, in and of itself will not prove useful unless it is tethered to the patient's experiential reality.

But what is the nature of this tethering? Certainly, it is not primarily intellectual coherence or legitimacy. The situation can be formulated in terms of the coupled oscillator model discussed in the previous chapter. Picture the underlying psychic content as a vibration and the interpretation as another vibration. For simplicity, imagine each as a vibrating string of a musical instrument. If the interpretation is exactly on target, analogous to a tone exactly at the pitch of the vibrating string, the two will resonate and the string will be activated. Beyond this, nothing very interesting will happen. An exact interpretation will produce nothing new, although it may intensify or bring out the underlying psychic process.

Now imagine an interpretation that is slightly "off," like a musical tone that is near enough to produce resonance but not identical to the psychic content. As discussed in the previous chapter, the result is something novel and interesting emergent from the interaction, something that in its psychological form would be regarded as creative as Winnicott suggested.

These ideas point again to the way in which the coupled oscillator model is consistent with the making of a new psychological configuration and clarifies the idea that the work of analysis is the co-creation of analyst and analysand. It is not the unearthing of a preexisting configuration. Work of this type is intrinsically nonlinear and involves the emergence of something that was not previously present.

Interpretations that work are good enough to stimulate new patterns of oscillation. They achieve more than amplification of the underlying oscillation but create something new and interesting precisely because they are somewhat off the mark while being sufficiently close to engage the original dynamic. A central feature of the coupled oscillator model is the emergence of something new and interesting, not simply the repair of the psychic apparatus to some predetermined point of excellence.

The model of development that Freud and many of his followers adopted included a picture of mature psychological functioning that was essentially unchanging once in place. In this model, pathology in the mature individual results from past developmental failures, which it may be possible to remedy through therapeutic regressions that allow for the reworking of aspects of development. Starting with the work of Erik Erikson (1963, 1968, 1973, 1986), analysts have increasingly recognized that development is ordinarily lifelong and that the idea of a developmental endpoint confuses the analytic understanding of normal psychological functioning (Galatzer-Levy and

Cohler, 1993). The psyche is a dynamic system, always changing and developing. The model of psychological function on which Glover based his idea of "inexact interpretations" is faulty in this regard and leads to concerns that are not appropriate for the dynamic that is an ever-changing, ever-evolving system that is human psychological functioning.

Note

1 Not all verbalizations or actions of the analyst are interpretations, and sometimes interpretations may be most effective when they are communicated in a very terse fashion that makes them difficult to see as interpretations. For example, a patient who was compulsively attracted to a certain kind of woman responded incredulously to a series of statements by the analyst about the motives for this attraction. Finally, the patient said in exasperation, "The next thing you're going to tell me is that I'm looking for the diamond in my mother's pussy." The analyst remained silent; the patient turned around on the couch, looked at the analyst, and gathered correctly from the analyst's facial expression that the analyst endorsed the patient's own interpretation, to which the patient responded by saying, "Oh, no!" and explored a previously unconscious fantasy very much along the lines of his statement.

Chapter 7

Prediction and Self-Similarity[1]

The empirical study of psychoanalysis has proven devilishly difficult. From his earliest investigation, Freud (1895b) tried to support his theories with data from the psychoanalytic situation, and, from that time until the present, this effort has foundered on recurring problems. The data is much too complex. Separating the signal from the noise is nearly impossible. In addition, the data is confidential and must be massaged in ways that are likely to distort it if it is to be made public (Galatzer-Levy, 2003). Aspects of nonlinear dynamics can help in the empirical study of psychoanalysis.

Insofar as psychoanalysis wishes to be a science in a traditional sense, we must address the problem of prediction since the most convincing demonstrations of the correctness of a scientific theory lie in its capacity to predict events that have not yet occurred, whether they be the results of an experiment or natural events (Waelder, 1963; Wallerstein, 1964; Sargent, Horwitz, Wallerstein, and Appelbaum, 1968). Some have argued that psychoanalysis should not attempt to be scientific in this sense; it should not attempt to predict the course of psychological events in the way physical scientists traditionally have predicted the evolution of physical systems. Elsewhere, Cohler and I (2007) present arguments for the position that psychoanalysis is a different kind of science than the physical sciences and should not try to attempt to ape them. In fact, the most valuable psychoanalytic contributions have been to clinical theory, the exploration of human meanings and motives (Klein, 1976).

At the same time, insofar as psychoanalysis can be a predictive science, that would certainly be to the good. Despite valiant efforts, theoretical work that does more than clarify clinical psychoanalytic concepts and goes on to make predictions of any kind is rare. Papers in which theoretical explorations lead to testable hypotheses are almost absent from the psychoanalytic literature (Edelson, 1983).

Furthermore, the notion that prediction is a uniquely appropriate measure of scientific status is faulty. It ignores the historical background of the prestige inherent of astrologers' and astronomers' capacity to predict (Schaffer, 1993). It also ignores accepted scientific disciplines, such as geophysics and meteorology, the study of which does not lead to satisfactory prediction. Conversely, prediction and understanding are not necessarily linked. Many statistically excellent but meaningless correlations are found in economic data (Silver, 2012). The most highly predictive science, quantum electrodynamics, capable of accurate predictions to seven decimal points, is said by its inventor to provide no understanding of the matters it so satisfactorily predicts (Feynman, 1985).

Nonetheless, where it is possible, the collection of meaningful, publicly communicable data is central to systematic investigations. The collection and communication of facts about analyses presents challenging problems. Many of them are inherent to psychoanalysis (Klumpner and Frank, 1991; Galatzer-Levy, *et al.*, 2000). They include:

- Psychoanalysis is thought to require confidentiality so that making an analysis public in any way distorts it.
- Psychoanalyses involve huge amounts of auditory and visual data whose recording and processing remains difficult, even though modern technologies make both easier than they were in the recent past.
- The internal state of the analyst, which many of us use as data in our clinical work, is at best difficult to capture and record.
- There is a huge problem with sampling.
- It is difficult to know in what sense, if at all, a particular analysis is representative of analysis in general, of a particular sort of psychoanalysis, or even of the work done with a particular patient.
- It is hard to know whether any portion of an analysis—say, a session or group of sessions—represents the whole analysis.

Many reasons have been suggested for this situation. Beginning with Freud (1920c), analysts have pointed to the insufficiency of quantitative data and inadequate means of measurement of psychological forces and energies as the source of difficulty. No matter how precise the theoretical formulations, they cannot predict outcomes without accurate measures of pertinent quantities. No one has found ways to quantitatively measure the forces and energies posited in metapsychology. For this reason alone, we would not expect quantitative prediction to be possible in psychoanalysis.

Robert Waelder (1963) understood that something even more fundamental was amiss. His insight that prediction of mental processes was intrinsically difficult or impossible, i.e. that prediction is difficult because of the very nature of the system under study, anticipates findings from nonlinear dynamics and complexity theory.

In the mid-1970s, many analysts repudiated traditional metapsychology and its project of reducing psychological phenomena to quantitative equations analogous to those of classical physics (Gill and Holzman, 1976; Klein, 1976). Some analysts sought other forms of reduction than to energy and force, including the study of brain mechanisms, ethology, developmental description, information processing and computer models, and revamping of older theories (e.g. Peterfreund and Schwartz, 1971; Basch, 1976a b, c, 1985; Rosenblatt and Thicksten, 1977; Bowlby, 1982; Galatzer-Levy, 1983, 1984, 1988, 1991; Reiser, 1984, 1985).

Others believed that reductionism is not an appropriate tack. They observed that the significant contributions of psychoanalysis are its clinical theories, its understanding of people in terms of meanings and motives. They suggested that attempts to replace metapsychology with a better reductionist framework only diverted psychoanalysts' attention from areas to which they might make real contributions, i.e. the hermeneutics of human action (Ricoeur, 1970, 1977; Schafer, 1976a, 1980, 1992; Klein, 1976; Spence, 1982, 1987, 1989). The hermeneutic trend in psychoanalysis embraces this abandonment of the reductionist program altogether (Ricoeur, 1970; Goldberg, 1988). They argued that the fantasy that one day analysts armed with good enough theories and methods of observation could, like the similarly armed physicist, make precise predictions and create useful interventions based on those predictions was not only impractical but also impossible for fundamental reasons, and even if not impossible, it was not the kind of understanding we seek in psychoanalysis.

Whatever the other merits of these arguments (and I think those merits are great), they are partly based on a picture of mathematical prediction that is no longer current. Nonlinear dynamics system theory suggests that the received version of mathematical-based prediction in the sciences is unduly narrow.

Classical Prediction

Part of the pessimism about the reduction of psychological to physical phenomena and physics-like laws originates in the received picture of the physical sciences. The working paradigm of modern physical science is the work of Newton. This is not to say that all of the content of Newton's theories continues to be seen as correct, but until the 1980s, Newton's model of how to do physical science was almost universally accepted in our society by all but a handful of philosophers (Toulmin, 1990).

In Newton's paradigm, scientists propose theories that, ideally, can be encompassed in mathematical equations. Quantitative predictions based on solutions of these equations are compared to experimental findings to confirm or disconfirm the hypotheses the equations embody. For example, based on his theory of universal gravitation, Newton predicted the moon's position in the heavens. The satisfactory comparison of his predictions with his (slightly fudged) observations was taken as confirmation of the underlying theory. Three centuries later, Feynman (1985), using essentially the same paradigm for scientific investigation, characterized his theory of quantum electrodynamics as successful because it predicts atomic spectra correctly to seven decimal points.

Newton introduced the main tool of theoretical physics, the differential equation, a mathematical statement that relates the rates of change of various aspects of a system to other aspects of a system. Saying the downward acceleration of a baseball is a constant is equivalent to writing a differential equation as follows:

The acceleration is the rate of change of velocity, which in turn is the rate of change of position. So if we call the height of the ball *e*, and indicate the rate of change by a dot above the variable (so that two dots indicate the rate of change of the rate of change), the equation for a falling baseball is

$$\ddot{e} = G$$

where G is the gravitational constant.

This is a "nice" equation in the sense that we can write its solution explicitly:

$$e = ½Gt2 + kt + h$$

where *k* is the initial downward velocity and *h* is the height from which the ball was thrown. So if we are given the time, initial position, and initial velocity, we can simply plug these numbers into the equation to compute the height of the ball from the ground. Fortunately for baseball fans, this equation provides a very incomplete description of the motion of a baseball. A real baseball is influenced by complex frictional forces as well as the force of gravity. But for situations where friction is a minor factor, such as the path of a bullet or the orbit of the moon, versions of this equation are adequate and lead to good predictions of motion.

Much of the physical world can be modeled using differential equations. The physical sciences were dominated by the search for appropriate differential equations to describe systems. This approach was so successful that by the 1950s, authors like physicist Eugene Wigner (1960) began to puzzle about the "unreasonable effectiveness of mathematics" in describing the physical world. Wigner wondered how such simple ideas and equations were so effective in clarifying a wide range of phenomena. The power of simple mathematical ideas in describing and predicting physical events is such that thinkers ranging from Descartes to Einstein believed that it suggested an intelligence behind the manifest universe.

Retrospectively, this "unreasonable effectiveness" resulted, in part, because theoreticians systematically ignored phenomena that could not be encompassed using the mathematical methods of their time (Thom, 1975) and because scientists chose problems that are mathematically tractable (Gribbin, 1994). If matters that are not well described by differential equations are ignored, it is not surprising that these equations appear to describe all phenomena. For example, surf and the physics of breaking water waves cannot be satisfactorily treated using differential equations. The definitive "comprehensive" treatise on water waves written by the world's leading expert on the topic in the middle of the last century simply omitted the obvious physical events of surf and breaking waves (Stoker, 1957). Researchers could maintain the illusion of the universal effectiveness of differential equations by simply ignoring phenomena for which differential equations were not useful.

Problems with the Classical Model and the Emergence of New Models

Mathematicians (and occasionally physicists) struggled with what at first seemed to be technical problems in the theory of differential equations. By the middle of the last century, a type of differential equation called linear differential equations was very well understood. In mathematics, the word *linear* means that the equation involves adding together derivatives (rates of change) that are multiplied by constants. None of the terms of a linear differential equation involve multiplying variables or their derivatives by one another. The word *linear* in this connection means nothing more or less. Mathematicians do *not* mean by linear that the solution is a line, is simple, proceeds step by step, or is easy to conceptualize. Nor do they mean by *nonlinear* anything mysterious, mystical, or related to "new age" thinking.[2] The equation for a spring's motion,

$$\ddot{e} - ke = 0$$

is linear because the position of the spring (e) and its derivatives do not appear as multiples of each other. In this case, the solution is a sine curve. If we add a term for friction that is proportional to the square of the velocity, the equation becomes

$$\ddot{e} + m\dot{e}^2 - ke = 0$$

where m is a constant associated with the elasticity of the spring. This equation is no longer linear because the velocity term appears multiplied by itself, squared.

Linear equations are "nice." Very well-developed methods exist for solving them and for describing their solutions. But they have an even more important feature. Insofar as phenomena are governed by them, the world is highly predictable, and predictions change in an easily comprehended way. A little bit of change in the initial conditions of situations governed by a linear equation results in a little bit of change in the behavior of the system. The idea that small changes in initial conditions cause small changes in outcome seems to correspond to our intuition. If I throw a ball slightly harder, I expect it will go slightly further. When I press the accelerator of my car a bit further down, I expect the car to go slightly faster.

This supposed intuition that, in the real world, small changes in the cause of an event will result in small changes in the event itself is not so much a reflection of reality as a result of our experience in which we systematically exclude data that does not fit with the idea of the proportionality of effect to cause. The fate of the pitched baseball is very different depending on minuscule differences in its velocity (e.g. a strike vs. a home run), and the additional gasoline flowing to the engine may make the difference between the car moving or stalling. The more we look at the idea that our experience of the physical world corresponds to the behavior predicted by linear differential equations that predict that effects will be proportional to their causes, the more it becomes apparent that this belief is achieved by systematically excluding the data of daily experience (Thom, 1975).

In addition, in our technological age, many of our experiences with machines that suggest the linearity of the physical world result from the careful design of those machines to behave in a linear fashion within the range of intended function. Imagine if automobile brakes always "grabbed" (i.e. the braking force was not smoothly related to the pressure applied to the foot pedal). Auto brakes are carefully designed to avoid this phenomenon. The speed of a gasoline engine is *not* proportional to the amount of fuel it receives, but the system linking the gas pedal to the engine is carefully designed so that it feels like the acceleration is proportional to the depression of the gas pedal.

Equations that are not linear are usually not "nice." Their solutions usually cannot be written down explicitly. In fact, they tend to be intractable. For many years, mathematicians did a bit of fudging to deal with this problem. They approximated the nonlinear equations by linear equations, and within a certain range these approximations were good enough for practical purposes.

Here is an example. (As is true throughout this book, readers who feel like, whenever mathematical formulae appear, they have landed in some foreign country whose language is somewhere between incomprehensible and something they vaguely learned decades ago should feel free to skip over these portions of the text. The central ideas do not require following every mathematical step.) Texts and teachers of elementary physics usually derive the equation for a pendulum's motion by first observing that the forces acting on the pendulum lead to the differential equation

$$\ddot{e} - k\text{sin}e = 0$$

Then the instructor observes that for small

$$e \cong \sin e$$

where ≅ means "is approximately equal to" so the equation becomes

$$\ddot{e} - ke \cong 0$$

This is a useful step because the instructor knows how to solve the last equation (it is a simple linear differential equation), but he does not know how to solve the equation involving the sine function. The only trouble is that the approximation is only good for small *e* and the difference between *e* and *sin e* becomes quite important without *e* getting very big at all (Figure 7.1).

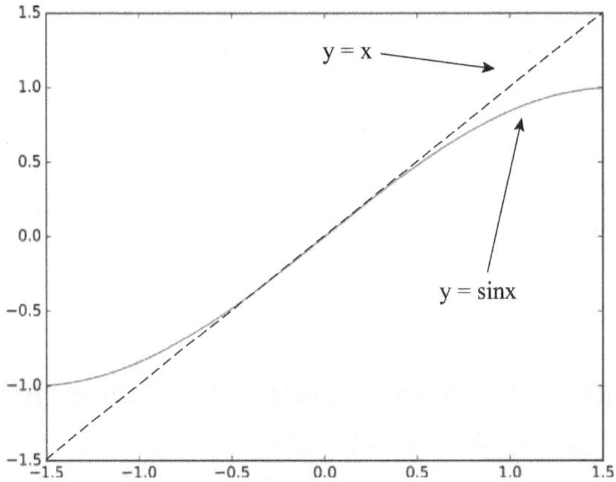

Figure 7.1 Comparison of $y = \sin x$ to $y = x$. Note the Approximation $x \gg \sin x$ is Only Valid for Small x. (Graph Courtesy of David Galatzer-Levy.)

The trend toward using linear approximation was so powerful that most physicists ignored phenomena that could not be approximated using it. Many mathematicians at best regarded the nonlinear realm as unusual or representing "pathological" variations. As mentioned before, major texts about water waves simply did not refer to breaking surf (Stoker, 1957). This was because there was no satisfactory mathematical method to deal with surf, so the phenomenon was ignored. René Thom (1975) observed the wide areas of physical phenomena that were ignored for this reason. This tendency was reinforced because technologists tried to design equipment governed by linear equations because, of course, when you build something you want to be quite certain what it will do. We are surrounded by a linear world created by technology, and this supports the impression (our seeming common sense) that the world is governed by linear differential equations.

Starting around 1970, computers became sophisticated enough that the properties of previously intractable equations could be explored through direct computation. It had been clear for many years that some of the linear approximations were simply inadequate and led to absurd predictions. But until new methods became available to examine the actual properties of nonlinear equations, these inadequacies tended to be treated as esoteric technical problems. With the development of the computer, it became possible to study the world of differential equations (or dynamic systems as they came to be called) in an entirely different way. At first, this required very sophisticated machines, i.e. the best technology of the day, but now the computers we have in our homes are quite adequate for many of these explorations. With the new computer technology, it became possible to experiment with differential equations and to produce pictures of the phenomena associated with them. A new world opened in these studies—a world much closer to our complex everyday reality.

At the turn of the century, the great French mathematician Henri Poincaré (see Kline, 1972) realized that the most important features of differential equations were not their solutions in numbers but the qualitative properties of those solutions. Typical questions in this context were: Would the system go on forever repeating the same states? Would it gradually damp down and come to a halt? Would it go into ever larger oscillation? What form would these changes take?

In the early 1960s, another French mathematician, René Thom, systematically explored the qualitative features of an important class of differential equations. He discovered two important facts:

- First, contrary to expectations, quite simple differential equations could lead to a variety of not only discontinuous solutions but solutions in which, for example, the final state of the system depends on its past history.[3]
- In addition, Thom was able to characterize all the types of abrupt changes that the kinds of differential equations he was studying could undergo. This new branch of mathematics was humorously labeled *catastrophe theory* because the abrupt changes can be thought of as catastrophes.

In this study of the simplest differential equations, Thom explored his model prediction that the system will be characterized by two distinct regimens with abrupt transitions between them (Figure 7.2). Unlike the situation that is described in older models in which the current forces acting on the system completely determine its current status, the models of catastrophe theory predict that the immediate past history of the system will shape the system's further evolution. If the system is in one state, it will tend to remain in that state until it abruptly shifts to the other. Figure 7.2 illustrates this. In the central part of the figure, we see two different outputs for a given input. Which of these outputs will occur depends on whether the input approaches its value from the right or the left. This property, called *hysteresis,* is actually observed in a number of physical systems. We can observe it easily when trying to push an object over a rough surface. If the object is not yet moving, considerable force may be necessary to get it going. But once in motion, the same amount of force will cause more change in position.

A common psychological situation is conscious ambivalence, which involves sharp, abrupt transitions from one state to another. At a given moment, the sum of current forces does not determine the ambivalent person's position but instead that we are dealing with a phenomenon (like the snapping of a twig) as a person moves from one position to another (Galatzer-Levy, 1976). In ambivalence, whichever position the person is in tends to continue until an abrupt change

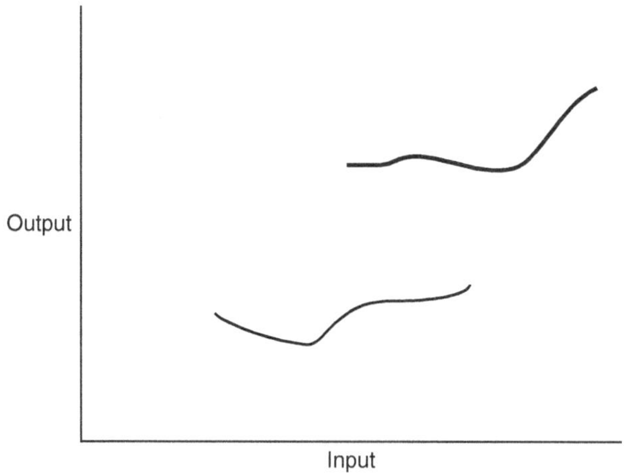

Figure 7.2 Hysteresis.

occurs, i.e. the person's current position is *not* determined by the forces acting on that person but also by the immediate past history. No intermediate states are apparent. Conscious ambivalence is thus governed by hysteresis.

Catastrophe theory models lead to specific predictions about how quantitative changes in intensity result in qualitative changes in a system's activity. At a minimum, the ideas of catastrophe theory lead to the recognition that apparently abrupt and discontinuous changes in a system are real phenomena and that qualitative changes in systems can arise from quantitative change.

Jerome Sashin (1985; Sashin and Callahan, 1990) began to explore the systematic application of catastrophe theory to psychoanalysis. His work went beyond generalized theorizing. On the basis of the study of a catastrophe theory model, he predicted a previously unobserved phenomenon. The prediction has not been verified because there has been no attempt to do so. This line of investigation was tragically interrupted by Sashin's death in 1990.

Despite its many promising features, catastrophe theory focused both on too narrow a range of systems and too specific qualitative features about systems to bring out the full fruit of the exploration of the qualitative features of differential equations. Extreme claims about the power of catastrophe theory by some of its students led to its being held in some ill repute. One proponent of the theory asserted that using it made it possible to predict prison riots. Although the underlying mathematics remained sound, exaggerated claims like this led to widespread skepticism about the theory. In recent years, a broader group of ideas about dynamical systems has come to prominence.

In the 1970s, mathematicians started experiments of a kind they had never done before. Computers made it possible to sit at a computer terminal and "fool around" with the graphic solution of differential equations. The resulting graphical displays are not only mathematically interesting but also aesthetically pleasing. Benoit Mandelbrot (2014) describes how the discovery of the beautiful structure named for him, the Mandelbrot set, emerged in printouts consisting of the letter *x* and blank spaces from the early IBM computers. The result was an empirically richer picture of the possibilities for dynamical systems. With this richer picture came a change in students' "intuition" about the possibilities of systems. Like the transformation of the worldview that resulted from Isaac Newton's work, the research of early dynamic systems theorists appeared to be about highly technical, even arcane, questions. But the results of their research reshaped the way we think about the world.

Greater computational power also made it possible to actually test the accuracy of predictions by using classical models from physics. These models often did not work well, particularly in predicting real world phenomena. Practical long-term weather forecasting, for example, was a complete bust. This failure occurred despite certainty that basic physical principles on which the forecasts were made were correct. Studies showed that the problem was not in the underlying physical concepts but in striking computational features of the equations generated from the physical theory. Most important, very small changes in the initial conditions of the system resulted in dramatic changes in predictions.

An important repercussion of the older idea that small changes should result in small consequences is that minor errors of measurement should not greatly affect the predictions derived from equations. If we put another straw on the camel's back, we expect the animal to bend very slightly further. The proverbial straw that breaks the camel's back takes us out of the linear world. The result is a seeming paradox. A system may be entirely deterministic in the sense that its future evolution is completely set by its features at a certain time, there are no random or probabilistic effects, the rules governing its evolution are entirely known, and still it remains impossible to predict its development (Kilert, 1993). This situation arises when small changes in initial conditions result in large changes in the final state of the system and, hence, any prediction about the system.

The problem is not resolved by making more precise initial measurements. The nature of the divergence of the predictions that results from the small differences in the initial condition is such that it grows very rapidly, no matter how small the initial deviation, so that while more precise specifications of the initial condition do result in better predictions, the investment in precision required to improve the predictions slightly becomes ever larger.[4] This phenomenon came to be known as the "butterfly effect" because it can be shown in studies of long-term weather forecasting that a butterfly flapping (or not flapping) its wings in Sumatra could result in a five-degree change in the temperature in Atlanta eight days later or the presence or absence of snowstorms in Chicago.

In the late 1970s, a British research group used equations of atmospheric dynamics that were known to be correct to make long-term weather forecasts. The results were appalling. They predicted five inches of snow in London in mid-July. Close inspection of the equations showed that their solutions were highly unstable in response to initial conditions. Even though the weather was completely determined and there was no thought of supernatural forces affecting it, it would be theoretically impossible to predict weather in detail over the long range. Thus, chaos theory was born out of the recognition of what could not be done. Any reasonably complex system is not predictable in its details over a long period of time. Certainly the human mind is at such a level of complexity.[5]

Chaos Leads to New Visions of Prediction

Our knowledge that the prediction of five inches of snow in London in midsummer is wrong points to the statistical or probabilistic prediction that we can make about systems. Though we cannot predict the weather in London at any moment, we can predict temperatures by time of year and time of day with a fair degree of confidence since their average values and the variation likely to occur around those average values are well known. In some sense, complex systems often seem to "average out." Such statistical prediction is also possible for matters involving people, including their psychological function. While such a prediction may be of more value to psychoanalysts than is generally believed, it remains distant from the type of statement we would like to be able to make about people. The likely accurate prediction that a person in midlife is likely to confront feelings about life's being finite is statistically accurate for many European and American populations, and even somewhat heuristically informative for psychoanalysts. Yet it is insufficiently detailed and not rich enough to be of much interest to the analyst working with a middle-aged person. We want richer, more precise statements about particular people.

At the same time that students of dynamic systems were discovering that certain kinds of predictions were not possible, explorations of dynamical systems showed that a different and surprising kind of prediction was possible. In complex systems, researchers were often able to discern well-defined tendencies within the system. The evolution of systems might, for example, tend toward stable, overall patterns with characteristic form, even though the precise position of the system was almost entirely unpredictable. For example, a system might go through many near repetitions of the same process without actually repeating the process. Many of the phenomena that had previously been described as the result of probability and chance, that somehow mysteriously resulted in a reliable statistical distribution, could now be reinterpreted as samplings of deterministic phenomena of this new, and hitherto unappreciated, type. These stable configurations of system evolution, called attractors of dynamical systems, have been classified with increasing clarity and thoroughness (e.g. Ott, 1993). The description of an ever-widening range of attractors has been the principal technical result of the study of chaos.

We are familiar with attractors where the particle follows a given path, or at least asymptotically approaches a stable orbit. For example, if we observe the motion of a pendulum, we see a regular progression of oscillations, which either repeat or, if we wait long enough, are gradually damped to no oscillation by the air's friction. Similarly, oscillators into which additional energy is placed—say, by a driving motor—evolve toward relatively easily described paths of motion.[6]

One of the major findings of research into apparently chaotic systems is the existence of "strange" attractors. Upon first examination, the motions in systems may seem random and disorganized, but after many repetitions, we can see that they tend toward a particular pattern—not in the sense that they settle down but rather that the apparently wild shifts in the motion represent tendencies to complex but representable patterns.

One of the first of these patterns to be discovered was the Lorenz attractor. As discussed earlier in this section, attempts at long-term weather prediction have proved impossible. Edward Lorenz (1963) used the equations of fluid dynamics to try to make long-term weather predictions based on the flow of the atmosphere as warm air rises and cold air falls. His computations showed him a new kind of attractor, one in which the observer could not predict the immediate movements of the system, yet an overall pattern emerged. (For an accurate, more detailed discussion that demands little mathematical background, see Stewart [1989] or numerous YouTube videos.)

The observation of these more complex forms of attractors was the first step in which students of dynamical systems discovered order in chaos. For psychoanalysts, these systems of attractors are important as possible models of the ways systems can evolve. Currently, much work is being devoted to the question of how empirical data can be matched with a known catalog of attractors (Morrison, 1991; Guastello *et al.*, 2011). The description of analytic data in a fashion that allows comparison with known descriptions of chaotic systems may result in the enrichment that comes when predictions can be made.

Let us look briefly at what behavior under the influence of a strange attractor might look like in the analytic situation:

> *A woman sought analysis for recurrent depressions accompanied with the desperate search for a man who would make things right. She believed that by associating with a handsome, brilliant man her own reputation would be enhanced. The man would give her ideas that would let her finish a doctoral dissertation. Sexual acts would magically give her his power. The analyst's every remark was, at best, useless and often made matters worse by reminding her of her problems. The patient seemed "set off" into inconsolable crying by the analyst's requests for clarification or the session's ending before the*

> *patient had come to a resolution of the topic she was discussing. All the people she discussed were petty, exploited her, and were the object of her angry contempt. The patient lived in a rageful world. Her major problem was to avoid being utterly plunged into its abyss. As had happened in previous psychotherapies, the patient experienced dramatic improvement in her symptoms after a few months of treatment.*
>
> *Now she appeared as a competent student. She had an ironic sense of humor and was compassionately interested in others. She sought men who liked and were interested in her. She thought of the men she had so desperately wanted as "narcissistic jerks." In the sessions, she worked with the analyst's interpretations. She could step back from and examine transference phenomena. She no longer panicked when the analyst did not immediately understand her or when it was necessary to continue a topic into another session. Her major concerns were those of a moderately inhibited student, combined with a mild fear that her depression would return.*
>
> *The analytic process centered on the movement between these two seemingly distinct states, which occurred in response to the analyst's availability. For example, the analyst's summer vacation regularly resulted in a panicked depression in the patient, and his sustained presence gradually relieved that depression. Early in the analysis, it was as if the patient had two distinct, noninteracting modes of psychological function. The transition between these modes occurred abruptly and for reasons that were obscure to the patient. The total pattern of the patient's psychological functioning was like a strange attractor with two basins. When in either basin the behavior was consistent (if sometimes distressing). At least as interesting as these stable states was that there were transitions between these two quite distinct major modes of functioning. The process of transition between the two required understanding.*

The vision of prediction that derives from the modern study of dynamical systems is different from classical prediction, in which investigators attempt to predict the state of a system at a given later time from data about the system's earlier state. Halley's Comet was predicted to appear in the heavens at a particular location and on a particular date based on previous observations of the comet and Newton's theory of gravitation. Its actual appearance at the right date and place was in itself dramatic and a great support for Newtonian science.

In the new vision of prediction, the investigator predicts patterns of change and stability of systems, not their moment-to-moment status. This type of prediction corresponds better to what we are often interested in when conducting psychoanalytic investigations than the older predictive goals. For example, we care much less which side of a predicament an obsessional person adopts at a particular moment than that he is likely to oscillate between two opposing positions. We are not so interested in the momentary level of regression of a patient as in his or her capacity to move in and out of regressed states in the course of the analysis. Predicting the form of evolution of a system is thus closer to our clinical interests than classical prediction was.

Self-Similarity

A second kind of order emerged through the study of chaotic systems. As we have seen, even in simple dynamical systems, initial conditions can grossly modify the results in the evolution of the system. Minute changes in the initial state of a system can result in qualitatively different regimes. A group of mathematicians inquired about the form of the sets of initial conditions that resulted in various regimens. Although some progress was made on this problem early in the century, the findings were abstruse and seemed to be mathematical oddities. With the development of increased computational capacity, the explorations of these odd and fascinating structures became possible. Among them, the Mandelbrot set has become the object of extensive study and fascination because of its aesthetic, as well as mathematical, features. The set is constructed as follows: Starting with a point in the plane, a simple rule is used to move to another point. The same rule is again applied at the new point, and this process is repeated indefinitely. For some initial points, this process results in a series of moves that makes an ever more distant path; starting from other points, the path is bounded. The initial point is colored or not depending on whether the path generated from the point is bounded or not. This coloring resulted in a startling map (see Figure 7.3).

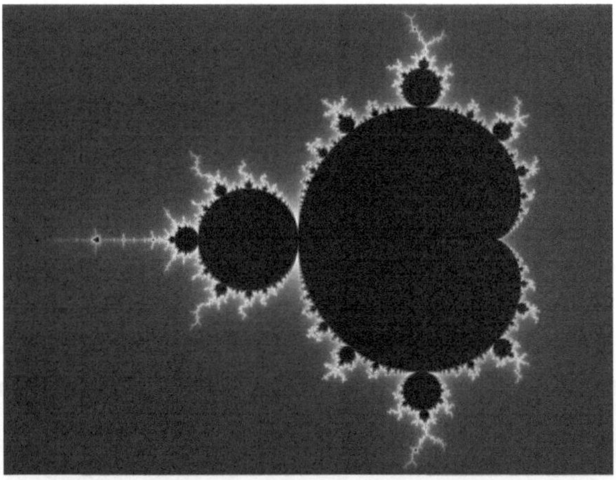

Figure 7.3 The Mandelbrot Set.

Figure 7.4 Magnified Area from Figure 7.3.

The resulting patterns are things of extraordinary beauty called *fractals.* They have many unusual mathematical properties, but in a sense, their most remarkable property is how strikingly they resemble natural forms, like the spray of surf, or coastlines (Barnsley, 1988).

For the purposes of this chapter, we will concentrate on just one feature of fractals. Looking at a series of pictures of progressively enlarged segments of the Mandelbrot set, we observe a remarkable property (see Figures 7.4, 7.5, and 7.6). We can zoom in on a small segment of the fractal—Figure 7.4 shows a picture of the small square

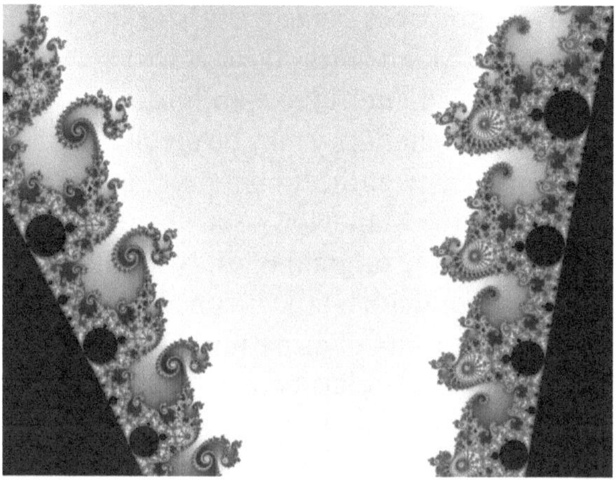

Figure 7.5 Magnification of Segment from Figure 7.4.

Figure 7.6 Magnification of Section of Figure 7.5.

outlined in the previous diagram.[7] At first, it gives the appearance of a wholly different landscape, but looking carefully, there appear to be little Mandelbrot sets in it.

Let's zoom in on another edge from this picture, again, magnifying a thousand times, a new and distinct landscape, but it too is populated by the Mandelbrot-like sets (see Figure 7.5).

This process can be continued indefinitely (see Figure 7.6), for we can compute the configuration of the Mandelbrot set to any magnification we wish. The result is always the same. At every level, new and distinctive landscapes appear, but at every level of magnification we find yet more Mandelbrot-like sets.

When a set is magnified and reveals an image of itself, again it is called "self-similar." Self-similarity may be precise—exactly the same set may reappear on each magnification—or it may be with modification, as is the case with the Mandelbrot set where the new images are similar but distinct from the original ones. Not only is self-similarity an inordinately powerful mathematical concept, but also it is at the core of much of what we think of as natural phenomena.

How is the concept of self-similarity of value to psychoanalysis? The central research problem for psychoanalysis is how to explore psychoanalytic work in an empirically rigorous but psychologically rich fashion. Any systematic investigation of psychoanalytic material quickly reveals that hours can be spent untangling a few minutes of interchange between analyst and patient. Investigators like Dahl (1974, 1988; Dahl, Teller, Moss, and Trujillo, 1978; Dahl, Kachele, and Thomä, 1988) have found it useful to explore psychoanalytic material on the level of words and sentences. Others, like Luborsky (Luborsky and Crits-Cristoph, 1990) and Gill (1982), examine single analytic hours in great detail. Yet while we all agree that analysis can go on only in the details of the interaction between patient and analyst, most analysts believe that psychoanalytic processes are best understood in terms of much longer intervals and that to understand an analysis we want to understand the analytic process in its entirety. Thus, investigating the analytic process appears to result in an enormous practical difficulty. To understand material well, one must study it in depth, but to capture analytic processes, one must explore material over extended periods of time. The study of analyses would then appear intractable simply in terms of the time necessary to investigate an analysis thoroughly.

Self-similar structures are important to empirical research because one can study the essential qualities of those structures, or at least some major aspects of them, by examining tiny portions of them microscopically. In an absolutely self-similar structure, such as the Sierpinski triangle,[8] looking at any subunit gives one essentially all the information that can be had about the system. For more complex systems, such as the Mandelbrot set, important qualitative elements can be found from arbitrarily small samples, but there are differences between the various levels of a Mandelbrot-like set within the Mandelbrot set. In natural occurring phenomena—for example, the growth of plants—obviously more significant samples are needed to be able to see the underlying structure. As the mathematician Fibonacci realized eight centuries ago, basic patterns of a tree's growth can be inferred from very small amounts of data about the underlying pattern of growth, and indeed on the computer, we can grow things like ferns and trees, not to mention realistic-looking coastlines, on the basis of specifying very few elementary features of the system.

Psychoanalytic material commonly has strikingly self-similar aspects. Here is an example taken from the analysis of an obsessional patient, looked at on several levels of magnification.

Yearslong Magnification

Mr. A first exhibited obsessional symptoms at age seven following his mother's remarriage. To others he seemed withdrawn, but, in fact, his time was spent fretfully counting objects in his room and worrying that something was missing. Psychotherapy helped relieve his symptoms. Although he remained inhibited and rather meticulous, he did fairly well until he was eleven. Then, apparently in response to puberty and tension in his mother's marriage, he again became symptomatic. He worried that he had not completed homework assignments and was so concerned to eat properly that charting the nutritional values of food disrupted his life. There were other less prominent obsessional symptoms. The patient interrupted a second round of psychotherapy by a conscious decision to suppress obsessional symptoms, which he did until he left home to go to college. In the uncontrolled, sexually liberal atmosphere of the college dormitory, Mr. A became anxious and severely obsessional, worrying that the cafeteria food might be bad for him, that he had prepared for his classes inadequately, and that he was dressed improperly.

Monthslong Magnification

Mr. A wanted very much to "do it [the analysis] right." In part based on his past therapeutic experience, he approached analysis by expressing jarringly intense feelings, something his first analyst had strongly encouraged. Both the patient and the analyst regarded these expressions as deeply authentic and representative of major analytic progress. Often, after several weeks of talking in this way, the affect intensified further. At these times, the patient demanded the analyst's direct assistance in managing the affects and, partly because the analyst did not know how to help him, became increasingly anxious. He feared going mad. This sense lasted for at most a couple of days. Then the patient regularly first became angry at the analyst for failing to manage some aspect of the analysis correctly (such as billing for missed sessions) and subsequently became enmeshed in sorting out the failing (e.g. developing elaborate moral arguments for and against charging for missed sessions).

Analytic Hours

Mr. A began most analytic sessions with some topic in mind about which he felt strongly. He developed it at some length. (For example, he would speak with rage about his father's departure.) After engaging the topic, the analyst often made a defense interpretation. (The analyst agreed that the patient was angry with his father for leaving but wondered whether his more immediate anger involved the analyst, who had recently returned from vacation.) At first, the patient engaged the interpretation vigorously. ("You always think it's you. You, you, you! But you don't think it's you enough not to go on your stupid vacations!") Then the patient began a much less effective, more intellectual discussion of why he had used the identified defense. ("I wonder why I use displacement so much. That is the right term, isn't it?") As the session grew to a close, the patient often felt it was urgent that he finish the discussion before the session's end. Frequently, he tried to get out a few more sentences as he left. The analyst encouraged him to leave and assured him that they could address the topic more fully in the next session.

Analytic Minutes

Attending closely to the patient's speech revealed that it was marked by constant interruptions either as dysfluencies or interrupting self-reference.

> *"I hate my, er, father because he, uh, he, uh, he, uh, he kinda doesn't, I mean didn't—I find this hard to say—he didn't, uh, do, uh—he*

> *didn't do what sorta what, er, he needed to do for me. [Pause.] You're going to ask what that was. Well, he didn't, uh, do it! I can't describe it. You know! He kinda didn't!"*

The obsessional phenomena described here are familiar to all analysts. No one of them is more essential than another. They can all be seen as aspects of the same self-similar structure view with differing temporal magnification.

Applying the idea of self-similarity to psychoanalytic data addresses one of the major problems of research—the intractable amount of data. The work of people like Dahl (1988), Bucci (1993), and Luborsky (Luborsky and Crits-Christoph, 1990) confirms our own clinical experience that psychoanalytic data is highly self-similar. This is not alien from the common clinical observation that careful enough attention to the material of single hours, or even fragments of hours, commonly reveals the way in which patients approach and work out difficulties on a larger scale, inside and outside of analysis. The "red thread" of a patient's interests and concerns and style is detectable in very small fragments of material because of the widely redundant self-similarity of the personality. It is common clinical wisdom that certain points in the analysis are particularly revelatory of the patient's underlying approach to issues; for example, the hour in which the first dream is reported, or the hour in which a termination date is set seem to be particularly informative. From this model, we can interpret this as reflecting times when we have chosen the right framework, which reveals a major chunk of a self-similar structure at once rather as though we had hit upon an area of the Mandelbrot set that was just right to include in one of the interior Mandelbrot sets.[9]

It remains uncertain to what extent it will be possible to find, in the self-similarity of analytic materials, elements that can be used to explore those materials in an empirically rigorous yet manageable fashion. However, we welcome the discovery of a conceptual framework that allows us to think about and formulate the clinical wisdom that much more information is packed into brief fragments of an analysis than one might guess. Currently, the discovery of self-similarity in natural systems occurs when researchers familiar with patterns of fractals and chaos recognize these patterns, often in the visual representation of their data. There is much to recommend analysts playing around with these ideas (which is easy to do using home computers) to get a feel for this sort of material. More sophisticated means of recognizing fractal patterns and chaos are emerging, and these will be applicable to psychoanalytic data.

Over the past quarter century, a new paradigm of scientific explanation has arisen that encompasses a far wider range of phenomena than had been capable of exploration using the Newtonian model of scientific explanation, including its variations, such as quantum mechanics and relativity theory. This group of explanations, which has globally been referred to as *chaos theory* or *nonlinear dynamic systems theory*, involves a qualitative as opposed to quantitative view of nature and addresses questions in a wholly different fashion from a traditional physical science investigation. Its capacity to deal with the intricacies of nature and the complexities of real systems—albeit in a different way from classical physics—makes it a promising candidate for a different form of theorizing than has previously been used in psychoanalysis. It brings a whole different meaning to the concept of prediction, one that is more in tune with what we as analysts expect, involving stable configurations over time as the unit of study as opposed to instantaneous snapshots of static situations. In categorizing the sources of configuration that are mathematically possible, it may well suggest an empirically explorable psychoanalytic hypothesis. A major feature of aspects of chaotic systems, the quality of self-similarity, suggests empirical approaches to the analytic situation that relieve us of the burden of analyzing intractable amounts of data, while still carrying the possibility of addressing genuinely psychoanalytically significant ideas.

Recent developments in the study of dynamical systems provide a new vision of what it means to predict the evolution of a system. Rather than predicting that the system will be in a particular state at a particular moment in time, they predict the form that this evolution is likely to take. For example, rather than predicting that Mars will be in a particular position in the sky at a particular time, they predict that Mars will follow an elliptical orbit around the sun.

Another example: In studying the flow of traffic, classical predictions might have focused on the number of cars at a particular moment, whereas a dynamical systems prediction would focus on whether and under what conditions traffic jams would occur. This description of a system's evolution is close to the kind of prediction most interesting to psychoanalysts who wish to understand characteristic patterns of response and coping rather than specific instances. The study of dynamic systems also suggests a theoretical grounding for the common psychoanalytic view that much information is contained in even small fragments of analytic material.

Although a better theory of psychoanalytic events is, of course, welcome, most analysts, being practical individuals, ask how these ideas might alter our technique of psychoanalysis. The next chapter addresses this question.

Notes

1 An earlier version of this chapter appeared in (1995). *Journal of the American Psychoanalytic Association*, 43:1085–1113. Reprinted by permission of SAGE Publications, Ltd.

2 Only confusion results when analysts and others borrow technical terms from other disciplines and use them in ways suggested by their common usage rather than their technical usage. The term *nonlinear* has a particularly unfortunate history in this regard, having been taken up as part of psychobabble to refer to nonpropositional thinking. Chaos theory is in the process of suffering a similar fate in which an admittedly suggestive technical term, *chaos*, is used to refer to notions suggested by the term but which refer to matters quite different from mathematical chaos. Confusion of technical terms and common usage leads to attributions to the mathematical theory that are not supported by its actual content.

3 Classical theory said that, at a given moment, if the positions, velocities, and forces in two systems were identical, the systems would remain identical going forward. Thom showed that in some instances what had happened in the systems before the moment of identity would result in the systems developing differently.

4 In this context, the phrase "growing very rapidly" has the specific meaning that the effect of a change in initial values on later conditions can be described as greater than some mathematical function of this change and the elapsed time. These findings often demonstrate that the difference in effect is exponentially related to the initial difference.

5 Given these results, the ideas of meaning and motive take on new predictive value for a complex system. Such systems can often in some sense be said to be "trying" to do something, including trying to remain stable. In this instance, prediction becomes more possible.

6 The description of these paths of motion is often facilitated by representing them graphically or by means other than depicting position as a function of time. For example, one might more clearly depict important

features of a planetary orbit by showing the relationship between velocity and position rather than position and time. Selection of appropriate graphic representation often results in deep insights into the nature of dynamical systems (Abraham and Shaw, 1992) and allows one to recognize regularities that would not be evident from direct observation or simple plotting of variables.

7 The fractal graphics in the paper were easily created on a home computer by using the shareware program Fractint, Version 15.0 (Tyler, Wegner, Peterson, and Branderhorst, 1990).

8 To make a Sierpinski triangle, start with an equilateral triangle. Draw lines connecting the midpoint of each side. This produces four new triangles. Color the central triangle (the one with the down-pointing apex) and repeat the process for the remaining three triangles. Continue this process, ad infinitum. The result is the Sierpinski triangle. Note: Except for size, each upward-pointing triangle is identical to all the others.

9 It should be noted that other factors may contribute to making such a strategy effective. The redundancy of analytic material mentioned earlier may reflect aspects of ordinary human communication in which the importance of getting across affectively important ideas results in their being communicated with high redundancy.

Chapter 8

Emergence

> Pip saw the multitudinous, God-omnipresent, coral insects, that out of the firmament of waters heaved the colossal orbs. He saw God's foot upon the treadle of the loom, and spoke it; and therefore his shipmates called him mad.
>
> —*Moby-Dick*

Pip, a seemingly minor character in *Moby-Dick*, realizes that the amazing structure of coral reefs was the product of the action of millions of independent organisms, each doing its own thing. These independent agents produced amazing coral reefs. Pip understood that this was the way God worked. His shipmates thought him mad, as indeed he appeared to be. But his madness included all sorts of changes in perspective that allowed him to see things in a way that today's reader recognizes as genius. Pip seems to have gotten hold of an idea that has fascinated students of complex systems, the question of how rich and amazing structure can appear, as if from nowhere, through the independent actions of many individuals.[1]

Emergence refers to situations in which it appears that one gets something for nothing. A phenomenon is emergent when it has significant aspects that are more than the sum of its parts. The term covers instances where joining components creates something that could not happen if they remained separate and situations where, from a common sense perspective, something new unexpectedly appears. This chapter explores the origins of emergence in complex systems and shows how an appreciation of emergence can inform psychoanalytic listening, understanding, and interventions.

The study of emergence is central to the difference between the reductionist program and the sciences of complexity. Whereas the central task of reductionism is to discover the components that make up a system, the central question of complexity theory is how the components interact to produce phenomena of importance. Let's look at how this happened in genetics. Following Mendel's demonstration that inheritance had a specific basis, the natural question was what was the material foundation of inheritance? It was in time recognized that the genetic material was located on a chromosome and then, with great difficulty, that the material was DNA, not proteins as it was initially thought. Analysis of DNA resulted in a further clarification. First, a quantitative relationship of the four components (bases) that are strung together to make DNA molecules was discovered. (The amount of adenine equals the amount of thiamine, and the amount of guanine equals cytosine.) So far, the process followed the reductionist program, finding out how something works by breaking it down into its components. Franklin, Watson, and Crick made a discovery in the direction of emergence, showing that these component bases in their quantitative relationship fit together in a specific form that emerged from their chemical properties—the double helix. In what is perhaps the single most pregnant sentence in science, Watson and Crick declared that they were "not unaware" of the biological consequences of their discovery. In other words, their thinking had turned a corner from exploring the components of the inheritance system to showing how, from the nature of these humble chemical compounds, the incredible complex phenomenon we call life could emerge.

Emergence is a concept from the study of complex and nonlinear systems that can reshape the way analysts think about therapeutic change and development. It is the way in which new, unexpected, and qualitatively new and distinct configurations suddenly appear in complex systems.

Shakespeare tells us, "Nothing can be made out of nothing" (King Lear, I.iv.126), and popular wisdom, less eloquently, says, "You can't get something for nothing." The idea that outcomes are in some way proportionate to what is put in is pervasive in moral, economic, and scientific thinking. This notion finds its clearest expression in the physical sciences as conservation laws, principles that state that despite apparent transformations in systems, some quantity is preserved. These laws have been central to the development of physics.

An example—gasoline is burned, releasing heat and gases whose expansion in the car's engine causes the motion of the engine's parts, which in turn rotates the car's wheels moving the vehicle forward. At each step, a certain amount of heat is produced and dissipated into the surrounding environment. The moving car appears to have little to do with the hydrocarbons of the gasoline and their chemical interaction with oxygen, nor with the heat that is generated in the process. But the law of conservation of energy applies to the entire system. The total amount of energy in the system is constant. The amount of chemical energy in the gasoline's hydrocarbons and oxygen at the beginning of the process is equal to the mechanical energy of the forward-moving car plus the energy of the heat generated in the process.

These powerful conservation laws include the conservation of mass and energy (or mass-energy in relativity theory), the conservation of momentum in mechanical systems, and the conservation of electrical charge. The laws are among the most successful tools for the rational comprehension of nature. Similarly, in economics, the idea that the result is generally proportionate to the investment, or, more practically, that if an economic proposition is "too good to be true" it probably is, pervades economic discourse from abstract theory to practical wisdom.

Contemporary moral discourse, strongly influenced by the Protestant work ethic, emphasizes how, through an input of personal work, rewards of spiritual, moral, and material well-being follow (Weber, 1905). In psychology, Freud attempted to develop conservation-like principles for mental function but with few exceptions (see, for example, French, 1952, 1954, 1958) the effort to develop a quantitative mental dynamics was abandoned, and psychoanalysts have generally discarded the effort as hopeless and antithetical to the major lines of advance of psychoanalytic thought (Gill, 1976). Nonetheless, in clinical work and theory, the theme that input in the form of effort or time will be roughly proportionate to rewards remains commonplace.

Sometimes the theme of the relationship of input to output takes a more gloomy form, suggesting an upper limit to outputs for a system. Boltzmann's dictum, "the energy of the world is constant; the entropy of the world tends toward a maximum," grimly suggests that not only can you not get something for nothing but that the inevitable decay of systems toward disorder and undifferentiated equilibrium implies input is needed to maintain order, and disorder is ever likely to emerge.[2]

These examples suggest conservation laws make their greatest contributions in the study of relatively simple physical systems. The value of the idea that you cannot get something for nothing remains persuasive in moral, psychological, and economic discourse. However, in these human contexts, this principle does not approach the power of quantitative conservation laws of physics. The principle becomes a rough heuristic for making decisions about action rather than a scientific principle. Anyone who has tried to use these ideas in a psychological arena knows that counterexamples readily leap to mind in which cleverness, or luck, contributed as much as effort to achieving desired goals. Wealth and hard work are only somewhat correlated. In general, as systems grow more complex, the principle that "nothing can be made out of nothing" proves ever less convincing.

The concept of emergence refers to those situations in which it at least appears that one gets something for nothing as the system evolves and unfolds. A phenomenon is emergent when it has significant aspects that are more than the sum of its component parts. The term is used to cover two instances: when bringing together component parts results in something that simply could not have happened, and situations where, from a human point of view, something novel and surprising appears from a situation that is not even suggestive of this novelty—something arrives, as it were, "out of the blue."

Certain phenomena depend on all the elements of a system being brought together to function as a system. Consider the Zen koan that asks, "What is the sound of one hand clapping?" While it is tempting to approach the question through a kind of reduction, attributing half of the clap to each hand, this is clearly not a satisfactory solution. Until a system consisting of two hands is considered, the question is either meaningless (i.e. a hand in isolation cannot clap) or is answered that there is no sound. An intrinsic aspect of clapping is that the property of clapping emerges only from the system of two hands in coordination.

An example of a system that is said to involve emergence because utterly surprising qualities appear in it is the Mandelbrot set, which was discussed in Chapter 7. The Mandelbrot set is a geometric configuration that is generated by extremely simple rules, yet its geometric structure is exceedingly complex (in some sense, infinitely complex). It contains many surprising qualities, which even the cleverest individual could not have surmised from the underlying equations. In fact, these properties were only appreciated when computer-generated graphics allowed Mandelbrot (1982) to see the geometric form of the set. Still, in some sense, the equations for the Mandelbrot set contain all the information about the system and so fully describe the set.

Many emergent phenomena were studied and puzzled about long before a unified conception of emergence became available. Adam Smith (1776) observed that when each individual in a community acts in his own self-interest, an economic system emerges in which the community succeeds in providing for a wide range of the needs of its members, even though there was no preexisting plan for that mutual provision. Smith referred to this phenomenon as an "invisible hand" because the economic structure occurring when many persons act in their own, seemingly uncoordinated, interests appears as if some force were coordinating and guiding their activities. (It is fascinating that, at the moment Smith discovered how the action's independent agents could result in what looked like a planned process, he felt the need to suggest the existence of such a planner, the "invisible hand.") Even more powerfully than Smith, Darwin observed that the biological process of evolution emerges from the very simple requirement that some characteristics of organisms be heritable and the tautology that more reproductively fit organisms reproduced more successfully.

Darwin was able to show that these simple rules were not only reasonably explanatory of the fossil record but that they generated surprising predictions about the nature of biological evolution. For example, Darwin (1859) showed that species that only mate with members of the same species are a predictable result of these elementary rules.

Although these and other brilliant examples of emergent phenomena were well known by the middle of the nineteenth century, the major forward movement of science came by way of the reductionist program, a program that moved in essentially the opposite direction. This program held that apparently complex phenomena were best explored by breaking them down to their component parts and showing how these parts resulted in manifestations such as biological life or overall psychological function.

Freud's teacher, Brücke, was among the four young scientists who, in 1848, swore an oath to reduce biology to physics and chemistry. That vision was among the most potent sources of Freud's scientific ideals (Jones, 1953) and led to the spectacularly successful scientific program that continues to this day in molecular biology. A disadvantage of the reductionist program is that it suggests that other forms of explanation are unworthy, that they are likely to reflect some form of mysticism or intellectual hand waving in that they posit processes that cannot be reduced to more elementary components.[3]

Starting during and after the Second World War, two factors led to increasing appreciation of the limitations of the reductionist program. First, attempts at technological advances and advances in fields like ecology that involve intrinsically complex nonlinear systems led to the recognition that important problems could not be adequately solved by reducing them to their components (Wiener, 1961; von Bertalanffy, 1968). At the same time, the development of computers simultaneously provided a new tool by means of which the very challenging mathematical equations could be explored and models for the mechanism of systematic explorations. Molecular biology itself represented a shift in point of view toward a systems perspective. Whereas traditional biochemistry focused on the description of the chemical components of biological systems, examining how they operated in the organism, molecular biology pointed to the qualities of chemical entities that make them functional within a biological system. For example, Watson and Crick (Crick, 1988) recognized from the start that they had achieved much more than a description of an important biochemical molecule in their double helix model of DNA. They recognized that their model was ideally suited to DNA's hereditary function in the organism.

Computer studies generated by these more complex models were explored, and, in addition, in the 1990s, computers provided a model of a complex system whose integrated operation and structure was clearly of equal importance to its component parts (Von Neumann, 1958, 1966; Goldstein, 1972; Stewart and Golubitsky, 1992). The recognition that systems have properties that depend primarily on their complexity, combined with the beautiful computer graphics that came from the study of complexity along with the evangelical enthusiasm of some of the proponents of these viewpoints led to important new developments. These appeared under such titles as chaos theory, complexity theory, and nonlinear dynamic systems and gained a widespread appreciation that complex systems have important properties that are not adequately described through reference to their component parts but, instead, are related to the structure of the systems themselves. Whole new systems for investigating complex systems developed. Among these, emergence is among the most important.

The Nature of Emergence

The formal properties of the system, or the poverty of our intuition regarding nonlinear systems, can lead to emergence. The simplest formal properties of a system concern its dimensionality, the minimum number of parameters needed to describe it fully in a non-redundant way. The concept of geometric dimension involves the minimum number of parameters needed to adequately describe the position of a point in a geometric space. A plane, for example, is two-dimensional in the sense that two parameters are necessary and sufficient to specify every point on a plane. The set consisting of vertices of the integer number points on a plane—points like (1,1) (–3,14)—is one-dimensional because, if one numbered these points starting at the origin and spiraling out, only a single number would be needed to specify each point. Of course, parameters can specify many other things besides physical position, for example, the intensity of the major effects or the rate of change of a variable, might be considered as a parameter so that spaces of varied kinds can be conceptualized and their dimensions considered.

One of the surprising results of topology, a field that studies the underlying properties of spaces, is that the dimension of a space determines many of its most important properties. Consider, for example, whether two points can be joined without crossing a given third point: on a line, a one-dimensional space, if the third point lies between the first two points, joining them without intersecting the third point will be impossible. In contrast, the same problem in a plane can be solved for any three points; the connecting curve is simply drawn to go around the point to be avoided. Having an additional dimension makes the problem entirely different. When an additional dimension is added to a system, qualitatively new phenomena may emerge simply by virtue of that change. For example, in neural networks, the interposition of a layer between the input and output layers creates novel forms of learning that are impossible in a two-layered system (Spitzer, 1999).

A second kind of emergence that results in the formal properties of systems has to do with the relationship of the system to chaotic states. In chaos, a system becomes entirely unpredictable because arbitrarily small changes in the parameters of the system result in drastic changes in the system's short-term evolution. In stable systems, changes in parameters lead to small changes in the system's evolution, and this changed evolution is qualitatively similar to what would have occurred without the change. Between chaos and stability are systems that are said to be "on the edge of chaos"—that is, they are in a state in which changes in the system's parameters can make significant changes in its evolution, but only a limited number of possible directions of change are available. This is likely to occur when bifurcations point out which slight change in parameters result in significant changes in the system's evolution if the paths available to the system are close at hand. Like Robert Frost's "Road Not Taken," being in a position where a choice between two alternatives leads to distinctly different outcomes can make "all the difference" in the system's evolution. Being in an area of the system's landscape where many bifurcations are possible is likely to lead to the appearance of emergent phenomena. These areas occur in regions between stability and chaos and are referred to as "on the edge of chaos."

This leads us to a third kind of emergence that seems to violate the something-for-nothing rule. When energy enters a system, new structures commonly appear in the system, even though no planned structure is introduced with the energy. For example, when a pan of water is heated on a stove, even though the heat under the pan is uniform, the water in the pan forms a new current, rising from the bottom center of the pan, moving outward from the top of the water and descending around the sides of the pan. Note that the input of energy, itself unstructured, results in the emergence of a new structure in the boiling water. This is an example of how structure may emerge in systems that are not at equilibrium without benefit of a model or prescription for that structure.

The second law of thermodynamics, that systems tend to increase in disorganization, in fact applies only in the long run to systems that are near equilibrium. John Maynard Keynes's observation, "In the long run we are all dead," suggests that in the system in which we are most interested, for living beings who are far from a state of chemical equilibrium and for whose actions we want to understand in the relatively short run, the second law of thermodynamics may offer us little that is useful. In fact, study of the thermodynamics of systems far from equilibrium shows that new structures often emerge in such systems (Glansdorff and Prigogine, 1971; Nicolis and Prigogine, 1977).

A particularly interesting example of self-organization that is pertinent to the development of psychological systems is seen in neural networks that are provided with random but active inputs (Spitzer, 1999). Neural networks that are given inputs designed to teach—that is, that allow the networks to discover relationships between the meaningful inputs—are observed to learn appropriate connections between elements of the inputs. Without input, the networks do not learn. But, surprisingly, given random inputs such that the network is active, the network develops additional structure, as if it were making sense of the nonsense input that it receives.

Another form of emergence relates to qualitative shifts in systems that occur in response to a change in some continuous variable. The most familiar of these is phase change in chemical systems, as when water freezes, melts, boils, or condenses. Continuous changes in the parameters of temperature and pressure lead (after equilibrium is established) to new forms of the substance in question, with distinctive qualities that could not easily have been anticipated from other forms. Even though the forces acting between the molecules remain exactly the same, and the rate of motion of the molecules changes only slightly, the molecules in an ice crystal form themselves into a significantly different configuration from those in water. Palombo (1999) has suggested that similar phase shifts can be observed within the psychoanalytic situation in the qualitatively different manner in which patients think and associate at various points in the analysis. Whether this is to be treated as an interesting and provocative metaphor or, in fact, individuals travel through abrupt transitions that can be equated with phase shifts, is a matter for empirical investigation. The discomfort with ideas of discontinuity in psychological life, and the heuristic that it is valuable always to look for continuities in psychological function, may interfere with noting phase shifts in psychological function when they are actually present.

Finally, we come to those situations where emergence results because of our poor capacity to intuit the qualities of complex systems. People appear not to be very good at anticipating and understanding the kind of discontinuous, jumpy behavior that occurs commonly in complex systems. This relative incapacity probably reflects the same sort of limitation of mental functioning manifest in most people's incapacity to reason well about probabilistic matters. These may arise simply because the needs of daily life, combined with the difficulty of such computation, have resulted in the human brain not evolving these abilities on a level that can be used without extensive recourse to conscious computation to solve such problems. Whatever the inherent limitations of human thought in this regard, those limitations are exacerbated in technologically advanced societies where an artificially created environment is carefully designed to avoid qualitative discontinuity, with controls on most devices being carefully designed to produce predictable, unsurprising results, and environments carefully designed to include few surprises.

For example, modern elevators are carefully designed to speed up and slow down in as smooth a function as possible, rather than abruptly jarring into and out of motion, which they would do if the sole task was to deliver their load to its appropriate location as rapidly as possible. The carefully designed, smooth elevator ride gives us the misimpression that this represents an expectable physical state, which it does not. In complex systems, one repeatedly has the experience of being surprised. New, unanticipated structures emerge from configurations in unanticipated ways. For example, systems referred to as cellular automata, or artificial life, are generated by sets of simple rules. Examined in isolation, these rules would seem unlikely to generate the complex structures and configurations that emerge when these rules are [instantiated] as computer programs (Levy, 1992). Similarly, the Mandelbrot set and fractal structures, generated by simple, well-defined rules, are a source of constant surprise and amazement even to those familiar with them. As discussed earlier, the discovery of major instances in which important and realistic qualities emerge from simple rules have been among people's greatest intellectual accomplishments.

It is interesting to compare the quality of surprise associated with emergent phenomena with the criteria proposed by Reik (1948) as indications of the successful progress of analysis. Reik observed that when analysis is going well, both analyst and patient are surprised by the material that comes forward. Reik argued that this surprise was both a marker of the material's authenticity (i.e. that the patient was not being indoctrinated by the analyst) and also an indication of the appearance of previously unconscious material into awareness. His numerous clinical examples strike the contemporary reader as remaining credible. However, within the context of the current discussion, some may wonder whether this quality of surprise may, on some occasions, result from the appearance of emergent phenomena within the psychoanalytic situation. This opens the question of how and whether it is possible to differentiate between genuinely emergent phenomena and situations in which what was previously present but outside of awareness has been brought into awareness.

The idea that there may be real discontinuities in psychological functioning, comprehensible as emergent qualities, is problematic in terms of a major means by which Freud and other psychoanalysts have comprehended psychological function. The idea that apparent discontinuity in psychological function disguises latent meaning was and remains a powerful tool in the development of psychoanalysis and clinical practice. It is, therefore, useful to explore the relationship of this idea to the concept of emergence discussed here.

Freud and the Problem of Rationality

Freud's confrontation with the problem of rationality was one origin of psychoanalysis. Economists and other social scientists, as well as common sense discussions, assumed that human action could be explained largely on the basis of reason. For example, it was assumed that people make relatively accurate computation of the likelihood of various outcomes for their actions. The notion of deviations from rationality in computations constitutes an interesting way of thinking about this material that has the advantage of avoiding the metaphor of hidden psychological content and issues having to do with thoughts that are not thought. However, maintaining the idea that there are two independent routes to surprise, emergence, and coming into awareness, we may achieve a richer picture of psychological function.

The idea of rationality dominated the intellectual thought from the Enlightenment until the end of the nineteenth century and proved particularly effective in explaining economic behavior. In this area, individual behavior could be explained by attempts to maximize personal wealth, which in turn could be explained by the anticipated biological rewards that came with that wealth. Thus, for example, Adam Smith describes a baker motivated to prepare good-tasting bread by the rational anticipation that others would purchase his product and allow him, on the basis of his skill in baking bread, to house himself and have other foods to eat.

Behavior that could not be understood as a consequence of rationality was regarded as deviant, unsuccessful, the consequence of failed personal or social development, or illness. Once so categorized, it needed little further explanation. British Common Law, for example, addressed only the behavior of a hypothetical "rational man." Those individuals who were not rational men were subject neither to the law's punishment nor to its protections but rather had inferior statuses that reflected the view that, in the absence of an adequate capacity for rational thought, these individuals were in need of tending and control by those who had this capacity. While some individuals in whom this incapacity was quite marked, such as lunatics and the feebleminded, were relieved of their legal responsibilities, whole classes of persons, including children, women, and people of color, were at various times assumed in English Common Law to lack the capacity for rationality and so to be appropriately controlled in ways that rational men were not.

Freud took three major steps in addressing the problem of manifest irrationality. First, he claimed that human actions that appeared irrational resulted not from some fundamental failure of a rational function but, rather, from parts of the rational process being barred from awareness because of the anxiety that would result from such awareness. Second, that the forms reason takes are more varied than suggested by ordinary experiences of avowed reasoning processes. In particular, reasoning may involve "primary process" mentation, which has rules that differ from those ordinarily accepted in conscious reasoning. Finally, even those processes that appear to have resulted from ordinary reasoning often, in fact, result from reasoning that is outside of awareness and that follows different rules from those that are avowed. Seemingly irrational behavior is continuous with rational behavior—irrational behavior has its reasons and reasoned behavior disguises disavowed processes that would be labeled as irrational.

Freud's discovery of pervasive non-rational processes in psychological function led to an attempt to develop a comprehensive theory of psychological function and development. Such a theory would include such novel elements and would, in particular, lead to a comprehensive description of the ways in which the psyche is transformed over time in a fashion that is actually orderly, even though it may appear manifestly disorganized.

Freud and his followers understood development as occurring as a sequential unfolding of steps that led to a final structure. Although Freud did not describe the mechanism by which this occurred, implicit in his conceptualization was the idea that these preprogrammed steps led to a final mature structure. And that structure, though varying from individual to individual, was, in a fundamental sense, common to all normal individuals; deviation from this fundamental normality resulted in pathology. The fundamental organizing principle of this development in Freud's view is the libidinal stages of development outlined in the *Three Essays*. Freud's recognition of the structures of the psyche led him to describe how the development of these structures occurred in concert with libidinal lines.

Anna Freud came to believe that while the various structures of the psyche followed a normative sequence, the overall function of the individual was shaped by the interaction of several independent sequences (developmental lines). Pathology could arise not only from the global interferences that resulted from disturbances in the libidinal sequence of development but also from incongruities between the essentially independent developmental lines that she described. Yet even within Anna Freud's model, normal development is characterized by expectable sequences occurring in a timely fashion, and pathology is generated when these preprogrammed sequences fail to occur in proper relationship to one another.

This formulation, based on the ideas of biological development that were so impressively coming to light during Freud's medical education and early career, continued to be the dominant theme of the study of biological development. Much of the elaborate work of molecular developmental biology has focused on the assumption that an organism's final structure reflects preprogrammed developmental sequences, and much of the investigation of biological development takes this idea as given. In particular, regularity of the emergence of structures is taken as an indication of their emergence being the result of a sequence of developmental steps specified in the genome.

Extended to psychology, this model of development carries with it natural consequences for psychotherapy. If psychopathology represents a flaw in the development of a predetermined scheme, two possibilities present themselves for its repair or management. The first, if possible, would be to undo development to the point where the flaw occurs, then to repair the flaw, and then to allow development to resume from that point, or, perhaps, having repaired the flaw and assuming that subsequent development has not been too distorted by its presence, to simply allow the patient with the now repaired flaw to proceed on his or her developmental course. Alternatively, if for whatever reason the fundamental repair appears to be impossible, some sort of prosthetic substitute for the lost function might be provided, allowing for the patient improved function, if not ideal function, despite the continued presence of the underlying difficulty. This, of course, is the distinction between psychoanalysis and suggestion that Freud originally introduced and the basis for his sharp distinction between the two procedures.

Another model of development, different from the one Freud presumed, could be considered if the nature of the mature organism were not formed in the prescribed developmental sequence at birth, subject only to an adequate environment in the form of a preset developmental program. Then the basic premise of Freud's formulation of the action of psychoanalysis comes into question. The major impediment to raising this question to begin with, however, is that clear indications show that many aspects of development are programmed in this fashion. For example, starting with Roger Sperry, investigators of connections of major areas in the nervous system were able to show that, contrary to previous belief, the pattern of connection was hard-wired into the system and not subject to correction through experience. Thus, for example, when a toad's eyes were reversed in their position in the orbit, the animal's optic nerves grew back in such a fashion that the connections were made in the same way as they would have been had the eyes not been reversed. The unfortunate consequent behavior, that the toad would, for example, attempt to capture an insect flying through the upper part of its visual field by moving its tongue as though the insect were in the lower part of its visual field, did not result in the correction of the wiring or even the correction of the behavior (Sperry, 1945).

Clearly, the idea that so complex a system must be the result of a preexisting program is comparable to an old argument for God's existence. The argument goes that were one to find a watch in the desert, one would assume there was a watchmaker because it seems obvious that such a complex structure could not occur by happenstance. The argument goes on to posit God's existence, since the entire universe or the creatures within it are clearly too complex to have originated without some sort of intentional activity of an intelligent being, a demiurge, who is equated with a deity. The fallacy of this argument is that certain qualities of the environment may result in the appearance of complex structures in a spontaneous fashion. Human intuitions about the way in which such things occur tend to be inadequate, partly because of the usefulness for everyday living of the position that events are caused by intentions, and partly because human appreciation of the time frame in which events occur tends to be badly constrained by our impressions from ordinary life. Probably the greatest investigation of the appearance of complex and diverse structure without a preexisting plan was Darwin's recognition that the complexity and diversity of life results not from some preprogrammed description or master plan for biological diversity but rather from the operation of natural selection on heritable features that are variable.

Limitations in the human capacity to anticipate the evolution of complex systems lead us to tend to believe that the complex forms we observe in the world must be the result of some sort of planning. The existence of complex biological entities was, until Darwin, taken as essentially irrefutable evidence of a demiurge who deliberately formed the structures we observe because no other plausible explanation seemed available. Using a similar implicit argument, the complexity of biological beings led to a belief that their development, structure, and function was encoded in the individual's genome, and that in the absence of significant insult, the program embedded in the genome is played out with slight variation resulting from environmental circumstances. Yet the environment does not seem to play a substantial role in the major thrust of this process. Enthusiasm for the idea that genetics fully determines human function has led to a vigorous effort to discover the genetic basis of psychological functioning, especially as it relates to psychopathology. With rare exception for significantly deviant behavior, the finding has been that some genetic contribution to disturbances occurs, but this contribution is limited and complex.

Indeed, now that a picture of the human genome is available, it is clear that insufficient genetic information is available to specify the wiring of even a fraction of the essential nervous system. Rather, what clearly is specified is the initial position of large numbers of neurons, possibly some of their connections, or at least the randomness of those initial connections, and the capacity of neurons to respond to experience through means that include forming or intensifying connections with other neurons, migration, growth, and dying off. In other words, at least a significant portion of brain function, probably that associated with "higher" mental functioning, results from the action of the environment on a neural network with the capacity to learn. We would expect in this obviously complex system that the phenomena typical of complex systems, and in particular, the phenomenon of emergence, would play a significant role. Emergence constitutes an alternative to preplanned development that is particularly likely to be active in the areas of brain function that interest psychoanalysts.

Emergence and the Technique of Psychoanalysis

The very different focus in understanding psychological function that results from taking emergence seriously has significant implications for psychoanalytic technique, including an altered view of how seriously to take certain happenings patients reported, how to understand the analyst's role in treatment, and ideas about the goals of analytic work. The construction of psychological events implicit in much of Freud's work is that they result from the step-by-step layering of slight changes, one on the other, to create a final psychological configuration.

With the exception of catastrophic breakdowns in psychological function, such as occur at the onset of psychosis (Freud, 1911), apparently abrupt, large scale changes in psychological function are treated by most psychoanalysts an epiphenomena. The analyst postulates that underlying such apparent abrupt changes and reorganizations is some continuous, orderly transformation. The only thing that is thought to change abruptly is manifest behavior or consciousness.

Elsewhere (Galatzer-Levy, in press), I have suggested that this assumption leads us to overlook real phenomena involving abrupt change. These phenomena are well documented in regard to general psychological development. For example, Thelen and Smith (1994) demonstrate that, while walking has precursors, the capacity to walk does not result from an epigenetic unfolding of these precursors but is an emergent property of the infant's engagement with them. Sometimes patients report, and analysts observe, similarly dramatic changes in psychological functioning, often occurring after a long, apparently fallow period of analytic work (Palombo, 1999). Rather than assuming an underlying continuity, and therefore, incidentally, being skeptical about the depth of the apparent change, the analyst might consider that the change in fact reflects a newly emergent aspect of the patient's psychological function. It could be that it is the product of a period of work "at the edge of chaos" in which that patient engaged in a state from which a genuinely new configuration could emerge. This shift in viewpoint would lead the analyst to look for evidence of such happenings, and appreciating this possibility, lead to examination of the conditions that enabled the patient to grow in this manner rather than exclusively searching for evidence for the motives and means by which the patient has attempted to hide the supposedly real process of change from himself and the analyst.

A second area in which the concept of emergence might inform analytic technique concerns the analyst's role in the treatment process. From its inception, the technique of psychoanalysis has been closely linked to theories about its mode of action. These theories initially focused on how the psychoanalytic process resulted in the undoing of the pathogenesis of hysteria and other neuroses, and only later, and only partially, shifted to how the process resulted in the modification and formation of psychological structures of a more satisfactory kind. (Throughout this book, the term *psychological structure* is used to refer to patterns of psychological activity that are relatively stable over time.)

It was understood from the beginning that the analyst's function in this process consisted in providing for the patient something that the patient could not provide for herself. Freud recognized that the analyst had a greater contribution than simply interpretation alone, although the analyst, less blinded than the patient by the needs of neurosis, could often understand phenomena that the patient could not. What it was beyond interpretation that the analyst could or should provide, however, remains today the subject of intense controversy. This controversy focuses primarily on the concern that non-interpretive or prematurely interpretive interventions may interfere with the analysand's full development of insight and deprive the analysand of the resulting deep changes in personality that are the rewards of properly conducted analyses.

Over the past three decades, analysts have become increasingly aware that concern to allow the patient an optimal experience of insight might interfere with other, less easily described benefits from the analytic situation. One of these involved the mutual influence of analyst and patient. Winnicott (1963–1965, 1965) and Benedek (1959; Anthony and Benedek, 1970) had shown that normal human development was best conceptualized as resulting from the mutual influence of child and caretaker. Racker (1968) had demonstrated that countertransference, formerly thought to be an impediment to the analytic process, not only was inevitable but, properly used, could facilitate analytic work. In recent years, many analysts have adopted the position, albeit to varying degrees, that analysis requires the mutual influence of analyst and analysand, and that the analytic dyad can be usefully thought of as a new entity with a life of its own. This new entity is an emergent property of the analytic setup.

The properties of the emergent dyad arise in part simply from its formal structure. Earlier in this article, I discussed the consequences for a system of simply having more dimensions. If we think of each participant in the analytic situation as bringing to it a personality that can be described in a certain number of dimensions, say n, the interacting system of any two persons can be described as having a dimension $2n$. This fact, in and of itself, introduces new possibilities for change. As discussed earlier, the possible paths between any two points in a system of lower dimension are increased if the system is joined to another to produce an overall system of higher dimension. In fact, looked at from the point of view of one component of the system, such changes might look like sudden jumps and discontinuities, though in the higher dimensional system the transition is smooth and continuous.

Another way to approach the analytic dyad is to conceptualize it as involving two coupled oscillators (Galatzer-Levy, 1997a; Palombo, 1999; Fajardo, 2001) where an "applet" allows experimentation with the simplest type of coupled oscillator. Modeling the analytic situation as a coupled oscillator suggests a variety of patterns of inaction that would be expected to emerge in the analytic dyad. For example, certain configurations lead to little significant change and damping of the overall system, perhaps analogous to an analytic stalemate; others lead to increasingly intense fluctuations that in practice would be seen as threateningly out of control; still others lead to gradual change in both oscillators viewed separately in a manner such that novel structure emerges, but disorganization does not occur. The exploration of these various configurations should be helpful in assessing and remediating problems that arise in the analytic dyad, particularly problems of stagnation or instability.

Finally, we come to the perennial problem of the goal of psychoanalysis (Sandler and Dreher, 1996). Anna Freud proposed that the goals of analysis of children should be the resumption of development toward a mature configuration of the personality. Because I believe that development is a lifelong process (Galatzer-Levy and Cohler, 1993), I have suggested an extension of Anna Freud's position to the effect that analysis allows the resumption of development across the course of life. This development is not aimed toward some final picture of ideal maturity; rather, the process in itself is the goal (Galatzer-Levy, 1988).

The idea of emergence and related ideas from nonlinear systems theory, however, suggest that the kind of development that we would expect to see if things go well is far from smooth. In many instances, it would involve qualitatively new configurations within the personality. Instead of being steady and ongoing, it might involve periods of rapid change and periods where little seemed to happen. What we would expect to see on an ongoing basis is that the individual was engaged in depth with the problems of development. Dreams and fantasies would be expected to be rich and changing, and the possibility of engaging novelty ever present.

Conclusion

The concept of emergence grows from the study of complex systems. It refers mostly to the qualitative changes that are intrinsic in complex systems and to the sense of surprise human beings experience in these difficult-to-anticipate developments. Situations that we now might classify as emergent have, in the past, been regarded as epiphenomena, to be explained by some underlying process in which the ordinary laws of continuity of change hold. In fact, proceeding in precisely that fashion has been a powerful means for the advance of psychoanalysis.

The idea of emergence from a state of complex systems suggests, however, that the possibility that what were thought to be epiphenomena constitute real change, not to be explained away by reduction to simpler steps or referenced to hidden factors, invites an appreciation of these phenomena in their own right. It opens the way for analysts to appreciate these phenomena when they occur and discourages distortion of them in mistaken attempts to reduce them to underlying continuities. It also suggests changes in the conceptualization of analytic technique in the direction of facilitating potentially emergent phenomena, with the recognition that the analytic setup may provide a situation where such transformations can occur. Understanding the environment needed for such transformations could inform the analyst's technique, first in appreciating that exploration near the edge of chaos is the manner in which ordinary development leading to emergence occurs so that the analyst will not interrupt such processes; and second, in appreciating that the insistence on creating an apparently coherent description of the process underlying the manifest, abrupt change may, in fact, interfere with or destroy that change.

Notes

1 In recent years, the specific situation of the production of complex systems by virtue of the actions of independent but interacting agents has become the focus of major research in the social sciences. See, for example, Epstein (2014).

2 The concept of entropy is simpler and less mysterious than it appears at first. Although the total amount of energy in a closed system is conserved when energy is transformed in the process of making it do work, a certain amount of it becomes heat due to friction and hence is lost to effective work. This "lost" energy is called entropy. Entropy is a measure of the degree to which a system loses its organization and efficiency. Boltzmann's law tells us that systems always move toward maximum entropy. Fortunately, Boltzmann's law has turned out to be less powerful than was imaged and later researchers have shown that it applied only to systems that are near equilibrium and then only over time, not complex systems, including living organisms, that are constantly taking in energy to maintain their structure and which are far from equilibrium (Prigogine, 1967, 1977).

3 In fairness to those who used the reductionist position to condemn other types of explanations, it should be observed that in the absence of a general concept of emergence, researchers who sought to explain phenomena like the existence of life often turn to *ad hoc* explanations, such as vitalism that posited mysterious forces or entities that gave a name to the phenomena in question but which were presented as explanatory. The various forms of vitalism are a good example (Hall, 1969).

Chapter 9

On Working Through

A Model from Artificial Intelligence[1]

> I have been obliged to adopt this order in my description; but what happens in reality is no doubt a simultaneous exploration of one path in another a swinging of the expectation now this way and now that, until at last it accumulates in the direction that is most opportune and one particular grouping becomes the permanent one.
>
> —(Freud, S. 1900 vol. 5, p. 76)

Freud's observation that working through is "a part of the work which effects the greatest changes in the patient and which distinguishes analytic treatment from any kind of treatment by suggestion" (Freud, 1914b, pp. 155–56) is still valid. Working through may be at the core of what is meant by psychoanalysis. Yet no satisfactory theory of this process is available. This chapter explores a model of working through based on concepts from artificial intelligence that are closely related to nonlinear dynamics systems theory.

Freud introduced the terms *wearing away* and *working over* in 1895 but first systematically examined the idea of working through in "Remembering, Repeating and Working-Through" (Freud, 1914b), where he defined working through as the arduous task of allowing "the patient time to become more conversant with this resistance" (p. 155). Freud also said that the need for working through was particularly prominent in those situations arising from "the compulsion to repeat" (1920a) and "id resistances" (1926) that result from the difficulty of detachment of the libido from previous objects and modes of discharge (1915a, b, c, d) and reflect such states as "psychical inertia" (1918), "adhesiveness of the libido" (1916–17), and "sluggishness of the libido" (1940).

Later authors discussed the clinical role of working through. This includes (1) the application of previously gained insights to a variety of situations (Fenichel, 1941), (2) achievement of multiple functions in a single psychological act (Fromm-Reichman, 1950), (3) the time "involved in actually experiencing and re-experiencing ... so as to bring about constructive change" (Novey, 1962), and (4) post-analytic structure building (Valenstein, 1962). Sandler *et al.* (1973) conclude that there is much agreement for the necessity of covering the same ground repeatedly with patients. There is a clinical consensus about the necessity of working through and its several functions in analysis.

Difficulties arise in attempts to explain these findings theoretically. Ideas based on libido theory have evolved little since Freud's time.[2] Precisely in the area of working through, libido theory is least satisfactory. Many attempts at a metapsychological explanation of working through are translations of clinical observations into metapsychological language that result in circular arguments. (What is the evidence of "adhesiveness of the libido?" It is the large amount of working through necessary to free libido from infantile objects. How is the need for extensive working through explained? By adhesiveness of the libido.)

Kohut's (1971, 1984; Kohut and Seitz, 1963) equation of working through with transmuting internalization provides another set of ideas. Optimal gratification and frustrations result in the formation of new structures through the microscopically fractionated internalization of the analyst's functions. This explanation is not tautological, but it implies that the major mode of action of all types of analysis is structure building. As Kohut pointed out, his views lead to quite different ideas from the "classical" idea. For example, the capacity for continued self-analysis is not regarded as central to a good analytic result (Kohut, 1984).

Ideas from Decision Theory and Artificial Intelligence

Here, I offer an explanation of the process of working through based on a model of mental function derived from the fields of artificial intelligence and computer science. These rapidly developing fields have much to offer the psychoanalyst in search of models of complex behavior. My goal is both to offer a specific model of working through and to whet the reader's appetite for the field of artificial intelligence.

Artificial intelligence has several advantages over previous sources of psychoanalytic theory. Ideas emerging in this context benefit from the needs of concrete implementation. This results in explicit formulation. Because the task is to design working machines that act intelligently, the ideas' validity is quickly put to empirical test. Unlike the models of mental function from classical analytic theory, ego psychology, cybernetics, systems theory, and information theory, the ideas of artificial intelligence tend to be explicit and testable.

Since the major activity of workers in artificial intelligence involves attempts to produce machines that behave intelligently (i.e. learn, find new solutions to problems, etc.), the models developed are appropriate for solving complex problems involving symbolic manipulation. This contrasts with classical analytic theory and ego psychology, which are modeled on the physics of forces and masses, anatomy, and embryology, and also cybernetics and information theory, which were developed to deal with goal-directed guidance systems and transmission of information, respectively.

General systems theory, while emphasizing the transfer of information and energy across the open boundaries of systems, does not attempt to address the question of how information is processed. (These remarks are not intended to denigrate the application of these fields to psychoanalysis but to indicate their probable limitations as a source for a comprehensive theory of mental functioning.)

Since action (internal or external) reflects decisions, much psychoanalytic study is devoted to how people reach emotionally important decisions. Freud explained observed choices of action in terms of quantitative intensities, cathexes of ideas. This formulation was plausible in that it corresponds to subjective experiences and is modeled on concepts of physics central to Freud's scientific ideals. These ideas have been rejected by many theoreticians (see, for example, Holzman and Gill, 1978), but there is no widely accepted theory to replace them.

A theory of decisions emerged following the Second World War. It has many sources, including computer science, artificial intelligence, and management. Important developments in this field result from attempts to build machines that make decisions. A popular misconception is that computers' central aspect is the ability to do rapid arithmetic. Though until the 1990s most applications of computers did center on this ability, computers are better thought of as processors of symbols and sequences of symbols of which arithmetic operations are but one example. (See, for example, Aho *et al.*, 1983; Simon, 1982.)

Two broad notions about decision processes are useful to our discussion. First, there must be a criterion for choosing among solutions to a problem. Second, there must be a method by which this criterion is applied. For example, if I am choosing a route from one place to another, in addition to the route having the correct endpoint, I might want it to be the fastest or the most scenic to meet some other criterion. Whatever criterion is selected, I must then find a way to discover the response that meets that criterion, e.g. to find the most scenic or fastest route between two points given the information available on those subjects.

The idea of psychic determinism can be restated in terms of decision processes. In this formulation, psychic determinism is simply that there is a criterion that selects among possible behaviors. The task of psychology is to describe this selection process. A potential source of confusion should be clarified now. When Freud spoke of "strict" psychic determinism (1901, 1935), he meant that psychological phenomena are lawful, not arbitrary. Psychic determinism is the idea that decision processes are orderly regardless of superficial indications to the contrary. Freud was not discussing deterministic as opposed to probabilistic behavior.

How criteria are applied is crucial to any model of decision making. Though not intuitively obvious, some ways of formulating decision problems are particularly effective to helping make decisions. In fact, there are whole disciplines devoted to decision theory and game theory, the study of decisions in the context of competitive interactions. Often, statements that some quantity is minimized or maximized can usefully express choice criteria. Each possible action is associated with a quantitative value. Actions can then be compared. In this context, an *action* is an entire action set, not some artificially delimited aspect of the action. The shortest route between cities is determined by the entire route traveled, not whether one turns left or right at a particular fork in the road. The best financial investment is not necessarily the one with the highest predicted return but for a particular investor may involve a combination the highest return with a factor based on the degree of risk involved. In psychoanalytic terms, this is the principle of multiple function—we must know all the meanings of an action to weigh its significance.

Many physical systems are most usefully characterized in terms of overall extremums (Courant and Hilbert, 1937; Goldstein, 1950). The actual path a physical system follows can be computed by calculating the value of some variable associated with the system and finding the form of the system that minimizes that value. For example, the actual shape of soap bubbles with defined edges can be determined by finding the shape that minimizes the surface area of the bubble and maintains contact with the defined edges. Freud's "regulatory principles" are applications of these methods. (The strategy of these principles does not rest on the details of the concept of psychic energy. The regulatory principles can be divided into two logically independent notions: a quantity may be associated with actions; that quantity is "psychic energy.") Such optimization is logically equivalent to virtually all decision processes, although it is not necessarily the actual method used in making decisions. I shall use the logical equivalent of such ordering to other decision procedures to simplify the discussion (Hartmann's [1958] concept of equilibria is another way of getting at the same idea).

The second aspect of decision problems is that of computation. Given a choice of criterion, the question remains of whether it can be implemented and the consequences of the implementation. This aspect of decision making has surprisingly profound effects. A classic example is the traveling salesman's problem, which illustrates its importance. A salesman going from city to city wishes to choose the route that minimizes the total distance traveled. An obvious solution is to examine all possible routes on a map and see which is shortest. Unfortunately, the number of possibilities rapidly becomes enormous, and the problem has been shown to be intractable in a fundamental sense, even with computers in the sense that as the number of cities and possible routes grows, the computational steps involved grow exponentially and it can be shown that no more efficient method can be devised (Fortnow, 2013). In actually planning the trip, the salesman must settle for less than perfect solutions if he is ever to leave home.

The study of the complexity of computation has blossomed in the last fifty years (Preparata, 1982). These inquiries show that some problems are unsolvable, others are inherently difficult (the computational resources required increase extremely rapidly with the situation's complexity), and specific estimates can be placed on the computational resources (time and/or equipment) needed to solve many types of problems. The important result emerges that the degree to which problems are solved is strongly determined by what computational resources will be devoted to them.

Choosing a method to solve a problem is itself a problem. Think of setting out to solve a problem as the equivalent to choosing a path along which to travel. The realization that the problem of choosing a method of solving a particular problem is not inherently different from problems of other types was the major step in the development of artificial intelligence. This basic idea antedates direct work on artificial intelligence (Gödel, 1931; Hilbert, 1929; Turing, 1936) and in fact led to the development of artificial intelligence (Hodges, 1983).

Solving Problems

Methods can be developed to find ways to solve problems. Finding general approaches to solving problems is difficult. The farther up in the hierarchy of generality, the more difficult it is to develop programming methods. Once the effort has been expended, unless the program works very poorly, developing other ways of solving the same problem is likely not worth the trouble. This is especially so when a significant investment in lower-order programs occurs, using the methods consistent with the high-level program. Since the development of new methods is difficult, they seldom appear.

In both emotional and intellectual human problem solving, using old methods is preferred to developing new ones. Even though doing arithmetic is fundamentally easier using 12 instead of 10 as the basis for computation, the likelihood of change in this regard is minimal because it would simply not be worth the trouble to try to convince everyone to adopt this more sensible way of doing things.

Old methods persist for additional reasons. A second source of conservatism is the difficulty of adapting to new programs. For example, QWERTY typewriter keyboards were set up to handle problems of long obsolete typewriter mechanisms (keys for each letter moving on individual levers became jammed easily so that it was desirable to place letters that commonly followed each other in writing as far apart as possible in the typewriter mechanism). When electronic mechanisms replaced traditional typewriter ones, as in the IBM Selectric and later in computer keyboards, the QWERTY keyboard based on avoiding jams of the typewriter mechanism no longer made sense. The arrangement is suboptimal for users. Yet these standard keyboards persist because of the investment required to retrain people to use other more rational keyboard arrangements (Pappert, 1982).

Having stable, preexisting solutions to problems is adaptive in and of itself. It not only spares an individual the energy involved looking for new methods to solve problems, but it is also useful to the individual to be able to predict his own response to a situation. In many contexts, the first concern of structures is their own stability. (The term *structure* refers here, not to the tripartite model, but simply to organized relationships of the mind, groups of people, etc.) Max Weber (1946) was the first to note the general tendency of organizations to perpetuate themselves. In fact, we observe such reluctance to change in psychology. Clinically, fear of loss of self-continuity is a significant source of resistance to change in almost all contexts.

Another reason for conservatism in program design is that programs designed for one purpose often prove useful for other purposes. Given a problem, it is efficient to use an available program (perhaps with slight modification) to solve the new problem. The loss of the opportunity to develop an ideal program is usually more than compensated by the time saved. This idea is also consistent with a developmental perspective on the "principle of multiple function" (Waelder, 1930). Significant psychological actions serve several purposes. Major psychological configurations, like character, combine numerous origins and current functions. Such an arrangement is a consequence of employing familiar methods, if possible, in problematic situations.

A major part of what we think of as psychopathology can be thought of as using methods appropriate for one situation in another situation where they are less appropriate. The ineffective and distressing overly emotional response of the histrionic individual, for example, can often be understood as resulting from using a solution of intense emotionality appropriate for the interaction of infant and parent in a situation, say an interaction between employer and employee, where it is likely to be less effective and even counterproductive.

Thus, it is not always possible or desirable to try to solve problems perfectly because the search for a method of perfect solution may itself be an intractable problem, or a problem that requires a disproportionate amount of effort, or a problem whose solution interferes with an existing solution, or a problem whose solution threatens personal stability and a sense of self. For actual problem solving, we need, and we would expect, mental actual functioning to be based on a more pragmatic concept than absolute optimization.

When the work in finding solutions is considered, it is useful to assume that a search is made, not for the problem's optimal solution, but rather for a "good enough" solution. Such solutions are said to "satisfice" (Simon, 1982). Consider the salesman problem—it really does not matter (at least to him) whether his route is absolutely the shortest. What matters is that it be within his budget and that it be nearly as cheap as possible, given the time he is willing to invest in exploring itineraries.

Most problem solving consists in recognizing the correspondence between the current problem and one previously solved, and applying the existing methods. (This is one of the first recommendations made in the study of heuristics—the study of workable methodologies for problem solving [Polya, 1954].) Solutions that satisfice will be accepted even though imperfect. Only in times of difficulty or when leisure is available are new methods likely to emerge. Abandoning old methods is impeded by the factors mentioned above. Thus, we expect and observe a conservative attitude in human thinking and are surprised by novel problem solving and creativity.

If most human functioning consists in recognizing previously solved problems and applying already formulated solutions to them, certain difficulties are predictable, including inappropriate application of the previously developed methods. Ordinarily, this creates no great problem. People learn to discriminate problems solvable by available methods. A cook might know that fish can be pleasantly prepared by poaching. Applying this general knowledge, he might attempt to poach a wild catfish. He soon discovers the error and excludes wild catfish from poachable fish. He has learned something new.

A special problem arises when such learning fails. Suppose that the criteria according to which the program is used are disguised. Learning—that is, modifying the criteria—becomes impossible.

Neurosis and transference involve this mechanism. The woman who desired her father as a child and represses that desire while being led to pick boyfriends who substitute for her father neither observes that her selection cannot get her what she wants nor reexamines the idea that her father is the only desirable man. Defenses make the material against which they defend inaccessible to learning through experience.

To defend against material is itself a decision. There are rules (and problems of modifying them) concerning defenses, as for other behavioral decisions. These rules must be inaccessible to scrutiny lest knowledge of their workings make them useless in keeping secrets (Freud, 1923a). Defense analysis consists of making as many of these schemas as possible available for reconsideration so that learning from experience can resume.

Let us examine more closely how choices among procedures are made. Given a situation, the individual reviews the repertoire of available procedures to determine whether they apply to that situation. (This idea can be formalized as a "production system" [Anderson, 1983], i.e. a group of rules of the form, if [conditional statement], then [a list of procedures].) In emotionally significant situations, the individual often feels impelled to do this rapidly. Consider an individual operating under the following rule:

> When in trouble, fear or doubt
> Run in circles
> Stamp and Shout—(Koestler, 1984)

He must decide whether he is "in trouble, fear or doubt," and apply appropriate action if he is. Two kinds of problems arise with this approach. First, the person may misjudge whether trouble, fear, or doubt applies. The information available to him, and the time he is willing to spend processing it, may lead to the ill-considered inclusion of a situation as an instance of one of these when it is not. (This is a typical transference situation.) Second, the procedure may itself be no good. Assuming a goal of ending dysphoria, even though the program may specify an action, that action may not achieve the goal well.

Analysis of an individual operating under this rule would, it is hoped, increase the accuracy with which he perceived situations and modify his responses to them. Both types of modification occur during psychoanalysis. These modifications are tied to several phenomena in analysis—the patient's having the experience in the analyst's presence, the patient's experiencing the situation with the analyst playing an important role, and the analyst and patient describing the situation verbally. How do these factors affect the rule?

Consider the possible origins of a procedure. It may be "wired into" the system—a biological given. It may be imported wholesale (for whatever reason) and slightly modified to suit the individual needs (analogous to purchasing software and corresponding to internalization). Or it may be developed from previously available procedures.

How does an individual develop new procedures from old? He may scan his repertoire and collect methods that seem relevant. He may use pieces of methods, putting them together to form partial solutions. As he develops procedures, he assesses whether they are closer or further from his goal. If one seems closer, he continues working with it, modifying it, and comparing it with other procedures until two criteria are met: the final procedure must satisfice (in the sense discussed above), and the development of a better solution must require significantly more work (time). Solutions found in this way depend significantly on time restrictions. One extreme will be the acceptance of solutions as soon as they satisfice, however satisfactory they are. Given more time, more elegant and satisfactory solutions are expected.

Consider, for example, two children suddenly confronted with death—one with the unexpected death of a sibling, the other with the anticipated death of a pet. The first child's situation demands a rapid solution. Few other criteria will be met besides reduction of anxiety. Often such a child denies any affective response and behaves as if the death had not occurred. The manifold problems involved, dealing with grief-stricken parents, the internal consequences of the loss (e.g. guilt) and intellectual activities (e.g. thinking about the meaning of death and one's own mortality) are put aside. Nothing new is learned, and ongoing learning is interrupted.

In contrast, the death of a pet may precipitate psychological and intellectual work. For example, fantasies of saving the pet may lead to ideas of being a veterinarian or physician. These fantasies, in turn, may lead to actual learning in those fields. The latter may fit with the child's sexual curiosity and simultaneously draw parental approbation. Furthermore, in the context of tolerable anxiety, mourning may occur, and with it the discovery that mourning is possible.

Thus, the situation that requires a less urgent solution permits not only an adequate resolution itself but other problems and developmental tasks as well. The more complex computation made possible by the less strenuous time constraints produces a more effective solution not only to the most pressing problem but also to related problems. (These issues are obviously related to the general problem of anti-developmental aspects of trauma.)

In addition to time, the availability of essential others, persons, and institutions that support development and provide need function for it (Galatzer-Levy and Cohler, 1993), or an adequate holding environment will make a substantial difference in the person's opportunity to search the field of possible solutions for ones that may be more sophisticated and effective than those that are initially evident.

Since past solutions are likely not to be optimal, mechanisms should allow for reexamining old solutions as well as for dealing with new situations. Mental functioning should have a primary tendency to evolve. Anna Freud (1965) described a "drive to the completion of development." Especially in children, but also in adults, there is a dramatic tendency to change. However, although certain developmental lines do recur, I believe that the "drive" is not toward "completion of development" to a predetermined endpoint; rather, the "drive" is for continued development and change. Less teleologically: the function of some mechanisms results in development. Successful analyses are characterized not only by the resumption of typical developmental lines but also by the emergence of solutions that surprise patient and analyst (Reik, 1948).

There are two fundamental ways of solving problems. In one, an endpoint is initially set, and the solution is gauged by its closeness to the endpoint. Another approach involves no predefined endpoint; possibilities are explored with a vaguer criterion for retaining solutions, for example, that the discoveries are in some sense "interesting" (Marsh, 1978). In human emotional problem solving, being "interesting" may involve solving outstanding problems, solving problems more efficiently, effectively, or elegantly, or improving efficiency through solutions compatible with one another (i.e. conflict resolution). Anna Freud (1965) proposed that pathology in childhood be defined as interferences in development. Age-appropriate norms are significant only because they point to developmental failures and irregularities. This idea can be extended to include all psychopathology.

The results of successful analyses are not the disappearance of conflict but the capacity to rapidly engage conflict and work on it effectively to resume development (Schlessinger and Robbins, 1983). This is precisely what the patient in need of analysis is unable to do by himself. The self-analytic function is the capacity to do independent developmental work. Adult and child analysis are the same in that the capacity for continuing development is restored. How does this occur? Further exploration of the modes of problem solving (the development of solutions) suggests an answer.

As discussed above, one way to think about problem solving is the determination of the extremum of some variable, i.e. most problems can be formulated as the problem of minimizing or maximizing some quantity. The identification of these extremes is a major undertaking of contemporary mathematics and computer science. Two major methods are available. One is to "divide and conquer," to break the problem up into smaller, more tractable problems. The second is the direct search for an extreme value.

To divide a problem into simpler problems requires that the components of the problem be separable from one another, i.e. subproblems can be independently solved and then patched together without loss of optimality. These modular approaches are powerful. For example, in writing computer programs, programmers use a "top-down" approach, where they break down the problem into successively smaller steps until they reach the level of statements in the programming language. Then they fit these steps together to create an overall program (Karp, 1977).

The modular approach's advantages include breaking problems down into smaller, more tractable units, allowing independent examination of each part of a solution and the rapid location of difficulties, and the ability, when interrupted, to save work to the end of a module and not have to start from scratch. Simon (1982) gives the example of two watchmakers, each of whose watches requires the same number of steps to construct. One of them works in a modular fashion, while the other requires that the entire watch be assembled in a continuous operation. If the watchmakers answer their own telephones, the second watchmaker will seldom complete a watch, while the first loses only the time required to remake the module he is working on.

A modular approach is not always appropriate or simple. In building a house, one would naturally divide the problem into subproblems, say, of building the walls and building the roof. Solving these problems independently results in walls and a roof, unattached. Obviously, the step of joining these partial solutions is not trivial. It would be more useful not to divide the problem, at least in this way.

When a modular approach is impossible or the problem cannot be further decomposed to subproblems, another method, called iterative search, is often employed. From an initial guess at the solution, some standard operation is applied until a rearranged configuration that improves the result is found (Dunham *et al.*, 1963; Lin, 1975). The process is repeated until no better solution is found. These methods have distinct disadvantages. When they reach a local minimum, they retain it as a solution, even though it is not optimal. To understand the idea of a local minimum, imagine a man trying to locate the lowest point on an island. By the method of iterative search, he begins at a point and looks in each direction. Seeing a lower point, he moves to it and looks from there, continuing in this way until he sees no lower points. This procedure finds the lowest point on the island only under special circumstances. If he started in a valley surrounded by mountains, he never examines points on the other side of the mountains. Only the valley's lowest point, the local minimum, is found. Iterative searches can be improved by widening the range of search, but the possibility of getting stuck in a local minimum always remains and fundamentally limits the method.

Simulated Annealing

Kirkpatrick *et al.* (1983) introduced a new approach to this important problem. They observed that the formal structure of such problems in large situations (i.e. situations involving a large number of factors) is analogous to the physical situations when metals or other substances are annealed.

In annealing, metals reach more stable structures by being heated to near melting and being slowly cooled. For practical reasons, this phenomenon is much studied. The states reached through perfect annealing, called ground states of matter, are the arrangements of the material with the lowest energy for the entire system. Low temperatures are not a sufficient condition for ground states. If freezing is too rapid, rather than reaching an overall ground state, local regions independently reach minimum energy values, usually at the expense of reaching minimal energy for the entire system. Once the system is frozen, change stops, and the less than optimal solution is preserved. Annealing prevents freezing at a less than optimal, and therefore unstable, point. In annealing, the temperature of the system is kept near freezing for long periods of time, so an overall optimal solution is likely. "If this is not done, the substance is allowed to get out of equilibrium, the resulting crystal will have many defects, or the substance may form a glass, with no crystalline order and only metastable, locally optimal structure" (p. 672). To find an overall solution to the problem of minimizing some function of a complex system, Kirkpatrick *et al.* propose that a process analogous to annealing be applied to the complex problem.

Does the intuitive analogy between annealing and analysis hold up? Do we "heat things up" in analysis and try to examine frozen psychological configurations that no longer fit together into an overall optimal solution?

Certain elements of the annealing problem seem readily translatable into the language of psychology. The minimized physical energy of the physical system can be replaced by an overall measure of goodness of a psychological situation. However, the concept of "temperature" has no obvious analogue in human psychology or in problem solving. Kirkpatrick *et al.* introduce the idea of *effective temperature* and show how a simulated annealing can be used in problem solving. They begin with an iterative approach. Improvements in a scheme are equated with reductions in energy, just as in the standard iterative approach. However, "... accepting only rearrangements that lower the cost function of the system is like extremely rapid quenching from high temperature to $T = 0$, so it should not be surprising that resulting solutions are usually metastable." (That is, not an overall solution but one that is only stable within a small range of variations. For example, if the problem was to find the shortest route from New York to Boston and one somehow got stuck looking only at routes that went through Providence, the process might give a solution that was the best among those that go through that city but would mistakenly present it as the best overall solution.)

Metropolis *et al.* (1953) first approached the problem of simulating annealing. The Metropolis algorithm is a method of simulating the behavior of a large group of atoms in equilibrium at a given temperature. In the algorithm, atoms are given small displacements, and the change in the overall energy of the system ΔE is computed. If the change decreases the total energy of the system (i.e. $\Delta E < 0$), the displacement is accepted, and further computation goes on from this point (so far, we have just a straight iterative procedure). However, if the energy of the system increases (i.e. $\Delta E > 0$), the situation is treated differently than in a straight iterative search. Instead of simply rejecting the solution, it is accepted with a probability that decreases sharply with the energy increases.[3]

Kirkpatrick *et al.* propose using this probability distribution in the search procedure, replacing temperature with a control parameter. The simulated annealing process consists of "first 'melting' the system being optimized at a high effective temperature, then lowering the temperature by slow stages until the system 'freezes' and no further change occurs. At each temperature, the simulating must proceed long enough for the system to reach a steady state" (pp. 672–73). One could also imagine that the process has no stopping point. It might reach a point that is sufficiently stable to be the basis for a decision to act, but the process of decision making could continue even after the action so that new and better solutions might be found and acted on later. One suspects that this is what sometimes happens in human decision making, where an adequate solution is put into action but the process of thinking about and accessing possible other solutions continues.

This process differs from ordinary iterative searches. It need never get stuck in relative minimum. The explorer in search for the lowest point on the island will not get permanently stuck at the lowest point in some valley with no likelihood of exploring what is on the other side of the mountains that surround it. Instead she will continue to have a certain probability of exploring a wider terrain albeit with rapidly diminishing likelihood as the surrounding mountains get higher. Transition from such a stuck position is always possible because even changes that would result in an increase in energy of the system remain possible, though increasingly unlikely as the energy increases.

The critical area in the annealing algorithm (as in the physical process of annealing) is near freezing. Below "freezing," change is unlikely. This is analogous to the physical freezing where, once it is frozen, little happens to a system. At high temperature, the system is disorganized. Near freezing, structures are more stable, but they are not fixed. When simulated annealing is actually used computationally, a "freezing point" can be observed—that is, a "temperature" below which there is little change. The reader will recognize that this situation in which a system has unstable structure and is located between a rigid regimen and a state of disorganization is in a state we have been referring to as at the edge of chaos.

Applications to Psychoanalysis

Analogies between psychoanalysis and simulated annealing are striking. Patients come "frozen" in important aspects of their development. The central problem of analytic work is to remobilize development. Patients' affective responses in areas where development is fixed are of inappropriate (either too great or too little) intensity. Analytic work aids the patient to experience these areas of difficulty with "optimal affective intensity." Affective intensity, particularly the intensity of anxiety, may be regarded as equivalent to the temperature parameter in simulated annealing.

The concept of "optimality" becomes clearer with this viewpoint. Discussions of "optimality" in psychoanalysis tend to become tautological. Thus, "optimal frustration" is "observed" to be necessary for growth, but the only specific marker of "optimal frustration" is the presence of such growth. Clinically, there is reasonable agreement on the range of intensity of frustration and anxiety that is useful to patients, but specific descriptions of that intensity are elusive. In the context of the present discussion, the idea of optimal frustration and anxiety can be reformulated in a specific, nontautological way.

"Optimal" anxiety is sufficient to strongly motivate change but not so great as to disorganize or demand emergency defenses that impede work. This corresponds to temperature in the vicinity of freezing where annealing occurs. Inadequately intense experience and anxiety are like frozen states in which significant change is impossible. Too intense experience results in disorganization, the loss of structure (the equivalent of melting), or, given the appropriate protective devices (defenses), the emergency cooling of the system and its consequent refreezing without the opportunity to develop optimal structures provided by annealing. A "good enough" environment is one in which reasonably good annealing can occur.

Aspects of the clinical situation can be described using these concepts. A characteristic of free association going well is the discovery of previously unappreciated connections between psychological schemata. This clinical observation can be described as the annealing of the system resulting in optima developing over large areas, i.e. optimization that now includes a wider range of interconnected problems.

An important aspect of the annealing algorithm is the way in which patterns of solutions emerge. These patterns were empirically discovered when the algorithm was used for the computer solution of technical problems. Gross outlines of the solution emerge as the system cools, followed by the refinement of these outlines as the system slowly is annealed toward freezing. At any point in the annealing schedule, there is both a changing level of refinement and a level of structure, laid down at a slightly higher temperature, that is unlikely to change further. Furthermore, once a level of structure stabilizes, even rapid cooling, while not resulting in an optimal solution, retains the developed structure.

This stability of structures, which takes place at temperatures above that at which the annealing is occurring, corresponds to two clinical observations. First, we know that satisfactory structures, once in place, are unlikely to change, even in analysis. People who have satisfactorily traversed a developmental phase do not change further in that regard. Clinically, attempts to engage such issues are generally futile. Second, the idea of the fixing of structure clarifies, in abstract and process terms, the appropriate endpoint for analysis. Annealing, like psychoanalysis, has no logical absolute endpoint, except that the work involved in further computation or analysis outweighs the anticipated benefits from continuing. The solution, in Simon's term, satisfices. However, it is possible to judge by lack of change in the system that it has come close to freezing. Relative lack of change with repeated application of the algorithm indicates that the system is frozen or nearly so. The desired outcome of analysis includes both a continued capacity for development (self-analysis) and indications that sufficient work has been done within the analysis so that continuing difficulties are no longer major interferences in living.

Major personality configurations have become relatively stable. In terms of the annealing algorithm, we are speaking of a point where freezing has not occurred, but there has been sufficient annealing so that major adaptive structures have developed and stabilized. In contrast, an analytic impasse reflects freezing of the system.

A Model of Working Through

To summarize the preceding discussion: Human problem solving, both cognitive and emotional, consists principally in employing preexisting methods, modified as needed. When these techniques prove inadequate, and if things are going reasonably well (i.e. if the person can tolerate the situation), a modified version of the annealing algorithm is employed. The likelihood that an old solution will be reworked using the algorithm increases when time is available for such recomputation. Reexamination of old solutions always remains possible (except in pathological situations, discussed below). The annealing schedule itself is a function of the time available for solving the problem and the danger (anxiety) associated with not solving it and reworking it.

Human use of the annealing algorithm involves a special group of conditions imposed by situations of danger (Freud, 1923b). These correspond to actual or potential destabilization of the system. Some of the danger situations correspond to temperatures high enough to threaten well-formed, stable structures. When such a condition occurs, the system acts to maintain stability. In terms of the annealing algorithm, there is very rapid cooling to avoid the loss of structure that would result from melting. Such emergency cooling typically results in unsatisfactory annealing. Less than optimal solutions are frozen, and further change is impossible at least until the annealing process can resume. The actuality or anticipation of trauma results in use of emergency defenses that remove aspects of the personality or experience from the area of change and reworking. The prototype of such a procedure is, of course, repression (Breuer and Freud, 1893a, b). Undoing these defensive operations so further work can be done is one of the functions of psychoanalysis.

These processes occur at all levels of function, but are most likely at lower levels of organization. Higher-level changes are more likely near the melting point and so precipitate emergency cooling (emergency defenses). Thus, I am more likely to consider the effectiveness of a particular intervention with an analysand than to re-explore the question of whether analysis is the treatment of choice for the patient, and I am more likely to consider the later question than to examine whether psychoanalysis in general is a useful procedure. This is a corollary of the fact that general outlines of structures emerge first, and the system is refined as it gradually cools, details being filled in as the cooling continues. This corresponds to analytic experience. Circumscribed areas of difficulty are far easier to rework than problems such as character pathology.

Two types of reasons to use the annealing algorithm correspond to the quite different adaptational heuristics discussed above. It may be used to solve a well-defined problem, or, alternatively, it may be part of a looser exploratory method where the direction of search is determined by vaguer factors (like "interestingness").

Naturally, the theory described here does not predict all the clinical details and complex processes observed in working through. Individual experience and endowment determine the defensive structures and problems that must be worked through in a particular analysis. However, the objection that a computer-based model fails to appreciate the richness of clinical experience is simultaneously accurate and misleading. Any theoretical statement, whether based on conflict theory, hermeneutic principles, models inspired by physics, or computer science, loses something of the phenomena themselves. A particular theory must be judged by how well it encompasses the data available, suggests further avenues for understanding, allows contact between various bodies of knowledge, and suits our esthetic values. The reluctance to think of human functioning as usefully modeled by studies in computers drives from the same narcissistic pain Freud encountered when he showed the closeness of our highest achievements to their irrational biological sources.

There are many indications that processes like the annealing algorithm are ongoing aspects of normal functioning and occur outside analysis. Freud (1926) refers to the ego's "impulsion to bind together and unify … this necessity to synthesize grows stronger in proportion as the strength of the ego increases" (p. 98) and goes on to describe a process consistent with annealing in symptom formation.

Nunberg's (1930) concept of a synthetic function of the ego points to the centrality of such integration in psychic functioning. Play, as described by Winnicott (1975) and Erickson (1950), has many aspects of this sort of activity. The states of mind of play, ritual, music, and theatrical performance, as well as in analysis and the liminal state (Turner, 1969), are special conditions allowing higher annealing temperatures than could otherwise be tolerated and so greater possibilities for novel solutions.

Another indication that processes like annealing are aspects of normal functioning is the appearance of distorted versions of the process in organic brain syndromes. Pollack (1981) describes a process in senile individuals in which old situations are repeatedly reexamined. Their ruminations, however, do not result in development because they are not remembered and so cannot move forward in any sense. However, their presence supports the idea that a part of normal brain function is the repeated reengagement of problems.

Spontaneous reworking through an annealing-like process occurs in dreaming, as described by Hobson and McCarly (McCarly and Hobson, 1977). They supply evidence that dreaming functions to work through the day's material. Furthermore, they contend, this results from the discharge of a specific brain center that stimulates this work, suggesting a primary biological function. This would constitute a third item of evidence for a central, naturally occurring role for a function like annealing.

People seek analysis when both old methods of problem solution and the spontaneous application of the annealing algorithm and other problem solving methods fail. This failure occurs for one of two reasons corresponding to the two major types of psychopathology—that resulting from intrapsychic conflict and that deriving from lack of structure (Tolpin, 1978; A. Freud, 1981). The pathology of absent or insufficiently stable structures corresponds to a system that is always too hot for structure adequately to develop and stabilize. The patient's clinical presentation either reflects directly the lack of structure or the defenses intended to deal with the potential emergency of disorganization (melting). For example, borderline pathology is characterized by the relative lack of stable structures, the failure of the emergence of structures as the system cools (Pine, 1974; Galatzer-Levy, 1980, see Chapter 2 of this volume). In conflict pathology, the danger of overheating has resulted in an interruption of the annealing algorithm and the introduction of emergency cooling, thus removing areas of the personality from further work in the algorithm and the interruption of development that is characteristic of neurosis.

Attempts to differentiate psychoanalysis from other psychotherapies often implicitly hinge on the idea of "working through." The use of transference and interpretation are not unique to psychoanalysis. But the depth and thoroughness of the process are uniquely psychoanalytic. Theoretical attempts to sharply differentiate psychoanalysis from other psychotherapies remain unsatisfactory, but there is consensus among analysts about the difference. The psychoanalytic setup permits a kind of change rarely seen in other contexts. Repeated failures in attempts to shorten analysis have clarified certain requirements of the analytic situation. Long periods (on the order of years) and frequent (approximately daily) sessions are both essential. There is also agreement that less prolonged and less intense treatments usually lead to different and less satisfactory results than analysis.[4] These less satisfactory results are not the consequence of the analyst's or the patient's ignorance of specific psychological facts. Nor are they explained by the distinction between intellectual and affective (or emotional) knowing.

Two specific findings that do not differentiate analysis from other therapies are important. The therapeutic process is incomplete both in analysis and psychotherapy. Nor do dynamics change fundamentally in analysis but not in psychotherapy. Essentially the same issues remain with a patient at the end of a successful analysis as at its initiation; the difference after analysis is the rapidity with which the patient resolves the problems confronting him (Pfeffer, 1961; Schlessinger and Robbins, 1983; Weiss, 1981). Furthermore, since continuing self-analysis is a hallmark of a successful analytic experience, no analysis is complete.

Analysis, then, may be viewed as a collection of methods to reinstate the working of the annealing algorithm when it ceases to operate—the reemergence of working through. The analyst provides an environment where it is safe to speak and think; he systematically examines and thereby disrupts interference with the algorithm (interprets defenses) in ways that avoid the evocation of emergency techniques of avoidance; and he allows himself to become the object of the patient's intense emotional responses without letting the patient or himself be overwhelmed by the experience.

The level at which the annealing reactivated in the analysis occurs is a function of the point in the hierarchy of structure at which the algorithm failed. The basic algorithm remains the same, regardless of where in the hierarchy this occurs. For example, a patient who was traumatized in the era when object constancy is established needs to reexamine affectively the unsatisfactory solution he achieved and to reactivate the annealing algorithm in the area of the pathology so generated—just as the patient whose difficulties arise from unresolved superego—id conflicts needs the opportunity to once again start the interrupted exploration and search procedure whose inadequate results are manifest in his pathology.

There is another function of the analyst in terms of the annealing algorithm. Clinically, the danger of examining and working on aspects of one's personality is decreased by the presence of a benign other. The transferential aspects of this situation are well known. While authors like Winnicott and Kohut have provided convincing descriptions of the subjective experiences involved, no satisfactory explanation exists of how the "facilitating environment" facilitates development. The mother's capacity to deal with the infant's danger situations—most obviously, her ability to reduce the child's physiological distress—clearly contribute. However, the situation can be viewed fruitfully in terms of the overall stability of the system and the relation of that stability to the functioning of the annealing algorithm.

The situation of instability is the first of the danger situations Freud describes. If two systems are joined, the likelihood of a specific change's destabilizing the overall system is decreased. This is the fourth function of the analyst (parent) in supporting the working of the annealing algorithm.

Conclusion

The annealing algorithm provides a plausible model for human emotional problem solving when the use of preexisting solutions must be abandoned for whatever reason. Failure to employ this normal psychological function is characteristic of psychopathology, and the function of analysis is to reestablish its use. The manifestation of this algorithm within analysis is the process of working through. The analyst functions to promote the reestablishment of this function.

The work described in this chapter illustrates the fruitfulness of applying ideas from artificial intelligence and related disciplines to psychoanalysis. Analysts are abandoning paradigms derived from Freud's scientific milieu and searching their own intellectual environment for appropriate concepts to describe the mind. Disciplines generated by scientific study of design, programming, and thought are promising sources for such ideas.

The model has many clinical consequences, consistent with modern analytic technique, but not adequately included in previous theories. The theory focuses attention on the process of exploring new pathways and associations rather than the emergence of specific content, a focus that is central to the points of view discussed in this volume. Whether the analyst is providing a "good enough environment" can be measured by specific process criteria other than the overall success of the analytic work. Normal development as well as analysis are conceptualized as having no absolute endpoint but rather as states of relative stability that include built-in mechanisms of continued evolution. The theory provides a rational basis for not disturbing genuinely satisfactory structures. It also implies that the basic analytic task, and consequently analytic technique, always involves the reemergence of normal processes of working over—that psychoanalysis does not differ in its basic methods as a function of the patient's developmental state.

Notes

1 First published as "On Working Through: A Model from Artificial Intelligence." *Journal of the American Psychoanalytic Association*, 36(1): 125–51, February 1988. Reprinted by permission of the journal and SAGE Publications, Ltd.

2 An important exception is the work of Solms (2013) on the "conscious id."

3 The likelihood of a change being accepted is $\Delta E = \exp(-E/\kappa bT)$ (where "exp" is the exponential function, κb the Boltzmann constant, and T the temperature of the system). This last function, the Boltzmann distribution, has been studied extensively. Its details do not matter greatly in this argument, but that its use leads to a stable configuration is important and has been demonstrated in a variety of situations.

4 As I suggested in Chapter 8, the frequency and intensity of analytic work simply increase the likelihood that truly analytic work will be possible. I believe that the apparent consensus about the desirability of intensive, frequent work along with an almost equally strong consensus that the essence of analytic work lies elsewhere points to the existence of a core of what it means to be analytic that is most easily achieved in intense, frequent work.

Chapter 10

The Nonlinear Clinician at Work on the Edge of Chaos

There is a place somewhere between living by routine automatic rules and psychological chaos. In this "edge of chaos," creative and new ways of being emerge. The core of psychoanalytic work occurs in the edge of chaos, and the work of analysis is to bring analyst and analysand there.

Over the past forty years, a small but ever-enlarging circle of psychoanalysts have come to believe that ideas from that field should inform psychoanalysis (e.g. Moran, 1990; Ruelle, 1991; Spruiell, 1993; Duke, 1994; Langs and Badalamenti, 1994; Boston Change Process Study Group, 2005; Marks-Turlow, 2008; and Guastello *et al.*, 2009). Over the last several decades, I have published a series of papers designed to show how important aspects of psychoanalysis can be conceptualized in the language of chaos theory (Galatzer-Levy, 1978, 1980, 1995, 1997a, 2002, 2004, 2009). In this chapter, I focus on three central ideas of the theory from a clinical point of view and show how they worked in an analysis.

But, first, we need some context for nonlinear dynamics systems theory.

Freud borrowed his worldview from nineteenth century natural science. This led him to the terrifying discovery of powerful forces within us that follow principles alien to the sense of being masters of our own minds. These forces are, however, as Freud described them, orderly and follow rules much like the machinery on which they are modeled. As we shift from the worldview that informed him, we should learn from him to take what is useful, discard what is not, and to avoid giving his ideas undue authority because of their scientific origins.

Newton created a fabulously powerful mathematical apparatus for understanding the world and, with it, a worldview implicit in that apparatus. The core of Newton's ideas is that the world can be described through mathematical formulae, now called linear differential equations. *Linear* refers both to the form of these equations *and* to a property implicit in that form, i.e. that small changes in one variable produce small changes in other variables. A ball thrown slightly harder will go slightly further. A little more electric current will make the bulb grow somewhat brighter. Generally small quantitative changes do not cause qualitative changes. The camel's back usually bends rather than breaks when a straw is added to its burden.

The enormous power of Newton and his descendants' mathematical tools and the associated worldview dominated Western scientific thought until the late twentieth century. It was this worldview, as handed down by his teacher Brücke, that informed Freud's central investigative tactic (Galatzer-Levy, 1976). The Newtonian view of the world as mechanism operating in a fundamentally linear way came to Freud, as it did to his contemporaries, indirectly, not so much from reading Newton and his physicist descendants, as through the ways that Newtonian ideals pervaded nineteenth-century science, including those of the biologists and clinicians who most directly influenced Freud. Starting with the *Studies in Hysteria,* Freud showed that when psychological material appeared to contain discontinuities and disconnections, we should look for the unconscious connections that bridge the apparent gap. In other words, Freud's assumption of continuous smooth linear development, based in a Newtonian worldview, produced the core of the psychoanalytic method.[1]

Scientists had long understood that many physical phenomena are not linear, but it was not until after the Second World War that several factors converged resulting in new sciences studying nonlinear phenomena.

The nonlinear world is radically different from the linear world. Ideas that have become so fundamental that they are confused with intuition do not apply in this world. For example, the assumption that where we find structure it must reflect a preexisting plan does not apply in the nonlinear world. Nor does the intuition that small changes in conditions yield small changes in outcome.

In order to talk about processes, generally mathematicians found it necessary to introduce new language. The idea of *attractors* is central to dynamical systems thinking. An attractor is a pattern of motion toward which a system tends. Kepler showed that ellipses are attractors for planetary motion. Freud showed that the phases of libidinal development are attractors for children's development, and defenses are attractors of psychological actions designed to protect against psychological distress. Melanie Klein showed that fluctuation between the overlapping paranoid-schizoid position and the depressive position is an ongoing attractor in human psychological functioning.[2]

We may speak of psychological well-being in terms of the sort of attractor under which a person is living. If the attractor is too simple so that the person lives according to a small number of rules regardless of the circumstances, it is unlikely that there will be either adequate richness or a capacity to adapt well to changing circumstances. On the other hand, if a person lives on an attractor that is overly complex, unpredictable, and erratic, life is constantly lived in the shadow of dangerous disorganization and chaos. In some sense, there should be an optimal sort of attractor that includes a wide range of possibility and creativity without undue risk of profound disorganization.

While many analysands fear disorganization, few of them are actually in this state in major aspects of their lives. They have instead moved to a region of the attractor too far from disorganization to allow for desirable complexity and richness. Here is the story of a man who had constricted his life to a tiny segment of possible attractors.[3]

Mr. Jones began analysis with a life dominated by a very simple attractor. In an important sense, almost nothing had changed for him between the time he was sixteen and when he was forty-four, when we first met. He was referred by a colleague who had been seeing him "temporarily" for eight years following the death of Mr. Jones's first analyst, who treated him for over twenty years. Mr. Jones continued to suffer from disabling obsessive-compulsive symptoms and irritable bowel syndrome. He still lived with his parents and was employed as a low-level civil servant. He spent most of his waking time in rituals and obsessional thinking, trying to avoid contaminating the world with feces. I was the twenty-second analyst to whom he had been referred.

Mr. Jones told me a remarkably simple story for a man who had decades of analysis. Bowel symptoms had plagued him all his life leading both to fears about being unable to get to a toilet and fears that he would contaminate things with his feces. His sole pleasure was collecting stamps, but fears that he would contaminate his collections interfered with any pleasure he might have had. His first analysis was with a "strict Freudian," but what this meant was unclear. The attractor that seemed to control Mr. Jones's life was a single, unmovable point, a place where he remained, repeating his rituals and worries, only to the slightest extent moved by the passage of time or experiences in the world.

Mr. Jones had interviews with many potential analysts. He liked each of them, but each had a flaw that made it impossible for Mr. Jones to work with them. One's office faced a busy street that made the consulting room too noisy. Another was too far from Mr. Jones's workplace. And so on and so on. As the end of our initial meeting approached, I suggested that we meet again, but rather sadly Mr. Jones declined. I asked why, and he pointed to a ventilation panel in my office ceiling. I said that I did not understand. He explained that the office was cold, that the air conditioning was too high. He could not return.

At this point, a fiercely competitive element of my own personality emerged. I told myself I could be more effective at engaging Mr. Jones than the twenty-two other analysts who had seen him. I said, "It is quite chilly (which it was), but you can come back."

He said, "Really?"

I said, "Yes."

After a bit of negotiation, the analysis began.

The session, which, of course could be described in terms of transference, countertransference, and enactment, can also be thought of in terms of an attractor, or unconscious fantasy, of Mr. Jones's that might be called, "the unfortunate flaw that makes working with this analyst impossible," an attractor of my own, a wish, "I want to be the best analyst in Chicago," and my intervention, an enactment, seen as a successful attempt to move Mr. Jones slightly off his attractor and have his action fit within mine. The phenomena referred to as attractors here (as well as "self-similarity," discussed in Chapter 7) could be discussed under the rubric of the repetition compulsion. The advantage of replacing this familiar psychoanalytic vocabulary with that of nonlinear dynamics is twofold. First, it underlines a fundamental relationship between these phenomena, albeit one that is generally recognized in psychoanalysis. Second, and more important, it points to the appropriateness of asking what part of the theory of attractors may be applicable to psychoanalytic phenomena. The awareness of previously unthought of psychoanalytic configurations that are known from the general study of attractors can call our attention to new clinical phenomena.

In 1665, Christian Huygens, the inventor of the pendulum clock, observed an "odd kind of sympathy" between clocks hung on the same wall. Their pendulums came, after a time, to move in synchrony. The observation that pendulum clocks hung on the same wall become synchronous pointed to how subtle an interaction was required for the clocks to influence one another. The pattern of motion of the pendulum is an attractor. Huygens's observation points to an important feature of attractors, namely that interacting attractors may require only very small interactions to have significant effects. If this idea is applicable to human psychological interactions, it implies that the intensity of effects may be out of proportion to the intensity of interaction.

Another feature of many attractors is the way in which a small part of an attractor resembles the overall attractor and, how, changing that small part of the attractor dramatically shifts the functioning of the overall attractor.

"The unfortunate flaw that makes working with this analyst impossible" was an aspect of a larger attractor that might be called "sadly nothing is possible except to do the same thing again and again," an attractor that dominated Mr. Jones's personality. This is an example of self-similarity, which is characteristic of many complex systems. When you examine a small portion of the attractor, it reveals information about the entire attractor. What is more, altering such small segments of the attractor may transform the overall attractor.

A common argument about analytic technique concerns how large a chunk of analytic material we should try to address—life narratives, material as it occurs as the analysis unfolds over, say, several weeks, the interpersonal transactions in the time frame of a portion of a session, a transaction of a few minutes- or even several seconds-long speech, act in the manner Paul Gray (1973, 1990) suggested. One implication of the self-similarity of attractors is that we cannot answer this question in a general way since the attractor is manifest at all levels *and*, more important, altering the attractor at a small level transforms the larger attractor. Of course, the attractor, "I want to be the best analyst in Chicago," can be seen as part of a general competitive and/or grandiose attractor.

Please notice that my attractor did not fit particularly well with the analysand and certainly had little to do with any deep empathy with him. The challenging nature of Mr. Jones's presentation happened to activate this attractor and supported a potential for interaction of some kind with the analysand's attractor. A tenuous connection thus emerged in which analyst and analysand used the bridge of the experience that the room was indeed chilly to bring their only slightly related attractors into contact. The result was a slight but significant modification of the attractors in both participants. Mr. Jones's "do the same things over and over attractor" came to include coming to analytic sessions, while my competitive attractor came to include trying to analyze Mr. Jones.

Many efforts to apply nonlinear dynamic systems thinking to the analytic process suggest that deep resonances between analyst and analysand, similar to that of an ideal mother-infant dyad, are necessary for analytic work. While such resonances are moving and may be important in particular cases, I do not see them as prerequisite for analytic work. In fact, nonlinear dynamics suggests even very tenuously connected attractors may profoundly influence one another over time. Thus, the nonlinear point of view opens up a clinical possibility that we would have been unlikely to contemplate without that theory. Whereas most current analytic thinking suggests that the analytic process proceeds by means of deep connections between analyst and analysand, nonlinear dynamics invites us to consider that in some instances seemingly slight connections may have profound effects, as I believe occurred in this case where my initial contact with the analysand seems to have rested on nothing deeper than a chance congruity between an aspect of his dynamics and my own.

When two attractors come into contact, they are likely to influence each other. One of the nonlinear ways I have come to think about psychoanalytic process is in terms of coupled oscillators (Galatzer-Levy, 2009). Oscillators are entities that move in a range between endpoints. The simplest oscillator is a pendulum, but far more complex oscillators are familiar to us all, including the gyrations of the stock market, the actions of a single neuron or group of neurons, or the movement between a sequence of defensive positions commonly seen in analysis.

When two oscillators are joined together, say by a spring attaching two pendulums, complex patterns of motion emerge, patterns which could not have occurred in either oscillator if not attached to the other. The joined oscillators may be thought of as forming a new oscillator that has richer capacities than either of its separate components and are far more than the sum of the two oscillators.

The analytic dyad that emerged from my initial meeting with Mr. Jones contained not only the features of each of us but also elements arising from the interactions of those features, elements more complex than a simple sum of the features that each of us brought to the interview. Please notice that the nature of the joining that initiated this analysis was simply the shared perception that the room was chilly. It was not some deep empathic making of contact nor any form of tender emotional response. I mention this here because the model of therapeutic action I propose is not based on any particular way that analyst and analysand come to be joined together. In particular, it does not require either empathy or insight, though either of these may facilitate the necessary joining.

The mathematical development of nonlinear dynamics included the study of many phenomena that appeared disorganized and intractable to previous mathematical approaches. The mathematician, Norbert Wiener, recognized that models systems that included feedback often gave rise to apparently disorganized behavior of great practical importance. At the same time, reconceptualizations of certain basic mathematical concepts, which I will not try to explain here, provided new tools for thinking about these problems. These seemingly disorganized phenomena were discovered to have an order of their own. The term *chaos theory* was introduced to describe a group of ideas that described this order in many phenomena that seemed incomprehensible and disorganized.

The single most important feature of this theory was to give shape to nonlinear phenomena. Remember that phenomena are called *linear* if in a very broad sense their outcome is proportional to the input. If I step on the gas a little harder, my car goes a little faster. If I have somewhat more libido, my fantasies become somewhat more erotic. But important aspects of the worlds are not linear. In nonlinear situations, qualitative or significant changes can result from small changes in underlying variables. I press on the gas a little harder and run into the car ahead of me, thus throwing the trajectory of my trip entirely off. My intensified libido suddenly becomes sufficient that my fantasies turn to manifest frustration and dramatically shift their content. A quantitative change has resulted in a qualitative change.

Mr. Jones and I began meeting regularly. Although I learned many more supposed facts about him, the sessions seemingly involved little change. He would describe how distressed he was by one of his symptoms and either by way of interpretation or questioning, I would link the symptom to some element of his history, a move that rarely met with any significant response. Although he sometimes responded to interpretations that some of his actions were related to the analysis, these were often manifestly ignored or led to such exacerbations of his symptoms that I felt I should avoid them.

On the one hand, we seemed to be operating chronically on the "sadly nothing is possible but to do the same thing again and again" attractor; on the other hand, we seemed to get to know each other better.

Every once in a while, I noted shifts in my own responses to Mr. Jones. These mostly took the form of greater empathy for his suffering. For example, he described how, during his childhood, the family regularly went to "fancy" restaurants for Sunday dinners. This invariably resulted in what Mr. Jones called a "gastric"—urgent diarrhea that forced the family to leave the restaurant early so Mr. Jones could get home to the toilet. Despite the regularity of this occurrence, the dinners continued unchanged for years. It became clear to me how distressing these episodes must have been, but not what they meant to him and how exactly they fit with his life. I also found myself increasingly irritated by him and sometimes acting on my frustration. For example, on occasion I would rationalize returning a phone call before his session in a way that cut into his time with the thought that, after all, he would merely use that time to recite a litany of complaints.

In retrospect, the analytic setup provided us an opportunity to become entangled, for the oscillators, which we each were, to come into contact at multiple subtle points so that the two of us formed a larger system together.

I believe that, regardless of their manifest content, in many analyses, the most important work is in the formation of such larger systems. I have argued that such systems of "coupled oscillators" are significant not only because they allow for mutual deep influence of the analyst and analysand but because the problems that can be solved by such a system are far more complex than either of the individuals involved could solve alone. Just as networks of computers can make computations that are qualitatively more complex than single computers, so too networks of minds can generate new types of functioning fundamentally different from those of single minds. In such coupled systems, the whole is indeed greater than the sum of its parts. The coupling of systems is subtle, occurs on multiple levels simultaneously, and is mostly unavailable to awareness.

Unfortunately, narratives of this process, in which many small connections are made, tend to distort the picture of the process itself because both as author and listener we tend to seize upon dramatic elements and look for a richer meaning than the simple making of a connection. If I tell you, for example, that some of Mr. Jones's stories of collecting at times reminded me of my own childhood stamp collecting, you are likely, as I did when I wrote this paper, to wonder why this particular example was chosen and so set off on a whole line of inquiry that misses the central point—that it was merely one of very many points of contact between us. Imagine a bridge held together with tens of thousands of bolts. We could tell a plausible story of what any one of the bolts did, but the more important story is one having to do with the entire ensemble of bolts. Thus, certainly in a paper such as this, it will have to suffice to say that very numerous connections manifest in such things as shared vocabulary, subtle rituals on entering and leaving the office, a rhythm of verbal exchanges emerged between us. (If one were able to do so, writing like Proust, capturing thousands of tiny details, would provide a better sense of what occurred than reference to punctate clinical events.) Recall that an important feature of nonlinear systems is that results are not proportional to causes. The strength and intensity of the connections to which I am referring tell us little about the significance of their effects. The manifest intensity of these connections tells us little about which will ultimately play an important role.[4]

My conversations with Mr. Jones followed a predictable format in which he began sessions complaining of a symptom, often repeating himself in exactly the same words with minimal elaboration.

He seemed to barely listen to any interpretation I made, although I realized after a time that he was telling me enough that my interpretations gradually grew richer and more precise. Despite the glacial pace of the work within the analysis, Mr. Jones's extra-analytic progress was impressive. Some symptoms seemed to melt away. New interests in other people appeared. Suddenly, there was a girlfriend—the first of his life—and then a marriage, and then a relationship with his stepson.

All of these came into the analysis primarily in terms of symptoms. For example, I first learned he was marrying because he came to a session with a new symptom, "doubt of love," which he eventually explained consisted of a fear that at the wedding ceremony he would doubt his love for his bride. Until he described the symptom in detail, I had no idea he was planning to marry. It was as if, clearly as a result of our analytic work, Mr. Jones's life included ever more possibilities that he was exploring in action, usually in a rewarding and sensible fashion. However, any connection to the analysis had to be by way of descriptions of symptoms. I chose not to interpret this behavior as acting out partly because similar interpretations by his previous analyst had served to shut down the behavior and partly because, from the point of view of nonlinear dynamics, it seemed to me important to interfere as little as possible with Mr. Jones's expanding landscape of possibilities for living. Mr. Jones was at the same time maintaining a major attractor for living, "I am a sick man who obsessively worries" and introducing important new elements into his life that might be thought of as making the attractor more complex and having greater possibilities. Although he did not experience it this way, Mr. Jones was beginning to live in a world in which he had ever more choices and possibilities and experimented with them.

Think of an attractor as a path along which a person travels. Sometimes the path divides or has offshoots. The analogy to a path is imperfect because the attractors for our lives consist in our own views of possible pathways rather than an external reality, but otherwise the analogy holds pretty well. Perhaps the simplest way to think of such a situation is a bifurcation like the two divergent roads in the Robert Frost poem where the poet's choice to take the less traveled road makes all the difference.

A slight change to the right or left at one point makes "all the difference" because it determines which one of two pathways that are quite divergent one pursues. Notice that this is a nonlinear process in the sense that a very small change in the initial action can produce a very large change in outcome.

Let us imagine a branching tree of such bifurcations, each one leading to significantly different plans or actions. As bifurcations become more dense, the system rapidly moves into a position in which the tiniest change sets one off into a significantly different course. No predictions can be made about how the system will evolve because to do so would require a perfect knowledge of its initial state. When this happens, the process is called chaotic.

Clearly, if a person functions in a way where the slightest perturbation causes a significantly different mode of functioning, no stability whatsoever would be possible. Life would be impossible. This is, I believe, the state Mr. Jones rigorously avoided. On the other hand, if a changed situation never results in an alteration in the mode of function, no development is possible. This is the stable state that Mr. Jones was in when he began analysis.

The situation in which significant but not necessarily overwhelmingly large changes lead to the exploration of new pathways is called the *edge of chaos*. It corresponds to what we think of as creative learning, the ability to at least mentally explore new possibilities with relative fluency and ease. It is somewhere in this region of the edge of chaos where the capacity for ongoing development and learning from experience occurs. It is where change, development, and creativity become possible. It is the place where the attractors for living can become richer and more complex. They are also more adaptive and capable of learning from experience.

In my view, the work of analysis is to bring the analysand into the realm of the edge of chaos. The analyst's role is to assist in this process. The analysand's main concern, not only in the sense of a fantasy but rather built into the functioning of any system that is to last for any significant length of time, is that he may become disorganized—that is, go beyond the edge of chaos into some form of a traumatic state. This tendency to stability is manifest by vigorous defenses against chaotic states and, more rarely, by tremendous anxiety when actual states of disorganization are approached.

I have suggested that the analyst's major role is to meet the patient in an emergent unity in which analysand's and analyst's capacities are joined. Analyst and analysand function as a single unit with capacities for solving problems that exceed that of either participant alone. In Chapter 5, on "good vibrations," I describe from the point of view of complex systems theory why it was that such a conjoint system could solve more difficult problems than any one of its members. Furthermore, this increasing capacity is not simply additive, not simply a matter of the knowledge of the two people bringing together what they know.

Think of individual minds as associative networks. Interaction with another mind is likely to involve the emergence of links between elements of the individual mind, which were not previously available and which gives them new meanings.

The extent and nature of the new dual unity of analyst-analysand is shaped by the qualities of the individuals and the nature of the connections between them. Because both people operate in some ways in a nonlinear fashion, the significance of these connections is not controlled entirely by their strength or intensity. Remember that in nonlinear systems, small changes can make "all the difference," and the difference they make can be hard to predict, at least beyond the fact that something has changed. Because the new system analyst-analysand can manage greater instability than either party could manage separately, both analyst and analysand can more freely explore the edge of chaos. This formulation suggests that it is the nature of the connections between analyst and analysand that is of critical importance to the analytic process. It is far easier to detect the consequences of these connections, e.g. Mr. Jones's growing life outside the analysis, than to specify the nature of the connections themselves.

One day, Mr. Jones had gone to the airport to pick up his thirteen-year-old nephew. He wanted to be sure to meet the boy and, realizing that he would not have time to park in a distant parking lot, he instead parked in front of the terminal. He was well aware that his car might be towed but had decided that meeting the boy promptly was more important and worth the risk. When the car was indeed towed, he was distressed but still satisfied with the decision he had made, even though it cost him $150.

On returning home, his mother yelled at him, "How could you think of such a thing?!" As he described it, the phrase "how could you think of such a thing?" was presented as a mere rhetorical flourish, a sort of explicative, but to me, the analyst, who was aware of the enormous extent to which Mr. Jones's thinking was inhibited, it precipitated an ah-ha moment in which then I realized that his mother had systematically prohibited him from thinking.

Retrospectively, I became aware of how difficult it was for me to think during many of the sessions with Mr. Jones. His loud complaints about how much he suffered often left me with little else than an urge to flee from him and pretty well paralyzed in terms of any ability to think about or understand the situation.

Mr. Jones initially resisted this interpretation, pointing out that the phrase "how could you think of such a thing?" is common. As he talked about this, he repeated the phrase numerous times, imitating his mother, each time more loudly and forcibly. I became aware of finding it difficult to focus on what he was saying and realized that I was wishing that he would just stop going on and on about the matter as I increasingly felt I could barely hear myself think as Mr. Jones, imitating his mother, seemed to be yelling over and over "how could you think of such a thing?" now meaning I must not even think that his mother could have prohibited his thinking.

Viewed in terms of an analytic process, we had entered new territory. While I, of course, had long entertained various genetic hypotheses about Mr. Jones, we now had, for the first time, a clear, intense engagement with an important early emotional interaction and a lively countertransference involvement in it. We were moving further into the edge of chaos in the sense that not only was something new happening but the possible directions it might go were increasingly unclear.

Viewed in terms of Mr. Jones's retreat from anything approaching the edge of chaos, his mother's prohibition on thinking helped explain both why the idea of playfully engaging different ways of looking at the world posed such a problem for him and also why the process of connecting with the analyst, the process of forming the connections needed to set up the analysand-analyst entity was so difficult for him.

And with this, we seemed to enter a new world. Suddenly, Mr. Jones, whose life had seemed frozen and to move forward only in a glacial pace, emerged as a man with passions and ideals, who understood that exploring his fantasies and the anxieties they stimulated was the direction in which he wanted to move.

It was as if a whole dimension of moral conduct suddenly became available to him. A cousin who had been hospitalized with chronic schizophrenia for over forty years had been avoided by the family for decades. Mr. Jones, in the full recognition that he was attempting to treat this cousin differently than he himself had been treated, started visiting him regularly, attempting to interact with him and taking note of every indication of the cousin's engagement. Mr. Jones held strong political views but limited them to polite conversation. His views were diametrically opposed to those of his father. Suddenly, Mr. Jones became politically active doing significant work for a candidate he supported. These shifts, despite their rapidity, were richly discussed in the analysis before Mr. Jones acted. Following the recognition of the prohibition on thinking and his motives for accepting that prohibition, a new capacity for meaningful thought emerged.

Note that, although Mr. Jones made substantial progress in the way he conducted himself outside the analysis before the piece of analytic work in which he engaged the prohibition on thinking, those earlier changes had not been clearly linked to analytic work. These newer changes had a particular quality—while they seemed in retrospect to be the logical outgrowth of elements that were already present, there was no way in which the analyst or analysand could have guessed their specifics. They did not seem to represent the liberation of previously repressed fantasies but were new constructions made possible by bringing together elements through thinking in a new way.

In complex systems, the phenomenon of surprising novelty that occurs when elements are placed together in particular contexts is called *emergence*. In emergence, qualitatively new aspects of systems appear, which are *not* reducible to the sum of the system's elements. They can be understood only in terms of the system as a whole.

Consider the freezing of water. Water molecules are dipoles—that is, each molecule of H_2O has relatively positive and relatively negative charged ends. Many of the properties of water are determined by the electrical forces between water molecules. These electrical qualities of the individual molecules do not change with temperature, but their effects on water molecules in aggregate do. At temperatures between 0° and 100°, water exists as a liquid, a substance that coheres to itself but whose coherence is relatively easily interrupted. At a molecular level, the H_2O molecules adhere to one another but can also slip by one another. Lower the temperature below freezing, and the water becomes a solid, ice, with properties distinctly different from those of liquid water. Notice that this shift occurs sharply—1° water is no more ice-like than 99° water, nor is –1° ice water-like.

Psychoanalysts have long been aware of emergence in certain contexts. For example, when Winnicott (1965) told us that there is "no such thing as a baby," he implied that it was impossible to understand babies without understanding the context in which they live. Extensions of this basic idea to the arena of psychoanalytic therapy, the appreciation of cultural and historical context and related developments, suggest that in many areas of psychoanalytic thought, we are becoming ever more aware that reducing phenomena to their components is incomplete and commonly misses central aspects of the phenomena. Many of these situations are well described in terms of how genuinely novel configurations can emerge in various contexts.

The concept of emergence does two things for us as clinical analysts. First, it allows us to recognize that something genuinely new can happen in psychological life and spares us the often counterproductive exercise of reducing every observed development into its component parts. Second, it suggests a means by which such transformations can take place and so allows us both to be at ease with the idea and to think about ways to facilitate development through attention to contexts.

I have suggested that change occurs on the edge of chaos and that the analytic context should assist the analysand in coming nearer to that edge. Much of the received wisdom about analytic technique suggests that the analyst should try to provide an extraordinarily stable, almost anti-chaotic environment. I believe this attitude arises first from the fact that many analysands' difficulties arose in contexts that threaten to force their development beyond the edge of chaos into traumatic disorganized states so that the analyst's reassurance that he will not simply reproduce these traumatic states in the analysis becomes very important. This is most convincingly done by acting in a way that is not only benign but also stable and predictable.

Another source of this attitude lies in the analyst's wish to be scientific in the sense of having a clear picture of at least what she is doing in the analytic sessions. The most rigid vision of analytic technique arose in American ego psychology during a time when analysts were working particularly hard to make their field scientific.

A nonlinear point of view appreciative of the reality of emergence and that emergence will be manifest on the edge of chaos suggests that the analyst must also operate appropriately close to the edge of chaos. Just as one could never learn about the remarkable transformations of which water is capable by always observing it at one temperature, so, too, analysands who are perpetually provided with the same context by the analyst are unlikely to discover or create new aspects of their personalities.

I hope not to be misunderstood as suggesting that the analyst should deliberately act in a way that is disorganizing or traumatizing. Some of the older ideas of analytic technique might be looked at as deliberately trying to disrupt chronic ways of living by having the analyst intentionally shock and break down the means by which analysands protected themselves—as it were, approaching the analysis from the chaotic side of the edge of chaos. This is not what I mean. What I am recommending is that the analyst feel free to come near an edge of chaos, to freely surprise himself and the analysand in ways that provide a sort of optimally unpredictable environment. When at the beginning of Mr. Jones's treatment I suggested he could return despite my office being chilly, I surprised both him and myself. I acted nearer the edge of chaos, and he was brought nearer that edge.

The story of the onset of Mr. Jones's symptoms could be heard in terms of the way in which life on the edge of chaos—that is, ordinary living—can become traumatic and lead to fixity. Until he was fourteen, Mr. Jones was, as he put it, "a punk." He enjoyed fighting with other boys, bullying them, and fantasied himself a rock and roll star. He was very attracted to a girl and arranged to visit her alone one afternoon. Wearing tight pants and a muscle shirt, he imagined he was Elvis Presley. He recalls a powerful erection when he came to the house. He could not remember exactly what happened between them, but he remembers leaving in great distress. Despite being quite sure that they never so much as undressed, he had an overwhelming fear, which became a preoccupation, that he had impregnated the girl. He later remembered how he had returned home from this episode feeling very "shaken up." He is sure that it must have been obvious that something was wrong, but no one inquired. The trauma of the event could equally well be understood in terms of an overwhelmed ego or an individual who could find no means to bring his nearly overwhelmed state into relation with others who could join him on the edge of chaos. It seemed to him that his life had changed so that ever since then he was drowned in obsessional worries and rituals, a dreadful but utterly stable existence far withdrawn from the possibility of chaos.

Let us turn to a final area in which a nonlinear worldview might help us clinically. Early in Mr. Jones's analysis, I had hypothesized various genetic roots of his difficulties and had sometimes offered those hypotheses as interpretations. Mr. Jones usually ignored these interpretations because he wanted to focus on some immediate problem that he faced, and, in fact, I could see no way in which the interpretations were particularly helpful. The first time that a genetic interpretation was either convincing or useful was the interpretation, described earlier, in which I described Mr. Jones's blocked capacity to think as a derivative of his mother's prohibitions on thinking. This interpretation derived from a combination of my countertransference responses, fragments of stories Mr. Jones had told me, and my particular interest in Bion's work. It was the first fragment of a narrative of Mr. Jones's development. It was like a small crystal forming out of a saturated solution. Around it, a story of recurring parental neglect slowly formed.

In particular, in many contexts Mr. Jones's parents blinded themselves to his distress, leaving him entirely on his own with overwhelming feelings. His mother's occasional active corrections of him, "How could you even think such a thing?" actually came as a relief compared to his father's seeming near total obliviousness.

As might be expected, Mr. Jones vigorously resisted the emerging story, especially as it supported a hostility toward his parents, which he had previously dealt with through reaction formation. "They did their best," "My father didn't really have a father to show him how to be a father," and "How were they to know I was suffering when I never told them?" This manifest resistance had a surprising effect in the analysis—the stories became ever more refined, complex, consistent, and, most important, functional in the sense that they became ever more useful for Mr. Jones's understanding of self and conduct of his life.

At many points where the narrative appeared well organized, Mr. Jones's manifest resistance would destabilize the story, lead to a struggle with it, and end in a reformulation in a more satisfactory narrative. I have discussed this process using another concept from nonlinear dynamics called *simulated annealing* (Galatzer-Levy, 1988), but for the purposes of this paper, I will summarize it by saying that the narrative was brought to the edge of chaos and lost substantial parts of its organization so that it might become reorganized in a new way.

The classical psychoanalytic understanding of symptoms as representations of elements of unconscious fantasy narratives emphasizes how the analytic process transforms these fantasies by bringing them into consciousness, allowing their transformation through contact with other aspects of experience to transform these overly stable configurations. The lifting of repression is not in itself primary or curative. It is the capacity to learn from experience unleashed by way of consciousness that makes change possible. Bringing the analysis to the region of the edge of chaos may be seen as a generalization of this principle and the means of doing it, the connection of analyst to analysand creating a new entity capable of communicating with and affecting overly stable narratives as its major tool.

Psychoanalysis may be seen as a method for freeing people from fixed patterns of thought, feeling, and behavior and allowing them to creatively learn from experience. Doing this requires a degree of disorganization sufficient to allow the exploration of novel possibilities while at the same time maintaining sufficient organization as to avoid the dual dangers of chaos or the precipitation of emergency rigid defenses against it. Such a state is called the *edge of chaos,* and that field's exploration of the edge of chaos and the possibilities it contains suggests an enriched way of thinking about psychoanalysis and its technique. Occupying the edge of chaos in a sustained way becomes possible through the joining together of analyst and analysand in a new system that is better able to live on the edge of chaos and thus allow the emergence of surprisingly novel ways of being that could not have been predicted.

I am, of course, aware that many of the phenomena I discuss in this paper have been observed and described by other analysts, using other metapsychological and clinical frameworks. It is legitimate to ask why I urge the introduction of a whole new point of view, what

I claim, in fact, to be a shift in worldviews into our already too complicated field.

I will use one example of analysts' efforts to deal with the phenomena studied in nonlinear dynamical systems theory without benefit of that theory. Let us refer to to Hans Loewald (1960) in his great paper on technique, which led to a major reconceptualization of the modes of action of psychoanalysis. Loewald discussed the problematic nature of the idea of the analyst as a traditional scientific observer. He wrote:

> The relationship between a scientific observer and his subject of study has been taken as the model for the analytic relationship, with the following deviations: the subject, under the specific conditions of the analytic experiment, directs his activities towards the observer, and the observer communicates his findings directly to the subject with the goal of modifying the findings. These deviations from the model, however, change the whole structure of the relationship to the extent that the model is not representative and useful but, indeed, misleading. As the subject directs his activities towards the analyst, the latter is not integrated by the subject as an observer; as the observer communicates his findings to the patient, the latter is no longer integrated by the "observer" as a subject of study.

Loewald does his best to deal with this problem within the context of ego psychology and suggests clinical formulations based in a recognition of the problem. But he has no larger conceptual framework within which to address his recognition that the received model of the analyst as a traditional scientific observer cannot be correct.

Had Loewald been schooled in nonlinear dynamics, he would have immediately recognized that what he was describing is two linked feedback systems, a configuration whose properties are well known under the rubric of coupled oscillators. He would have known that such coupled systems can bring each of its elements into states they never could achieve independently, in fact states on the edge of chaos and beyond. He would have known that a grave problem for such a system is that it can become chaotic and that it would be likely that the system would have built in breaks to keep it from doing so. In other words, a nonlinear model would have pointed him to centrally important aspects of the analytic system that could have enriched his understanding. We can hardly fault Loewald for knowing none of this; the progenitors of nonlinear dynamics had only started to emerge in mathematics a decade earlier, and the robust worldview we now have emerged thirty-five years after he wrote. But we do have this different worldview available to us.

Freud used the scientific worldview of his times as a guiding lamp in his exploration of the psyche. It helped him see deep into what had before him been nearly incomprehensible.

That worldview focused on the reduction of observations to a small number of underlying causes, which operated through mechanistic connection that linked cause and effect in rough proportionality. Yet it left him and his followers in the dark about some of the most important aspects of human psychology, such as the nature of trauma or the structure of interpersonal influence. We are fortunate to live in a time when a new scientific worldview has come to prominence. This worldview, under labels like *chaos theory* and *complexity theory*, describes the world of interacting systems, transformation where effects are related to each other in disproportionate and rich ways, where surprise becomes an expectable feature of the system.

I believe that the obvious application of these ideas goes beyond providing a more satisfactory theoretical underpinning for psychoanalysis. I believe that, just as Freud's scientific worldview shaped his practice, so, too, a nonlinear worldview can reshape our practice. I have attempted to demonstrate this reshaping by indicating how several ideas from nonlinear dynamics allow ways of thinking about important clinical phenomena and by providing a point of view for examining them allow us to more fully appreciate those phenomena. I have tried to show how this background provided a useful context in which to think about the clinical work with a challenging and rewarding analysand. I am well aware that in doing so I am inviting you to join me at the edge of chaos. I have tried to let you know that the world is more interesting, surprising, and rewarding, if a little scary, from here.

Notes

1 Just as in reading Freud today it is possible to recognize the centrality of hermeneutic method to his work, it is also possible to read Freud as anticipating some of the most exciting elements of nonlinear dynamics. For example, in Chapter 7 of *The Interpretation of Dreams,* following ideas first laid out in *On Aphasia,* Freud brilliantly anticipates network theory, which would not see its full development until almost a century later. Such retrospective readings of Freud would be misleading if they led to a view that Freud was not highly linear in his worldview. In a sense, this becomes most evident in his later writings when he had developed multiple theories of mental function. In general, he attempts to show how each theory separately is useful but does not attempt to integrate them into a single conceptualization since they cannot fit together in a linear fashion.

2 A perceptive editorial reader for the *International Journal of Psychoanalysis,* in which an earlier version of this chapter appeared, observed that the idea of attractors described here seems to include little about the person who creates, evaluates, and experiences them (albeit indirectly). This objection could be extended to include the objection that although the mechanisms involved are somewhat different from those of classical analysis, the nonlinear viewpoint appears to be fundamentally mechanistic and lacking in a hermeneutic dimension.

This valid objection should be thought of in the context of the whole discussion of the role of psychoanalytic theories, from drive theory to contemporary neuroscience, in all of which the step from underlying non-psychological process to subjectivity is difficult or impossible to trace. (This difficulty appears to be greater for conceptual frameworks like nonlinear dynamics that refer to abstract concepts with unfamiliar names. But I contend that the problem is even greater when the abstract concepts are disguised by seemingly familiar names like "self," "object" or "person.") In other words, I think that the ideas presented here are not much worse in this regard than most generalizing psychoanalytic thinking and are subject to similar limitations to those lines of inquiry.

Elsewhere in this book, I argued that nonlinear thinking provides a potential bridge between subjectivity and psychoanalytic theorizing by virtue of its recognition that the configurations that matter in psychoanalysis are manifest in multiple ways and that, in particular, they are manifest in narratives. When we talk about the structure and configuration of narratives, we abstract from their specifics structures whose dynamics are attractors. The language of nonlinear dynamics seems to include a natural bridge between subjectivity and narrative on one hand and mechanisms, whether abstract or neuroscientific, on the other. Obviously, the elaboration of these ideas takes us beyond the scope of this paper. Here, I would argue only that the nonlinear viewpoint can aid psychoanalytic practice.

3 The work described here is presented with the patient's permission. Identifying details have been removed. The treatment lasted approximately two decades during which the patient was seen with varying frequency (from two to four times each week), and the couch was used during most of it.

4 Another editorial reader pointed out that these ideas run contrary to known "clinical facts," such as the centrality of empathy for analytic work. While I have no doubt that empathy is a highly visible component of many analyses and often seems to analysts and analysands to be of central therapeutic value and that, further, thinkers like Kohut (1959) see empathy as the core methodology of psychoanalytic investigation, I do not take it as a demonstrated fact that empathy is always a central curative factor in analysis. That, in recent years, empathy appears in this light as a central fact to many analysts has many sources. One of these is the absence of a good alternative explanation of the effectiveness of psychoanalysis. Nonlinear dynamics provides alternative explanations and thereby opens up the possibility of observing a wider range of "facts."

Chapter 11

Afterwards and Forwards

Forty years or so after coming across René Thom's masterpiece *Structural Stability and Morphogenesis: An Outline of a General Theory of Models,* I remain informed by the worldview embodied in it and continue the attempt to integrate it with my ever-deepening commitment to psychoanalysis with delight.

This book is an attempt to describe where I have gotten so far in this project. My hope is that it has communicated some particular ideas about how nonlinear thinking can contribute to psychoanalysis. But more important, I hope the reader will take away from it a feeling for how a nonlinear worldview can enrich psychoanalytic thought.

The project of bringing nonlinear thought to psychoanalysis is only beginning. It would be silly to end a book largely devoted to the impossibility of meaningful prediction for any reasonably complex system with predictions of where we will go from here. At the same time, it is my hope that readers will have a sufficient sense of what has been learned so far that the incompleteness of the development of ideas of nonlinear dynamic systems theory in psychoanalysis and the potential value of further developing these ideas will be equally obvious. This final chapter, then, describes some areas of exploration and some questions that I find particularly interesting and would like to learn more about in the coming years. At the same time, I would be even more pleased at the discovery of new and surprising directions of the kind one would say, "I never thought of that!" i.e. a nonlinear development.

By the time I began my psychoanalytic studies, it was clear that the linear mechanistic worldview foundational to traditional psychoanalytic theorizing until well into the 1970s constricted analytic thinking, but, at the same time, the more romantic worldview, content to point to significant psychological experiences and try to grasp them through nonsystematic similes and metaphors, left too little room for the sort of critical thinking that most serious students of psychoanalysis feel is essential to the well-being of the field.

In the intervening forty years, the scope of psychoanalytic thinking has widened enormously. It has expanded simultaneously in several major directions coming to include a range of methods from literature and philosophy. It has increasingly drawn on empirical observational studies of human development. The importance of cultural and group phenomena and, to a lesser extent, historical contingency have become ever more apparent, while at the same time Freud's dream that neuroscience could inform psychoanalysis has become an emerging reality. As was already evident in Freud's writing, this ever-expanding psychoanalytic landscape was ever less well encompassed by mechanistic metapsychology.

Systems and Reduction

The strain observed in psychoanalysis paralleled and was part of a strain seen in many disciplines where the reductionist program that attempted to dissect phenomena into their component parts and to explain the phenomena as summation of these parts broke down as the situations under study became more complex. Even at the simplest levels, greater complexity pointed to the limitations of traditional conceptual and mathematical techniques. For example, while it had been possible in the seventeenth century to give a complete description of the motion of two bodies operating under the force of gravity, the same problem for three bodies remained fundamentally intractable and only approachable by approximation in combination of two body solutions, an approach that was recognized from the beginning as fundamentally flawed.

This book itself is a history of two developmental processes. One was the emergence in psychoanalytic thinking of a nonlinear dynamical systems approach to that field, a development to which I had the pleasure of contributing. The other was my own personal development, which at age eighteen included two of those events that, depending on how you viewed them, could be seen either as a major discontinuity, a shift from one attractor to another, or as the unfolding of a continuous coherent narrative. One of them occurred in a dreary Quonset hut converted to classrooms that graced, or perhaps disgraced, the north end of the NYU Uptown campus. There, I was introduced to ordinary differential equations by a depressed-appearing graduate assistant, Mr. Goodman, and I first saw the stunning beauty of mathematical thought. Somewhere around the same time, on the other end of campus, I consulted with a Dr. Robert Averbach in the student mental health service for the miseries suffered by a large proportion of the New York Jewish boys of my generation and had the good luck to be referred for analysis, a step that sent me off in the dominant theme of my adult life. It is hardly a surprise then that the convergence of the themes of mathematics and psychoanalysis should have continued to weave themselves into the work described in this book.

It would be tempting to say that the ideas in this book (or my thinking) could be reduced to two major themes, mathematics and psychoanalysis, and indeed a great deal about its history and content could be clarified by studying each of these sources separately. This would constitute a classical reductionist approach. A distinctly different approach would focus on how these two groups of ideas interacted and might claim that, insofar as I have achieved anything of value, it is through the interaction of these ideas, a systems approach.

Throughout this book, in my attempt to emphasize the role of nonlinear thinking, I have underemphasized the significance of classical systems thinking for psychoanalysis. I did this for several reasons. The most important of these is simply that my focus was elsewhere. Another factor is that classical systems thinking (von Bertalanffy, 1968), in its attempts to mathematize within the confines of linear mathematics, got caught up in a swamp of complicated appearing but not very helpful equations. Norbert Weiner's cybernetics met with a similar fate. The result was that the most useful findings of both general systems theory and cybernetics lay in their appreciation that some of the phenomena that arise in any system of interest have characteristics that we would now recognize as nonlinear. The recognition that systems thinking required a new mathematics awaited the appreciation that the systems that are of interest are complex.

Complex Systems

In modern science, reductionist approaches have until recently proved more fruitful because the methodology of reduction was so much better developed. To discover the elements that made up a chemical compound or the forces at play in a market, though at times technically difficult, was conceptually straightforward and has an armamentarium of techniques at hand. Until the last half-century, there were only the beginnings of a methodology for studying systems so that while occasional brilliant discoveries appeared in this area, it was not until recently that systematic methodologies for studying systems became common.

Yet even so, the potential richness of a systems approach often remains underdeveloped because the interactions of systems on different scales are seldom considered. One area where an understanding involving very different scales of interaction is investigated in depth is molecular biology, and this has been true from its very beginnings. In fact, an argument could be made that what differentiates molecular biology from biochemistry is the shift that instead of asking, "What are the component parts of chemistry of biological systems?" the question in molecular biology is, "How are fundamental life processes shaped by the chemistry that generates them?"

This change is perhaps best epitomized in two sentences of Watson and Crick's 1953 paper describing the double helical structure of DNA, "This structure has novel features which are of considerable biological interest" and "It has not escaped our notice that the specific pairing we have postulated immediately suggests a possible copying mechanism for the genetic material" (p. 737). The body of the paper concerns a classical, if difficult, chemistry problem, deciphering the structure of a complex organic molecule, DNA. But the significance of the paper lies in these two sentences, which point to the awareness that the structure is significant as it relates to the function of the molecule within the complex life of the cell and organism. This was to become the central strategy of molecular biology—showing how the structure of molecules resulted in functions within biological systems. These studies ranged from genetic transmission, to the regulation of metabolism, to the transport of oxygen by hemoglobin.

The direction of science is not only the discovery of the elements that make up a system, i.e. a reductionist approach, but also the direction of understanding how these elements interact to form a system. Fields like molecular biology suggest that in important systems the interacting elements of the system are often of different types and their interactions far richer than additive functions. Sometimes these elements are conceptually so far apart that only the reality that they are connected in real systems convinces us that there is any connection. Although the most brilliant minds of the first half of the twentieth century, including Linus Pauling and Erwin Schrodinger, tried to imagine how genetic information could be passed between generations, none came up with anything resembling the way in which DNA actually transmits information. As an example of emergent properties reflecting different orders of magnitude and different arenas of function, consider the structure of ant colonies and the volatility of pheromones, the chemical traces left by the ants as they move about. The structure of the colony is, in fact, highly contingent on the volatility of these substances. Intuition boggles, at first, at the idea that the shape of ant colonies derives from the volatility of some organic compound.

The study of complex systems increasingly sheds light on important processes in systems, ranging from the Internet and ecosystems to brains and markets. The conceptual and material internal connections of complexity often do not fit with our "common sense" of what would produce order but nonetheless result in these and many other functioning processes. The study of such interactions has led to vast empirical and theoretical developments.

The objects of study of psychoanalysis are obviously complex systems in this sense. Difficulties in psychoanalytic study often arise when attempts are made to integrate viewpoints on similar or related subject matter from differing perspectives. For example, psychoanalytic processes explored on various time scales must be related to one another. The process observed in five years of analysis is, after all, composed of a long series of thirty-second long processes. But it seems very unlikely that the five-year process is simply the sum of very many thirty-second processes. Another example concerns the relationship of psychic structures to objects. Although it is evident that the development of stable patterns of psychological actions (psychic structures) is closely tied to representations of environmental figures, the nature of this connection, though central to many psychoanalytic theories, remains conceptually incomplete despite enormous efforts of researchers from Freud to Melanie Klein to Daniel Stern. Both of these problems are precisely the kind of issue best formulated and engaged through complexity theory.

The relationship of complexity theory to nonlinear mathematics is that the latter is the appropriate mathematical approach to many of the problems of the former. In other words, complexity theory is in many ways logically preliminary nonlinear mathematics, but its historical development largely followed that of nonlinear mathematics. This is typical of the development of many sciences. The central subject emerges only after mathematical methods of studying it have been developed.

If we think of the human mind and its environment, including the brain in which it resides and the world of other minds with which it interacts, as a complex system, it becomes obvious that ideas from complexity theory should inform its study and that methods of complexity science should help shape psychoanalysis. Thus, nonlinear psychoanalysis will need to extend its boundaries to include complexity theory.

Abstraction—Thinking about Thinking about Thinking

A second important area of nonlinear psychoanalysis in need of development concerns how general nonlinear theories relate to the particulars of psychological life.

Starting with clinical papers, including "Attacks on Linking," Wilfred Bion attempted theoretical formulation of "thinking" based in an attempt to abstract, and hence make mathematical, the nature of thought and thought-like processes (Bion 1958a, b, 1959, 1962a, b, 1965, 1963, 1967, 1983). He started with the Kleinian notion that not only was the mind modeled on the alimentary canal but also that metaphors like mouth, breast, filled, empty, expelled, broken into or existing in pieces, applied well to mental entities. He explored the metaphors further assuming that the mind, in fact, acted in the manner they implied. For example, in projective identification, some element of mental function is pictured as being split off from oneself and attributed to another, where it may undergo some transformation and be returned to its originator. Bion indicates this is not merely a fantasy in the sense of being an image that serves primarily a defensive function. The fact that the individual is committed to this metaphor means that it will actually operate on and transform the mental content in a manner consistent with the metaphor. For example, the idea that one has removed an element of mental life from one's own mind means that in significant ways it is no longer in the mind and its absence may have significant consequences. This very plausible model of information processing in the mind, which is quite analogous to the idea that it is the computer program rather than the machinery in which it is instantiated that is most important (assuming the machinery is adequate) leads to a genuinely novel theory of mind determined by autonomous elements whose intrinsic nature and links to one another result in overall mental function. The overall effect is to create a picture of the mental apparatus as a group of abstract processes and entities instantiated in the mind(s) of those under study. What Rapaport and Gill (1959) complained of as an "id mythology" (as compared to their own "ego psychology") is, in fact, a computational model based on the function of autonomous agents. The study of the emerging processes involving autonomous agents has, in recent years, been given enormous power by virtue of the recognition of the computational capacities of systems of autonomous agents (see, for example, Epstein, 2014). Abstractly, mathematicians demonstrated that a collection of autonomous agents interacting using very simple rules is capable of any computation any computer might be able to perform. Autonomous, but linked organisms, such as bees, can and do build vastly complex structures, even though each bee appears to be "doing its own thing." Neurons, each capable of very limited forms of action, by virtue of their connections to other neurons, each with similarly limited capacities, carry out all the activities that we experience as mental life and much else. On a different level, the fundamentally independent, though, again, to varying degrees linked, functions of the cellular metabolic apparatus produce the emergent structure we call life.

As Bion sought to explore thought and related mental activity, he realized that there was no adequate vocabulary for describing thought and thought-like processes. He recognized that available language was not only inadequate but actually obfuscated the very issues he was trying to attack. Correctly recognizing that the problem requires attention to matters that can only be addressed at an appropriate level of abstraction, Bion explored these issues through a classifying scheme he called "the grid" and to a lesser extent through models derived from a form of mathematics called "the theory of complex variable" that studies linear transformation. His basic strategy was to abstract aspects of mental processes from the welter of material constituting ordinary mental life as manifest in psychoanalytic sessions, to then explore the resulting abstract system, and finally to return to the clinical material with an eye to seeing whether the abstraction proved useful to its understanding.

An aspect of Bion's genius was his recognition that the very research in which he engaged could be described and explored as a form of thinking and, consequently, could be investigated using its own methods. For example, the formulation of the "grid" could be located on the grid. Bion thus recognized that there were multiple useful directions of psychoanalytic theorizing and that their relationship to one another could be characterized. In *Learning from Experience,* he emphasizes that abstraction itself carries with it, on one hand, the power that comes from being able to manipulate clear elements and, on the other hand, inevitably loses the richness of particular situations. If I employ the abstraction that $2 + 1 = 3$ in certain circumstances, such as computing the amount of grass seed needed for planting a lawn, I spare myself the difficulty of discovering how much grass seed I need by other means and lose little of value in understanding the situation. On the other hand, if abstraction led one to treat the mystery of the Holy Trinity being one God as an arithmetic problem, it would be impossible to feel that the abstraction had been helpful.

The further steps of understanding psychoanalytic matters through abstractions by way of mathematics will require constant attention both to the ways that abstraction can enrich understanding and the ways in which it can impede appreciation of a particular situation. Nonlinear psychoanalysis involving abstraction must therefore be subject to constant interrogation as to what may be lost as well as what may be gained through its use. As Bion suggested of his own theorizing, it is probably generally best left behind as a conscious activity while doing analytic work. But he also emphasized sufficient familiarity with how it alters one's spontaneous thinking while doing analysis—opening the possibility of appreciating a wider landscape of analytic material.

Hermeneutics and Nonlinear Dynamics

A third area of interest is the relationship between nonlinear psychoanalysis and psychoanalysis as the study of meaning making. A matter that seems to be the subject of endless debate is whether psychoanalysis is or should be a discipline that attempts to use the methods of natural science investigation or should approach matters in the manner that has been designated as the human sciences, i.e. through the study of personal motives and the construction of personal meanings. This problem has confronted psychoanalysis since Freud demonstrated the power of each in the foundational chapters (4 and 5) of *The Interpretation of Dreams*.

As with most such questions in scholarly investigation, principled arguments have and will be made on either side. However, the outcome of these arguments as manifest in the position adopted by working psychoanalysts and psychoanalytic thinkers will almost certainly focus on the pragmatic question of which approach is most useful for the researcher and context of the research. In the case of psychoanalysis, this usefulness will include the capacity to relate to other disciplines and viewpoints. For example, although research on the efficacy of psychoanalysis and psychodynamic psychotherapy using traditional methods of efficacy research has contributed little to psychoanalytic practice or theory, many psychoanalysts continue to value these studies because of their potential to maintain engagement with mainstream mental health investigations. It is almost always the case that the fruitfulness of results proves more powerful than logical arguments in deciding what methods are adopted by a discipline.

If one compares the discussions in Chapters 4 and 5 of *The Interpretation of Dreams*, the first being entirely hermeneutic and the later highly metapsychological, it is apparent that the interpretations offered in Chapter 4 are much more complex than those of Chapter 5. A diagram of the interconnected ideas and associations of the dream of Irma's injection, even limited to those that appear in the text of the book, reveals a vast array of interconnected ideas linked to each by bonds of quite different and varying intensities. In contrast, the metapsychological explanations of Chapter 5 are simpler and relate to far less material. The hermeneutic explanations generally tend to be vastly more complicated than metapsychological ones. As many authors have noted, the metapsychological points of view are modeled on the abstractions of physics, embryology, and common sense, while the hermeneutic explanations are of a qualitatively different type. All the metapsychological viewpoints, at least at the time of their formulation, could be well encompassed in a linear worldview. This worldview gained its power because it made computation and hence useful prediction possible, albeit at the price of simplifying assumptions that put the complexities of systems to one side. Nonlinear dynamic systems theory has taught us that discarding complexity is truly *over*simplification—that is, a simplification that is made at the expense of excluding essential features of the situation.

Thus, while there are those who argue on philosophical grounds that the hermeneutic and natural scientific approaches are intrinsically alien from one another, whatever the validity of their arguments, in practice what will matter is whether the richness present in psychological events can be captured only through hermeneutic methodologies or whether the abstractions characteristic of natural science can provide a useful method for approaching these questions. It seems likely that a mathematical worldview developed specifically to deal with complex systems and to incorporate the phenomena associated with complexity will include many of the features that we seek to achieve through hermeneutic methodology.

Another way in which hermeneutic and nonlinear approaches overlap concerns the nature of satisfactory narratives. Insofar as the world is seen as linear narratives with nonlinear elements, the nonlinear elements are regarded as fantastic or otherwise unsatisfactory. When their images of causality, for example, do not correspond to a presumptive linear worldview about causation, narratives will seem unrealistic and not convincingly applicable to real lives. These narratives may seem satisfactory as instances of magic realism or science fiction but not as description of how ordinary people, including analysands, conduct mental life. Analysts have long dealt with the situation that people actually conduct their lives differently from the way they believe they do in the sense that unconscious mental processes play a major role in human lives. Analysts' familiarity with unconscious processes and the resistances to acknowledging them allow us to point to their presence and to help analysands understand their role in psychological life.

As we become increasingly familiar with the realistic but rich narratives implicit in a nonlinear worldview, we will be in a position to help our patients and ourselves recognize their presence and usefulness. The nature of the interference in recognizing nonlinear processes to that involved in recognizing dynamically repressed processes differ in many ways. The unawareness of nonlinear processes is not necessarily as motivated by traditional sources of anxiety as by simple ignorance of the possibilities implicit in them. But both awareness of dynamically unconscious processes and nonlinear processes are at least in part blocked by the narcissistic injury involved in recognizing the presence of mental processes that do not conform to visions of rational thought.

The enriched picture of possible mental processes that nonlinear dynamic systems theory brings will enrich the hermeneutic possibilities available to analysts, and attempts to abstract features of the hermeneutics of mental life will point to nonlinear configurations that are particularly important to examine. This process is well underway in works like Harris's (2005) study of gender but has very far to go.

Nonlinear Geometry and Fractals

From its earliest beginnings, psychoanalytic discourse has employed spatial metaphors to explore psychological phenomena. These metaphors describe situations in which entities are separated into groups by boundaries or barriers. Within the boundaries such things as information, energy and functions are freely exchanged, and activities are easily coordinated. Exchange across boundaries is limited and, if permitted at all, requires more or less elaborate processes. The repression barrier of classical psychoanalysis separates the dynamic unconscious from the preconscious through active and motivated processes of repression and, at the same time, allows the passage of unconscious material into the preconscious, provided that material is appropriately transformed through such mechanisms as transference, symbol formation and sublimation. Passage in the other direction is not symmetrical, but generally requires some kind of stripping of the links between entities that move from the preconscious to the dynamic unconscious, such as the logical connection to one another.

There are many other examples of boundaries of various types that have proved more or less useful in analytic thought.

It is striking that despite the extensive use of the boundary metaphor, the concept of boundary in psychoanalysis itself remains ill explored and the metaphors of boundary significantly limited. Often boundaries are implicitly likened to geopolitical boundaries, and approaches to thinking about them and their desirable features are based on notions that have been developed in association especially with problematic geopolitical boundaries. For example, in the arena of overt sexual interaction between patients and therapists, which is almost universally regarded as highly undesirable, attempts to deal with this problem often begin with an assertion of the absoluteness and rigidity of a boundary separating permissible and impermissible actions and then continue with the development of means to ensure that this boundary is never crossed by the development of means to keep the analytic couple at a significant distance from it altogether (Guttheil and Brodsky, 2006).

Such widely divergent topics as the ethics of physical intimacy between analyst and patient and the nature of gender rest on notions about the nature of the separation between various psychological and material states. Whereas fifty years ago the idea that gender was essentially a binary function and states of gender ambiguity were rare and pathological, today it is increasingly recognized both that gender is multidimensional and that in the multidimensional space of gender complex combinations of what used to be thought of as masculine and feminine commonly exist side by side, with the boundaries separating them recognized in some senses as far less clear and defined than they once seemed. In an entirely different area, the boundaries separating analyst from analysand, the clear separation of two individuals is no longer an underlying presumption of psychoanalytic technique in practice. Circumstances are increasingly recognized where the assumption of separateness fails and is replaced by something ranging from psychological unity to a complex intermingling of psychological functions.

At the end of the nineteenth century, mathematicians began to realize that the idea of a boundary needed clearer definition and further exploration. A particularly important group of questions concerned situations in which conditions of a process were predefined at a boundary. For example, imagine studying the vibrations of a drumhead. Will the boundary of the drumhead, the shape of the drum, determine those vibrations and hence the resulting sound? A more abstract group of questions concerning the nature of boundaries themselves was first explored in the early twentieth century, but lacking the tools necessary for this exploration did not fully engage mathematicians until the last decades of the twentieth century.

The most important of these new tools was the computer that provided the computation muscle to create pictures of complex boundaries and forms that arose from nonlinear processes. By a happy convergence, Benoit Mandelbrot came to work at the IBM laboratories just as computers had reached the point where they could begin to produce graphics adequate to literally get some picture of the more complex types of boundaries, the equivalents of rough surfaces, that he wanted to study. Mandelbrot not only recognized both the major features of such boundaries and provided a sophisticated mathematical approach to their description but also recognized a vast range of practical problems, from stock markets to plant growth, that could be approached using fractal geometry (Mandelbrot, 1982, 2014).

The nature of boundaries implicit in fractal geometry is complex and rich in a manner that suggests that it would introduce new possibilities into our thinking about psychoanalytic boundaries were analysts to explore conceptualizing boundaries using fractal geometry. Other mathematical models of boundaries included fuzzy set theory, and concepts from network theory may also be useful.

The study of fractal boundaries constitutes a third direction for the advance of nonlinear psychoanalysis.

Empirical Quantitative Study

A fourth area of advance in nonlinear psychoanalysis concerns empirical study of psychoanalysis.

The empirical study of psychoanalytically significant phenomena is difficult. Quantitative empirical study works best when a small number of variables can be found that encompass important phenomena and when these variables can be adequately measured in a way that both provides sufficient data to allow correlations between the variables and gives quantitative estimates of both the reliability of the data and their correlations.

For example, the foundation of modern chemistry was the discovery that when chemicals react, the same proportional weight of each chemical is involved. If a reaction is complete when 5 grams of compound A reacts with 8 grams of compound B, then the reaction between 5 kilograms of A and 8 kilograms of B will also be complete. The molecular hypothesis that followed from this discovery, i.e. that matter is made up of tiny particles that combine with one another in fixed proportions, became so fundamental to chemistry that students of the subject are often not even exposed to the quantitative empirical finding that led to the hypothesis. Each experiment of this type involved the measurement of the quantity of the interacting compounds and the products of the reaction. Since weighing substances may give different results because of limitations in the accuracy of scales, weights are usually given not as absolute values but as a weight and a range within which the true weight is likely to fall (e.g. 14.5 ± 0.2). The variation in measured weights was conceptualized as an "error" of measurement.

In the late nineteenth and early twentieth centuries, quantitative studies extended to include matters in which variations in measurement clearly resulted not from experimental errors but variations in things measured. Consider, for example, corn plant heights. A certain amount of variation will occur in any population of corn plants. If a particular fertilizer seems to cause the distribution to shift, how is the researcher to know whether the change results of random variation or was an effect of the fertilizer? Statistics came to the rescue. It provided quantitative estimates of how likely it was that the differences were the result of chance.

But statistics often involve underlying and untested assumptions about the subject being studied. In particular, it was common to assume that the variation within populations fell on a bell (or normal) curve. As Cramer (1946) pointed out long ago, theoretical statisticians claimed this was because empirical researchers had said this distribution was very common, while empirical researchers claimed that the distribution is theoretically justified. The belief in the bell curve was reinforced when researchers, assuming that data must be distributed in this way, designed tests in such a way as to actually produce a normal distribution. For example, assuming that "intelligence" is normally distributed, tests were designed so that the average score was 100 and that surrounding scores followed a bell curve, so that now everyone knows intelligence is so distributed.

In fact, many real-world phenomena are not normally distributed. An academic parlor trick is to ask a group of academics to write the number of their publications on a piece of paper and to calculate the mean (the total number of publications divided by the number of academics) for the entire group. Often there are one or two people present who have written hundreds of papers, while most have written fewer than ten. The result—almost everyone present is "below average" in the number of publications. In the last decade, the recognition that the bell curve and similar distributions do not accurately capture the reality of many situations has come into particular focus in the study of economics where the enormous weighting of wealth among the very rich, the 1 percent phenomenon, has enormous economic consequences (Piketty, 2014). Normal distributions are not to be expected in nonlinear processes so that if the main hypothesis of this book, that many important psychological processes are in essence nonlinear is correct, it is not to be expected that common statistical methods will prove useful in their study.

Since the questions one hopes to answer through data about nonlinear processes are often quite different from those about presumptively linear processes, the methods used to explore these questions should be different. Consider the research problem of studying the effectiveness of a treatment for anxiety attacks. The typical approach to the problem would be to ask, for example, the effect of the treatment on the frequency with which patients had these attacks. A nonlinear approach might conceptualize the problem as involving two mental state attractors, one of which included anxiety attacks and the other of which did not. The question would then be what is the pre- and post-treatment nature of the transition between the two attractors. The comparison would have to start with an analysis of the distribution of the transitions between the two attractors and proceed to describe how they changed following treatment. It would then ask how likely it is that the observed change resulted from a fluctuation in the initial modes of transition rather than being a specific response to treatment. The statistical methods appropriate to answering this question are very different from those of traditional statistics.

Students of nonlinear systems have begun to describe specific methodologies for analyzing nonlinear data (Guastello and Gregson, 2011). If, as seems clear from the discussions in this book, psychoanalysis is a fundamentally nonlinear discipline, meaningful empirical studies of its processes must use methods appropriate to studying nonlinear phenomena.

Psychoanalysis has not fared well as an empirical discipline. This is at least in large measure because approaching analytic material empirically from the point of view of the richness that makes analysis so appealing to many seems technically extremely difficult, but breaking it down into smaller more empirically tractable problems omits certain core features of analytic problems. Put differently, if you attempt to study a nonlinear complex system (psychoanalysis) with linear methods, you either end up with intractably difficult problems or with researches that fail to include the most important aspects of the system. Psychoanalysis needs nonlinear methodology.

Final Remarks

In this chapter, I have outlined four major themes of nonlinear psychoanalysis that seem likely to develop in coming years. A vast amount of work remains to fill in the details of the themes I outline elsewhere in this book. Nonlinear psychoanalysis has an exciting future.

The introduction to this book started with the idea that my researches in nonlinear psychoanalysis in many ways could be seen as part of an, albeit nonlinear, narrative that included my father and continues in my family, students, and professional community. The reflexive nature of the process both gives it its fascination and its nonlinear character. It is an outgoing adventure in which I have been lucky to play a part.

Bibliography

Abraham, K. (1924). "A short study of the development of the libido, viewed in the light of mental disorders." In: *Selected Papers of Karl Abraham, M.D.* London: Hogarth Press, 418–501.

Abraham, R. and Shaw, C. (1992). *Dynamics: The Geometry of Behavior.* 2nd ed. Redwood City: Addison-Wesley.

Aho, A., Hopcroft, J. and Ullman, J. (1983) *Data Structures and Algorithms.* New York: Addison-Wesley.

Anderson, J. (1983). *The Architecture of Cognition.* Cambridge: Harvard University Press.

Anthony, E. and Benedek, T. (1970). *Parenthood, Its Psychology & Psychopathology.* Boston: Little Brown.

Anthony, E. J. (1975). "Childhood depression." In: E.J. Anthony and T. Benedek, eds., *Depression and Human Existence.* Boston: Little Brown, 231–77.

Arbib, M. (1972). *The Metaphorical Brain: An Introduction to Cybernetics of Artificial Intelligence and Brain Theory.* New York: Wiley.

Arlow, J. and Brenner, C. (1969). "The psychopathology of the psychoses: A proposed revision." *International Journal of Psychoanalysis,* 50:5–14.

Bakhtin, M. M. (1981). *The Dialogical Imagination: Four Essays,* ed. M. Holquist. Trans. C. Emerson and M. Holquist. Austin: University of Texas Press.

Barnsley, M. (1988). *Fractals Everywhere.* Boston: Academic Press.

Baron-Cohen, S. (1995). *Mindblindness: An Essay on Autism and Theory of Mind.* Cambridge: MIT Press.

Basar, E. (1998). *Brain Function and Oscillations.* Heidelberg: Springer.

Basch, M. (1976a). "Psychoanalysis and Communication Science." *Annual of Psychoanalysis,* 4:385–422. New York: International Universities Press.

Basch, M. (1976b). "The concept of affect: A re-examination." *Journal of American Psychoanalysis Association*, 24:759–77.

Basch, M. (1976c). "Theory Formation in Chapter VII: A Critique." *Journal of American Psychoanalysis Association*, 24:61–100.

Basch, M. (1985). "Interpretation: Toward a developmental model." In: A. Goldberg, ed., *Progress in Self Psychology*, Vol. 1. New York: Guilford, 33–42.

Becal, H. and Carlton, L. (2011). *The Power of Specificity in Psychotherapy.* New York: Aronson.

Benedek, T. (1959). "Parenthood as a developmental phase." In: *Psychoanalytic investigations.* New York: Quadrangle, 378–401.

Bergler, E. (1956). *Homosexuality: Disease or Way of Life.* New York: Hill and Wang.

Bion, W. (1958a). "On Hallucination." *International Journal of Psychoanalysis*, 39.

Bion, W. (1958b). "On Arrogance." *International Journal of Psychoanalysis*, 39.

Bion, W. (1959). "Attacks on Linking." *Internation Journal of Psychoanalysis*, 40:308–15.

Bion, W. (1962a). "A Theory of Thinking." *Internation Journal of Psychoanalysis*, 43(4–5).

Bion, W. (1962b). *Learning from Experience.* Northvale: Jason Aronson.

Bion, W. (1965). *Transformations: Change from Learning to Growth.* London: Heinemann.

Bion, W. (1977). *Seven Servants.* New York: Aronson.

Blos, P. (1941). *The Adolescent Personality: A Study of Individual Behavior for the Commission on Secondary School Curriculum.* New York: Appleton-Century-Crofts.

Blos, P. (1962). *On Adolescence: A Psychoanalytic Interpretation.* New York: Free Press of Glencoe.

Blos, P. (1967). "The second individuation process of adolescence." *Psychoanalytic Study of the Child*, 22:162–86.

Blos, P. (1968). "Character formation in adolescence." *Psychoanalytic Study of the Child*, 23:245–63.

Bohm, O. (1957). *Causality and Chance in Modern Physics.* New York: Van Nostrand.

Boston Change Process Study Group (2005). "The 'something more' than interpretation revisited: Sloppiness and co-creativity in the psychoanalytic encounter." *Journal of the American Psychoanalytic Association*, 32:693–729.

Bowlby, J. (1969). *Attachment and Loss, Vol. 1: Attachment.* New York: Basic Books.

Bowlby, J. (1973). *Separation, Anxiety and Anger: Attachment and Loss, Vol. 2*. New York: Basic Books.

Bowlby, J. (1982). "Attachment and loss: Retrospect and prospect." *American Journal of Orthopsychiatry*, 52:664–78.

Bowlby, J. (1988). "Developmental psychiatry comes of age." *American Journal of Psychiatry*, 145(1): 1–10.

Brenner, C. (1979). "The components of psychic conflict and its consequences in mental life." *Psychoanalytic Quarterly*, 48(4): 547–67.

Breuer, J. and Freud, S. (1893a). *Studies in Hysteria*, Standard Edition, 2:1–305. London: Hogarth Press.

Breuer, J. and Freud, S. (1893b). "On the psychical mechanism of hysterical phenomena: preliminary communication." S. E. 3:27–39.

Bruner, J. (2011). *Making Stories: Law, Literature, Life*. Cambridge: Harvard University Press.

Bucci, W. (1993). "The development of emotional meaning in free association." In: J. Gedo and A. Wilson, eds., *Hierarchical Conceptions in Psychoanalysis*. New York: Guilford.

Bulmer, M. (1984). *The Chicago School of Sociology: Institutionalization, Diversity, and the Rise of Sociological Research*. Chicago: University of Chicago Press.

Callebau, W. and Rasskin-Gutman, D. (2005). *Understanding the Development and Evolution of Natural Complex Systems*. Cambridge: MIT Press.

Case, R. (1992). *The Mind's Staircase: Exploring the Conceptual Underpinnings of Children's Thought and Knowledge*. Hillside: Erlbaum.

Cicchetti, D. (1996). "Developmental theory: Lessons from the study of risk and psychopathology." In: S. Matthysse and D. Levy, eds., *Psychopathology: The Evolving Science of Mental Disorder*. New York: Wiley, 253–84.

Cicchetti, D. and Rogosch, F. (2002). "A developmental psychopathology perspective on adolescence." *Journal of Consulting and Clinical Psychology*, 70:6–20.

Cohen, P. (1966). *Set Theory and the Continuum Hypothesis*. New York: W. A. Benjamin.

Cohler, B. and Galatzer-Levy, R. (1990). "Self, Coherence and Meaning in the Second Half of Life." *New Dimensions in Adult Development*. R. a. C. C. Nemiroff. New York: Basic Books, 214–59.

Cohler, B. and Galatzer-Levy, R. (2007). "What kind of Science is Psychoanalysis?" *Psychoanalytic Inquiry*, 27(5): 547–82.

Condon, W. and Sander, L. (1974a). "Neonate movement is synchronized with adult speech: Interactional participation in language acquisition." *Science*, 183:99–101.

Condon, W. and Sander, L. (1974b). "Synchrony demonstrated between movements of the neonate and adult speech." *Child Development*, 45:456–62.

Courant, R. and Hilbert, D. (1937). *Methods of Mathematical Physics*. New York: Interscience, 1953.

Cozolino, L. (2014). *The Neuroscience of Human Relationships*, 2nd Edition. New York: Norton.

Cramer, H. (1946). *Mathematical Methods of Statistics*. Princeton: Princeton University Press.

Crick, F. (1988). *What Mad Pursuit*. New York: Basic Books.

Dahl, H. (1974). "The measurement of meaning in psychoanalysis by computer analysis of verbal contexts." *Journal of the American Psychoanalytic Association*, 22:37–57.

Dahl, H. (1988). "Frames of mind." In: H. Dahl, H. Kächele, and H. Thömä, eds., *Psychoanalytic Process Research Strategies*. New York: Springer-Verlag.

Dahl, H., Kächele, H., and Thomä, H. (eds.) (1988). *Psychoanalytic Process Research Strategies*. New York: Springer-Verlag.

Dahl, H., Teller, V., Moss, D., and Trujillo, M. (1978). "Countertransference examples of the syntactic expression of warded-off contents." *Psychoanalytic Quarterly*, 47:339–63.

Darwin, C. (1859). *On the Origin of Species by Means of Natural Selection*. London: Murray.

Deutsch, H. (1945). *The Psychology of Women*. New York: Grune & Stratton.

Devaney, R. and Keen, L. (1989). *Chaos and Fractals: The Mathematics Behind the Computer Graphics*. Providence: American Mathematical Society.

Duke, M. (1994). "Chaos theory and psychology: Seven propositions." *Genetic, Social, & General Psychology Monographs*, 120(3): 267–86.

Dunham, B., Fridsahl, D., and North, J. (1963). "Design by natural selection." *Synthese*, 15:254–59.

Dusheck, J. (2002). "The interpretations of genes." *Natural History*, 111:52–59.

Edelman, G. (1987). *Neural Darwinism: The Theory of Neuronal Group Selection*. New York: Basic Books.

Edelson, M. (1983). "Is testing psychoanalytic hypotheses in the psychoanalytic situation really impossible?" *Psychoanalytic Study of Children*, 38:61–112.

Einstein, A. (1931). *Relativity: The Special and General Theory*. New York: Crown.

Emde, R.N. (1995). *Diagnosis, Assessment, and Individual Complexity. Archives of General Psychiatry*, 52:637–38.

Emde, R.N. and Spicer, P. (2000). "Experience in the midst of variation: New horizons for development and psychopathology." *Development and Psychopathology*, 12:313 31.

Epstein, J. (2014). *Agent Zero: Toward Neurocognitive Foundations for Generative Social Science.* Princeton: Princeton University Press.

Erikson, E. (1950). *Childhood and Society.* New York: Norton.

Erikson, E. (1958). *Young Man Luther: A Study in Psychoanalysis and History.* New York: Norton.

Erikson, E. (1963). *Childhood and Society*, 2nd Edition. New York: Norton.

Erikson, E. (1964). *Insight and Responsibility.* New York: Norton.

Erikson, E. (1968). *Identity Youth and Crisis.* New York: Norton.

Erikson, E. (1978). *Adulthood.* New York: Norton.

Erikson, E. (1982). *The Life-cycle Completed: A Review.* New York: Norton.

Erikson, E. (1984). "Reflections on the last stage—and the first." *Psychoanalytic Study of the Child*, 39:155–65.

Fajardo, B. (2001). *The Therapeutic Alliance: Coupled Oscillators in Biological Synchrony.* Presented at Chicago Psychoanalytic Society, Sept. 25.

Fenichel, O. (1941). *Problems of Psychoanalytic Technique.* New York: Psychoanalytic Quarterly Inc.

Feynman, R. (1985). *QED.* Princeton: Princeton University Press.

Fisher, R. A. (1951). *The Design of Experiments.* Edinburgh: Oliver & Boyd.

Fonagy, P. and Target, M. (2003). *Psychoanalytic Theories: Perspectives from Developmental Psychopathology.* New York: Brunner-Routledge.

Fonagy, P., Gergely, G., Jurist, E., and Target, M. (2002). *Affect Regulation, Mentalization and the Development of the Self.* New York: Other Press.

Fortnow, L. (2013). *The Golden Ticket: P, NP and the Search for the Impossible.* Princeton: Princeton University Press.

Frazier, E. (1948). *The Negro Family in the United States,* Revised and abridged ed. Chicago: University of Chicago Press.

Freeman, W. (2000). *How Brains Make Up Their Minds.* New York: Columbia University Press.

French, T. (1952). *The Integration of Behavior, Vol. 1: Basic Postulates.* Chicago: University of Chicago Press.

French, T. (1954). *The Integration of Behavior, Vol. 2: The Integrative Process of Dreams.* Chicago: University of Chicago Press.

French, T. (1958). *The Integration of Behavior, Vol. 3: The Reintegrative Process in Psychoanalytic Treatment.* Chicago: University of Chicago Press.

Freud, A. (1958). "Adolescence." In: *The Writings of Anna Freud*, Vol. 5. New York: International Universities Press, 136–66.

Freud, A. (1965). *Normality and Pathology in Childhood: Assessments of Development.* New York: International Universities Press.

Freud, A. (1967). *Comments on Psychic Trauma*. New York: International Universities Press.

Freud, A. (1981). "The concept of developmental lines: Their diagnostic significance." *Psychoanalytic Study of the Child*, 6:129–30.

Freud, S. (1895a). "Project for a scientific psychology." In: *Standard Edition*, Vol. 1. London: Hogarth, 281–397.

Freud, S. (1895b). "Studies on hysteria." In: *Standard Edition*, Vol. 2. London: Hogarth.

Freud, S. (1900). "The Interpretation of Dreams." In: *Standard Edition*, Vol. 4, 5. London: Hogarth Press, 1953:76.

Freud, S. (1901). "The Psychopathology of Everyday Life. In: *Standard Edition*. London: Hogarth.

Freud, S. (1905a). "Fragment of an Analysis of a Case of Hysteria." In: *Standard Edition*, Vol. 2. London: Hogarth Press.

Freud, S. (1905b). "Jokes and Their Relation to the Unconscious." In: *Standard Edition*, Vol. 8. London: Hogarth.

Freud, S. (1905c). "Three Essays on the Theory of Sexuality." In: *Standard Edition*, Vol. 7. London: Hogarth, 125–243.

Freud, S. (1908). "Character and Anal Erotism." In: *Standard Edition*, Vol. 9. London: Hogarth.

Freud, S. (1909a). "Analysis of a Phobia in a Five-Year-Old Boy." In: *Standard Edition*, Vol. 10. London: Hogarth.

Freud, S. (1909b). "Notes upon a Case of Obsessional Neurosis." In: *Standard Edition*, Vol. 11. London: Hogarth.

Freud, S. (1911). "Psycho-Analytical Notes on an Autobiographical Account of a Case of Paranoia (Dementia Paranoides)." In: *Standard Edition*, Vol. 12. London: Hogarth, 3–82.

Freud, S. (1912). "Recommendation to Physicians Practicing Psychoanalysis." In: *Standard Edition*, Vol. 12. London: Hogarth, 109–22.

Freud, S. (1914a). "On Narcissism: An Introduction." In: *Standard Edition*, Vol. 14. London: Hogarth, 73–104.

Freud, S. (1914b). "Remembering, Repeating and Working through: Further Recommendations on the Technique of Psychoanalysis II." In: *Standard Edition*, Vol. 20 London: Hogarth, 146–56.

Freud, S. (1915a). "A Case of Paranoia Running Counter to the Psychoanalytic Theory of the Disease." In: *Standard Edition*, Vol. 14. London: Hogarth.

Freud, S. (1915b). "Observations on Transference Love." In: *Standard Edition*, Vol. 12. London: Hogarth.

Freud, S. (1915c). "The Unconscious." In: *Standard Edition*, Vol. 14. London: Hogarth, 159–215.

Freud, S. (1915d). "Introductory Lectures on Psychoanalysis." Part I and II. In *Standard Edition*, 15. London: Hogarth.

Freud, S. (1916–1917). "Introductory Lectures on Psychoanalysis." Part III. *Standard Edition*, 116. London: Hogarth Press, 1963.

Freud, S. (1917). "Mourning and Melancholia." *The Standard Edition of the Complete Psychological Works of Sigmund Freud.* J. Strachey. London: Hogarth Press.

Freud, S. (1918). "From the History of an Infantile Neurosis." In: *Standard Edition*, Vol. 17. London: Hogarth.

Freud, S. (1920a). "Beyond the Pleasure Principle." In: *Standard Edition*, Vol. 18. London: Hogarth, 3–64.

Freud, S. (1920b). "The Psychogenesis of a Case of Homosexuality in a Woman." In: *Standard Edition*, Vol. 18: London: Hogarth, 145–72.

Freud, S. (1920c). "Group Psychology and the Analysis of the Ego." In: *Standard Edition*, Vol. 18. London: Hogarth.

Freud, S. (1923a). "The Ego and the Id." In: *Standard Edition*, Vol. 19. London: Hogarth.

Freud, S. (1923b). "Two Encyclopedia Articles." In: *Standard Edition*, Vol. 18. London: Hogarth, 235–62.

Freud, S. (1926). "Inhibitions, Symptoms and Anxiety." In: *Standard Edition*, Vol. 20. London: Hogarth.

Freud, S. (1935). "The Subtleties of a Faulty Action." In: *Standard Edition*, Vol. 22. London: Hogarth.

Freud, S. (1940). "An Outline of Psychoanalysis." In: *Standard Edition*, Vol. 23. London: Hogarth.

Fromm-Reichmann, F. (1950). *Principles of Intensive Psychotherapy.* Chicago: University of Chicago Press.

Gabbard, G. and Westen, D. (2003). "Rethinking therapeutic action." *International Journal of Psychoanalysis*, 84:823–41.

Gaddis, J. (2002). *The Landscape of History: How Historians Map the Past.* Cambridge: Harvard University Press.

Galatzer-Levy, R. and Cohler, B. (1990) "The developmental psychology of the self: A new worldview in psychoanalysis." *Annual of Psychoanalysis*, 18:1–43.

Galatzer-Levy, R. and Cohler, B. (1993). *The Essential Other: A Developmental Psychology of the Self.* New York: Basic Books.

Galatzer-Levy, R. (1976). "Psychic energy: A historical perspective." *Annual of Psychoanalysis*, 4:41–64.

Galatzer-Levy, R. (1978). "Qualitative change from quantitative change: Mathematical catastrophe theory in relation to psychoanalysis." *Journal of the American Psychoanalytic Association*, 26(4): 921–35.

Galatzer-Levy, R. (1980). "Characterizing Our Ignorance." *Annual of Psychoanalysis*, 8:77–82.
Galatzer-Levy, R. (1983). "The regulatory principles of mental functioning." *Psychoanalysis and Contemporary Science*, 6:255–89.
Galatzer-Levy, R. (1984). "Perspectives on the regulatory principles of mental functioning." *American Journal of Psychiatry*, 134(11): 1211–21.
Galatzer-Levy, R. (1988). "On working through: A model from artificial intelligence." *Journal of the American Psychoanalysis Association*, 36:125–51.
Galatzer-Levy, R. (1991). "Computer models and psychoanalytic ideas." *Bulletin of the Society for Psychoanalytic Psychotherapy*, 6:23–33.
Galatzer-Levy, R. (1995). "Psychoanalysis and Dynamical Systems Theory: Prediction and Self Similarity." *Journal of the American Psychoanalytic Association*, 43:1085–1114.
Galatzer-Levy, R. (1997a). "On studying an overly complex interaction: The psychoanalytic process and chaos theory." The Edith Weygert Memorial Lecture, Bethesda, MD.
Galatzer-Levy, R. (1997b). "The Witch and Her Children: Metapsychology's Fate." *The Annual of Psychoanalysis*, 25:27–48.
Galatzer-Levy, R. (2002). "Emergence." *Psychoanalytic Inquiry*, 22(5): 708–27.
Galatzer-Levy, R. (2003). "Psychoanalytic Research and Confidentiality: Dilemmas." In: *Ethical Perspectives and Clinical Dilemmas.* Hillsdale: The Analytic Press, Inc., 85–106.
Galatzer-Levy, R. (2004). "Chaotic possibilities: Toward a new model of development." *International Journal of Psychoanalysis*, 85:419–41.
Galatzer-Levy, R. (2009). "Good Vibrations: A Non-linear Dynamical Systems Model of the Action of Psychoanalysis." *International Journal of Psychoanalytic Psychotherapy*, 90:983–1007.
Galatzer-Levy, R. (2014). "Exploring a Complex Systems Map of Gender: Commentary on Saketopoulou." *Journal of the Amaerican Psychoanalytic Association*, 62:815–21.
Galatzer-Levy, R., Bachrach, H., Skolnikoff, A., and Waldron, S. (2000). *Does Psychoanalysis Work?* New Haven: Yale University Press.
Gallese, V. (2003). "The roots of empathy: The shared manifold hypothesis and the neural basis of intersubjectivity." *Psychopathology*, 36:171–80.
Gedo, J. and Goldberg, A. (1973). *Models of the Mind: A Psychoanalytic Perspective.* Chicago: University of Chicago Press.
Gedo, J. (1979). *Beyond Interpretation.* New York: International Universities Press.
Gibbons, S. (1932). *Cold Comfort Farm.* New York: Longmans, Green and Company.

Gilbert, O. (1993). *The Narrative of Sojourner Truth.* New York: Vintage.

Gill, M. (1976). "Metapsychology is not psychology." In: M. Gill and P. Holzman, eds., *Psychology versus Metapsychology. Psychological Issues,* 9(26): 71–105.

Gill, M. (1982). *Analysis of the Transference.* New York: International Universities Press.

Gill, M. and Holzman, P. (eds.) (1976). *Psychology versus Metapsychology.* New York: International Universities Press.

Glansdorff, P. and Prigogine, I. (1971). *Thermodynamic Theory of Structure, Stability and Fluctuations.* New York: Wiley-Interscience.

Glover, E. (1931). "The therapeutic effects of inexact interpretation." In: *Techniques of Psychoanalysis.* New York: International Universities Press, 353–66.

Gödel, K. (1931a). "On formally undecidable propositions of Principia Mathematica and related systems, I." In: J. van Heijewoort, ed., *From Frege to Gödel.* Cambridge: Harvard University Press, 592–617.

Gödel, K. (1931b). "Über formal unentscheidbare Sätze der Principia Mathematica und verwandte Systeme I." *Monatshefte für Mathematik und Physik*, 38:173–98.

Goldberg, A. (1988). *A Fresh Look at Psychoanalysis.* Hillsdale: Analytic Press.

Goldstein, H. (1950). *Classical Mechanics.* Reading. New York: Addison-Wesley.

Goldstein, H. (1972). *The Computer from Pascal to Von Neumann.* Princeton: Princeton University Press.

Gottman, J., Murray, J., Swanson, C., Tyson, R., and Swanson, K. (2002). *The Mathematics of Marriage: Dynamic Nonlinear Models.* Cambridge: MIT Press.

Gould, S. (1977). *Ontogeny and Phylogeny.* Cambridge: Harvard University Press.

Gray, P. (1973). "Psychoanalytic technique and the ego's capacity for viewing intrapsychic activity." *Journal of the American Psychoanalytic Association*, 21(3): 474–94(0003–0651. H9Z).

Gray, P. (1990). "The Nature of Therapeutic Action in Psychoanalysis." *Journal of the American Psychoanalytic Association*, 38:1083–96.

Green, A. (1975). "The analyst, symbolization and absence in the analytic setting (on changes in analytic practice and analytic experience). In memory of D. W. Winnicott." *International Journal of Psychoanalysis*, 56:1–22.

Greenacre, P. (1967). "The influence of infantile trauma on genetic patterns" In: *Emotional Growth.* New York: International Universities Press, 260–99.

Gribbin, J. (1994). "The prescient power of mathematics." *New Scientist*, 14:256.

Grinker Sr., R. R. and Holzman, P. S. (1973). "Schizophrenic pathology in young adults: A clinical study." *Archives of General Psychiatry*, 28:168–75.

Guastello, S. and Gregson, R. (2011). *Nonlinear Dynamical Systems Analysis Using Real Data.* Boca Raton: CRC Press.

Guastello, S. *et al.* (2009). *Chaos and Complexity in Psychology: Theory of Nonlinear Dynamics.* New York: Cambridge University Press.

Gutheil, T. and Brodsky, A. (2008). *Preventing Boundary Violations in Clinical Practice.* New York: Guilford.

Haken, H. (2002). *Brain Dynamics: Synchronization and Activity Patterns in Pulse-Coupled Neural Nets with Delays and Noise.* Berlin: Springer.

Hall, T. S. (1969). *Ideas of Life and Matter.* Vols. 1 and 2. Chicago: University of Chicago Press.

Hardy, G. (1967). *A Mathematician's Apology.* Cambridge: Cambridge University Press.

Harris, A. (2005). *Gender as Soft Assembly.* Hillsdale: Analytic Press.

Hartmann, H. (1939). *Ego Psychology and the Problem of Adaptation.* New York: International Universities Press.

Hartmann, H. (1950). "Comments on the psychoanalytic theory of the ego." In: H. Hartmann, ed., *Essays on Ego Psychology.* New York: International Universities Press, 113–41.

Hartmann, H. (1958). *Ego Psychology and the Problem of Adaptation.* New York: International Universities Press.

Heisenberg, W. (1930). *The Physical Principles of the Quantum Theory.* New York: Dover.

Henderson, J. (1980). "On fathering (the nature and functions of the father role). Part II: Conceptualization of fathering." *Canadian Journal of Psychiatry* 25:413–31.

Hilbert, D. (1929). "The foundations of mathematics." In: J. van Heijewoort, ed., *From Frege to Gödel.* Cambridge: Harvard University Press, 464–79.

Hodges, A. (1983). *Alan Turing: The Enigma.* New York: Simon & Schuster.

Holzman, P. S. (1976). "Theoretical models and the treatment of schizophrenia." In: M. M. Gill & P. S. Holzman, eds., *Metapsychology versus Psychology.* New York: International Universities Press, 134–57.

Holzman, P. S. and Gill, M. (1978). "Psychology versus Metapsychology." New York: International Universities Press.

Hume, D. (1739). *A Treatise on the Nature of Human Understanding*, ed. L. A. Selby-Bigge. Oxford: Oxford University Press.

Hurewicz, W. (1958). *Lectures on Ordinary Differential Equations.* Cambridge: MIT Press.

Huygens, C. (1665). "Letter to his father, dated 26 February 1665." In: *Oeuvres complets de Christian Huygens*, vol. 5, 243. The Hague: Société Hollandaise des Sciences.

Jones, E. (1953). *Life and Works of Sigmund Freud.* New York: Basic Books.

Jung, C. G. (1933). *Modern Man in Search of a Soul.* New York: Harcourt, Brace and World.

Jung, C. G. (1954). *The Development of Personality.* Princeton: Princeton University Press.

Kagan, J. (2000). *Three Seductive Ideas.* Cambridge: Harvard University Press.

Kagan, J., Kearsley, R., and Zelazo, P. (1978). *Infancy: Its Place in Human Development.* Cambridge: Harvard University Press.

Kanwisher, N., McDermott, J., and Chun, M. (1997). "The fusiform face area: A module in human extrastriate cortex specialized for face perception." *Journal of Neuroscience*, 17:4302–11.

Karp, P. (1977). "Probabilistic analysis of partitioning algorithms for the traveling-salesman problem in the plane." *Mathematics Operations Research*, 2:209–24.

Kernberg, O. (1975). *Borderline Conditions and Pathological Narcissism.* New York: Jason Aronson.

Kilert, S. (1993). *In the Wake of Chaos.* Chicago: University of Chicago Press.

Kirkpatrick, S. *et al.* (1983). "Optimization by simulated annealing." *Science*, 220:671–80.

Klein, G. (1970). "Two theories or one." In: *Psychoanalytic Theory.* New York: International Universities Press, 41–71.

Klein, G. (1976). *Psychoanalytic Theory: An Exploration of Essentials.* New York: International University Press.

Klein, M. (1923). "The development of a child." *International Journal of Psychoanalysis*, 4:419–74.

Klein, M. (1928). "Early stages of the Oedipus conflict." In: *Love, Guilt and Reparation and Other Works, 1927–1945.* New York: Delacorte Press.

Klein, M. (1935). "A contribution to the psychogenesis of manic-depressive states." In: *Love, Guilt and Reparation and Other Works, 1927–1945.* New York: Delacorte Press.

Klein, M. (1937). "Love, guilt and reparation." In: *Love, Guilt and Reparation and Other Works, 1927–1945.* New York: Delacorte Press, 344–69.

Klein, M. (1945). "The Oedipus complex in the light of early anxieties." In: *Love, Guilt and Reparation and Other Works, 1927–1945.* New York: Delacorte Press, 370–419.

Klein, M. (1957). *Envy and Gratitude.* London: Tavistock.

Klein, M. (1969). *The Psychoanalysis of Children*. London: Hogarth.
Kline, M. (1972). *Mathematical Thought from Ancient to Modern Times*. New York: Oxford University Press.
Klumpner, G. and Frank, A. (1991). "On methods of reporting clinical material." *Journal of the American Psychoanalytic Association*, 39:537–51.
Koestler, A. (1984). *Arrow in the Blue*. New York: Holt.
Kohler, E., Keysers, C. *et al.* (2004). "Hearing sounds, understanding actions: action representation in mirror neurons." *Science*, 297:846–49.
Kohut, H. (1959/1978). "Interspection, empathy, and psychoanalysis: An examination of the relationship between mode of observation and theory." In: P. Ornstein, ed., *The Search for the Self: Selected Writings of Heinz Kohut, 1950–1978*. New York: International Universities Press, 205–32.
Kohut, H. (1966). "Forms and transformations of narcissism." *Journal of the American Psychoanalytic Association*, 14:243–72.
Kohut, H. (1971). *The Analysis of the Self*. New York: International Universities Press.
Kohut, H. (1977). *The Restoration of the Self*. New York: International Universities Press.
Kohut, H. (1984). *How Does Analysis Cure?*, eds. A. Goldberg and P. Stepansky. Chicago: University of Chicago Press.
Kohut, H. and Seitz, P. (1963–1978), "Concepts and theories of psychoanalysis." In: P. Ornstein, ed., *The Search for the Self: Selected Writings of Heinz Kohut, 1950–1978*. New York: International Universities Press, 337–74.
Krafft-Ebing, R. V., *et al.* (1939). *Psychopathia Sexualis: A Medico-Forensic Study*. New York, Pioneer Publications, Inc.
Langs, R. and Badalamenti, A. (1994). "Psychotherapy: The search for chaos and the discovery of determinism." *Australian & New Zealand Journal of Psychiatry*, 28(1):68–81.
Langston, C. (1990). "Computation on the edge of chaos: Phase transition and emergent computation." *Physica D Nonlinear Phenomena*, 42:12–37.
LeDoux, J. (1996). *The Emotional Brain*. New York: Simon & Schuster.
Levy, M. (1952). "Metabolic Patterns in Embryonic Development." *Annals of the New York Academy of Sciences*, 55:51–56.
Levy, S. (1992). *Artificial Life*. New York: Pantheon.
Lewis, C. (1964). *The Discarded Image: An Introduction to Medieval and Renaissance Literature*. Cambridge: Cambridge University Press.
Lewis, M. (1997). *Altering Fate: Why the Past Does Not Predict the Future*. New York: Guilford.
Lichtenberg, J. (1975). "The development of the sense of self." *Journal of the American Psychoanalytic Association*, 23:453–84.

Lichtenberg, J. (1979). "Factors in the development of the sense of the object." *Journal of the American Psychoanalytic Association*, 27:375–86.

Lichtenberg, J. (1983). *Psychoanalysis and Infant Research.* Hillsdale: Analytic Press.

Lin, S. (1975). "Heuristic programming as an aid to network design." *Networks*, 5:33–43.

Llinás, R. (2001). *I of the Vortex: From Neuron to Self.* Cambridge: MIT Press.

Loewald, H. (1960). "On the therapeutic action of psychoanalysis." *International Journal of Psychoanalysis*, 41:16–33.

Lorenz, E. (1963). "Deterministic nonperiodic flow." *Journal of Atmospheric Sciences*, 20:130–37.

Luborsky, L. and Crits-Cristoph, P. (1990). *Understanding Transference: The Core Conflictual Relationship Theme Method.* New York: Basic Books.

Luthar, S., Cicchetti, D., and Becker, B. (2000). "The construct of resilience: A critical evaluation and guidelines for future work." *Child Development*, 71:543–62.

McCormmach, R. (1991). *Night Thoughts of a Classical Physicis.* Cambridge: Harvard University Press.

Mabee, C. (1993). *Sojourner Truth: Slave, Prophet, Legend.* New York: New York University Press.

Mahler, M. (1952). "On child psychosis and schizophrenia: Autistic and symbiotic infantile psychoses." *Psychoanalytic Study of the Child*, 7:286–305.

Mahler, M. (1958). "Autism and symbiosis: Two extreme disturbances of identity." *International Journal of Psychoanalysis*, 39:77–83.

Mahler, M. (1968). *On Human Symbioses and the Vicissitudes of Individuation, Vol. 1.* New York: International Universities Press.

Mahler, M. (1971). "A study of the separation–individuation process and its possible application to borderline phenomena in the psychoanalytic situation." *Psychoanalytic Study of the Child*, 26:403–24.

Mahler, M. (1972). "On the first three sub-phases of the separation–individuation process." *International Journal of Psychoanalysis*, 53:333–38.

Mahler, M., Pine, F., and Bergman, A. (1975). *The psychological birth of a human infant.* New York: Basic Books.

Mandelbrot, B. (1982). *The Fractal Geometry of Nature.* San Francisco: Freeman.

Mandelbrot, B. (2014). *The Fractalist: Memoir of a Scientific Maverick.* New York, Vintage.

Marks-Turlow, T. (2008). *Psyche's Veil: Psychotherapy, Fractals and Complexity.* London: Routledge.

Marsh, J. (1978). "Bounded rationality, ambiguity and the engineering of choice." *Bell Journal of Economics*, 9:587–608.

Matte-Blanco, I. (1988). *Feeling, Thinking and Being.* New York: Routledge.

McCarly, M. D. and Hobson, J.A. (1977). "The neurobiological origins of psychoanalytic dream theory." *International Journal of Psychoanalysis*, 40:153–62.

Mead, G. H. (1934). *Mind, Self and Society.* Chicago: University Chicago Press.

Meehl, P. (1962). "Schizotaxia, schizotypy and schizophrenia." In: T. Millon, ed., *Theories of Psychopathology.* Philadelphia: Saunders, 59–72.

Meltzoff, A. and Moore, M. (1977). "Imitation of facial and manual gestures by human neonates." *Science*, 198:75–78.

Metropolis, N., Rosenbluth, A.W., Rosenbluth, M.N., Teller, A.H., and Teller, E. (1953). "Equation of state calculations by fast computing machines." *Journal of Chemical Physics*, 21:1087–92.

Mitchell, S. (1988). *Relational Concepts in Psychoanalysis: An Integration.* Cambridge: Harvard University Press.

Moran, M. (1990). "Chaos Theory and Psychoanalysis." *International Review of Psychoanalysis*, 18:211–22.

Morrison, F. (1991). *The Art of Modeling Dynamic Systems: Forecasting for Chaos Randomness and Determinism.* New York: Wiley.

Mullahy, P. (1970). *The Beginnings of Modern American Psychiatry: The Ideas of Harry Stack Sullivan.* Boston: Houghton Mifflin.

Needham, J. (1959). *A History of Embryology*, 2nd Edition. New York: Abelard-Schuman.

Newman, M. (2013). *Networks: An Introduction.* New York: Oxford.

Nicolis, G. and Prigogine, I. (1977). *Self-Organization and Non-Equilibrium Systems from Dissipative Structures to Order through Fluctuations.* New York: Wiley.

Novey, S. (1962). "The principle of 'working through' in psychoanalysis." *Journal of the American Psychoanalytic Association*, 10:658–76.

Nunberg, H. (1930). "The synthetic function of the ego." In: *Practice and Theory of Psychoanalysis Vol. I.* New York: International Universities Press, 120–36.

Oberman, L., Hubbard, E., McCleery, J., Altschuler, E., Ramachandran, V., and Pinella, J. (2006). "EEG evidence for mirror neuron dysfunction in autism spectral disorders." *Brain Research. Cognitive Brain Research*, 24:190–98.

Ott, E. (1993). *Chaos in Dynamical Systems.* New York: Cambridge Univeristy Press.

Painter, N. (1996). *Sojourner Truth: A Life, a Symbol.* New York: Norton.

Palombo, S. (1999). *The Emergent Ego: Complexity and Co-evolution in the Psychoanalytic Process.* Madison: International University Press.

Panel (1973a). "Separation– individuation: Maturity, senescence." *Journal of the American Psychoanalytic Association*, 21:633–45.

Panel (1973b). "Separation–individuation: Adolescence, maturity." *Journal of the American Psychoanalytic Association*, 21:155–67.

Pappert, S. (1982). *Mind Storms.* Cambridge: MIT Press.

Park, R., Burgess, E., and McKenzie, R. (1925). *The City.* Chicago: University of Chicago Press.

Peterfreund, E. and Schwarz, J. (1971). *Information Systems and Psychoanalysis and Evolutionary Biological Approach to Psychoanalytic Theory.* New York: International Universities Press.

Pfeffer, A. (1961). "Follow-up study of a satisfactory analysis." *Journal of the American Psychoanalytic Association*, 9:698–718.

Piketty, T. (2014). *Capital in the Twenty-First Century.* Cambridge: Harvard University Press.

Pine, F. (1974). "On the Concept 'Borderline' in Children—A Clinical Essay." *Psychoanalytic Study of the Child*, 29:341–68.

Poincaré, H. (1886). "Sur les intégrales irregulières des equations lineaires." *Acta Mathematica*, 8:295–44.

Pollack, G. (1981). "Reminiscences and Insight." *Psychoanalytic Study of the Child*, 36:274–87.

Polya, G. (1954). *Mathematics and Plausible Reasoning.* Princeton: Princeton University Press.

Pontryagin, L. S., Boltyanskii, V. G., Gamkrelidze, R. V., and Mischenko, E. F. (1962). *The Mathematical Theory of Optimal Processes.* New York: Wiley.

Preparata, F. (1982). *Computational Complexity.* In: S. Pollack, ed., *Studies in Computer Science.* Washington: Mathematical Association of America.

Prigogine, I. (1967). *Introduction to Thermodynamics of Irreversible Processes.* Wiley Interscience.

Prigogine, N. and Prigogine, I. (1977). *Self-Organization in Nonequilibrium Systems: From Dissipative Structures to Order through Fluctuations.* New York: Wiley.

Quinodoz, J. (1999). "Dreams that turn over a page." *International Journal of Psychoanalysis*, 80:225–38.

Racker, H. (1957). "The Meanings and Uses of Countertransference." *Psychoanalytic Quarterly*, 26:303–57.

Racker, H. (1968). *Transference and Countertransference.* New York: International Universities Press.

Rangell, L. (1989). "Rapprochement and other crises. The specific and nonspecific in analytic reconstruction." *Psychoanalytic Study of the Child*, 44:19–39.

Rapaport, D. (1960). *The Structure of Psychoanalytic Theory Psychological Issues*. New York: International Universities Press.

Rapaport, D. and Gill, M. (1959). "The points-of-view and assumptions of metapsychology." *International Journal of Psychoanalysis*, 40:153–62.

Reich, W. (1924). "On genitality: From the standpoint of psychoanalytic prognosis and therapy." In: *Wilhelm Reich: Early Writings*, trans. P. Schmitz. New York: Noonday.

Reich, W. (1949). *Character Analysis*, 3rd Edition. New York: Farrar, Straus and Giroux.

Reich, W. (1975). *Early Writings*. New York: Farrar, Strauss, and Giroux.

Reik, T. (1948), *Listening with the Third Ear*. New York: Farrar, Straus and Giroux.

Reiser, M. (1984). *Mind, Brain, Body: Toward a Convergence of Psychoanalysis and Neurology*. New York: Basic Books.

Reiser, M. (1985). "Converging sectors of psychoanalysis and neurobiology: Mutual challenge and opportunity." *Journal of the American Psychoanalytic Association*, 33:11–34.

Ricci, J. (1966). *The Phase Rule and Heterogeneous Equilibrium*. New York: Dover.

Ricoeur, P. (1970). *Freud and Philosophy: An Essay on Interpretation*. New Haven: Yale University Press.

Ricoeur, P. (1977). "The question of proof in Freud's psychoanalytic writings." *Journal of the American Psychoanalytic Association*, 25:835–72.

Rizzolatti, G. and Craighero, L. (2004). "The mirror-neuron system." *Annual Review of Neuroscience*, 27:169–92.

Rosenblatt, A. and Thickstun, J. (1977a). "Energy, information and motivation: A revision of psychoanalytic theory." *Journal of the American Psychoanalytic Association*, 25:537–58.

Rosenblatt, A. and Thickstun, J. (1977b). "Modern psychoanalytic concepts and a general psychology, Part I: Principal concepts and principals; Part II: Motivation." *British Journal of Medical Psychology*, 12:91–108, 199–233.

Ross, W. D. (ed.) (1928). *The Works of Aristotle Vol. 1 Logic: Categoriae*, trans. E. M. Edghill. New York: Oxford University Press.

Ruelle, D. (1991). *Chance and Chaos*. Princeton: Princeton University Press.

Saketopoulou, A. (2014). "Mourning the Body as Bedrock: Developmental Considerations in Treating Transsexual Patients Analytically." *Journal of the American Psychoanalytic Association*, 62:773–806.

Sameroff, A. (1995). "General systems theories and developmental psychopathology." In: D. Cicchetti and D. Cohen, eds., *Developmental Psychopathology, Vol. 1: Theory and Methods*. New York: Wiley, 659–95.

Sameroff, A. and Fiese, B. (2000a). "Models of development and developmental risk." In: C.H. Zeanah Jr., ed., *Handbook of Infant Mental Health*, 2nd Edition. New York: Wiley, 3–19.

Sameroff, A. and Fiese, B. (2000b). "Transactional regulation: The developmental ecology of early intervention." In: J. Shonkoff and S. Meisels, eds., *Handbook of Early Childhood Intervention*, 2nd Edition. New York: Wiley, 135–59.

Sander, L. (1969). "Regulation and organization in the early infant caretaker system." In: R. Robertson, ed., *Brain and Early Behavior*. London: Academic Press, 128–52.

Sander, L. (1989). "Investigation of the infant and its caregiving environment as a biological system." In: S.I. Greenspan, ed., *The Course of Life, Vol. 1: Infancy*. Madison: International Universities Press, 359–91.

Sander, L., Stechler, G., Burns, P., and Julia, H. (1970). "Early mother–infant interaction and 24 hour patterns of activity and sleep." *Journal of the American Academy of Child and Adolescent Psychiatry*, 9:103–23.

Sandler, J. and Dreher, A. (1996). *What Do Psychoanalysts Want?* New York: Routledge.

Sandler, J., Dare, C., and Holder, A. (1973). *The Patient and the Analyst: The Basis for the Psychoanalytic Process*. New York: International Universities Press.

Sargent, H., Horwitz, L., Wallerstein, R., and Appelbaum, A. (1968). *Prediction in Psychotherapy Research: A Method of the Transformation of Clinical Judgments into Attestable Hypotheses*. New York: International Universities Press.

Sartre, J. P. (1943). *Being and Nothingness*, ed. H. Barnes. New York: Washington Square.

Sashin, J. (1985). "Affect tolerance – a model of affect-response using catastrophe theory." *Journal of Social and Biological Structures*, 8:175–202.

Sashin, J. and Callahan, J. (1990). "A model of affect using dynamical systems." *Annual of Psychoanalysis*, 18:213–31.

Saunders, P. (1980). *An Introduction to Catastrophe Theory*. Cambridge: Cambridge University Press.

Schafer, R. (1973). "Concepts of self and identity and the experience of separation–individuation in adolescence." *Psychoanalytic Quarterly*, 42:42–59.

Schafer, R. (1976a). "Concepts of self and identity in relation to separation–individuation." In: *A New Language for Psychoanalysis*. New Haven: Yale University Press.

Schafer, R. (1976b). *A New Language for Psychoanalysis*. New Haven: Yale University Press.

Schafer, R. (1980). "Narration in the psychoanalytic dialogue." *Critical Inquiry*, 7:29–53.

Schafer, R. (1992). *Retelling a Life: Narration and Dialogue in Psychoanalysis*. New York: Basic Books.

Schaffer, S. (1993). "Comets and the world's end." In: L. Howe and A. Wain, eds., *Predicting the Future*. Cambridge: Cambridge University Press.

Schlesinger, J., dir. (1996). *Cold Comfort Farm*. London: BBC.

Schlessinger, N. and Robbins, F. (1983). *A Developmental View of the Psychoanalytic Process*. New York: International Universities Press.

Schreber, D. (1988). *Memoirs of My Nervous Illness*. Cambridge: Harvard University Press.

Searles, H. (1979). *Countertransference and Related Subjects*. New York: International Universities Press.

Seligman, S. (2006). "Dynamic systems: Theories as a metaframework for psychoanalysis." *Psychoanalytic Dialogues*, 15:286–319.

Shapiro, T. and Perry, R. (1976). "Latency revisited. The age 7 plus or minus 1." *Psychoanalytic Study of the Child*, 31:79–105.

Silver, N. (2012). *The Signal and the Noise: Why So Many Predictions Fail – but Some Don't*. New York: Penguin.

Simon, H. (1982). *Science of the Artificial*, 2nd ed. Cambridge: MIT Press.

Singer, T., Seymour, B., O'Doherty, J., Kaube, H., Dolan, R.J., and Frith, C.D. (2006). "Empathy for pain involves the affective but not sensory components of pain." *Science*, 303:1157–62.

Smith, A. (1776). *An Inquiry into the Nature and Causes of the Wealth of Nations*. Dublin: Whitestone.

Smith, H. (ed.) (2007). "Comparing theories of therapeutic action." *Psychoanalytic Quarterly*, 76 Supplement.

Snodgrass, M., Bernat, E. and Shevrin, H. (2004). "Unconscious perception at the objective detection threshold exists." *Perception & Psychophysics*, 66:888–95.

Snow, C. (1961). *The Two Cultures and the Scientific Revolution*. New York, Cambridge University Press.

Solms, M. (2013). "The Conscious Id." *Neuropsychoanalysis*, 15(1): 5–19.

Spence, D. (1982). *Narrative Truth and Historical Truth*. New York: Norton.

Spence, D. (1987). *The Freudian Metaphor*. New York: Norton.

Spence, D. (1989). "Narrative appeal vs. historical validity. Scientific Symposium: Clinical controversies and the interpersonal tradition." *Contemporary Psychoanalysis*, 25:517–24.

Sperry, R. (1945). "Restoration of vision after crossing of optic nerves and after contralateral transplantation of eye." *Journal of Neurophysiology*, 8:17–28.

Spitzer, M. (1999). *The Mind within the Net*. Cambridge: MIT Press.

Spitzer, R.L. and Robins, E. (1978). "Research diagnostic criteria: rationale and reliability." *Archives of General Psychiatry*, 35(6):773–82.

Sprott, J. (2002). *Sprott's Fractal Factory*. http://sprott.physics.wisc.edu/fractals.htm.

Sprott, J. (2003). *Chaos and Time-Series Analysis*. New York: Oxford University Press.

Spruiell, V. (1993). "Deterministic Chaos and the Sciences of Complexity: Psychoanalysis in the Midst of a General Scientific Revolution." *Journal of the American Psychoanalytic Association*, 41:3–44.

Stern, D. (1985). *The Interpersonal World of the Infant*. New York: Basic Books.

Stern, D. (2004). *The Present Moment in Psychotherapy and Everyday Life*. New York: Norton.

Stewart, I. (1989). *Does God Play Dice?* New York: Blackwell.

Stewart, I. (2001). *Flatterland*. New York: Perseus.

Stewart, I. (2002). *Does God Play Dice?* 2nd Edition. New York: Blackwell.

Stewart, I. and Golubitsky, M. (1992). *Fearful Symmetry*. Oxford: Blackwell.

Stockmeyer, L. and Chandra, A.K. (1979). "Intrinsically difficult problems." *Scientific American*, 240:140–54.

Stoker, J. (1957). *Water Waves. Pure and Applied Mathematics Series*. New York: Wiley.

Stolorow, R. and Atwood, G.E. (1979). *Faces in a Cloud*. New York: Jason Aronson.

Strachey, J. (1934). "The nature of the therapeutic action of psychoanalysis." *International Journal of Psychoanalysis*, 15:127–59.

Strogatz, S. (1994). *Nonlinear Dynamics and Chaos: With Applications to Physics, Biology, Chemistry and Engineering*. Cambridge: Westview.

Strogatz, S. (2003). *Sync: The Emerging Science of Spontaneous Order*. New York: Theia.

Sullivan, H. (1940). *Conceptions of Modern Psychiatry*. New York: Norton.

Sullivan, H. (1964). *The Fusion of Psychiatry and Social Science*. New York: Norton.

Sulloway, S. (1979). *Freud, Biologist of the Mind: Beyond the Psychoanalytic Legend*. New York: Basic Books.

Thelen, E. and Smith, L. (1994). *A Dynamic Systems Approach to the Development of Cognition and Action.* Cambridge: MIT Press.

Thom, R. (1975). *Structural Stability and Morphogenesis* (trans. D. H. Fowler). New York: Benjamin.

Tolpin, M. (1978). "Self-Objects and Oedipal Objects—A Crucial Developmental Distinction." *Psychoanalytic Study of the Child*, 33:167–89.

Tomasello, M., Carpenter, M., Call, J., Behne, T., and Henrike, M. (2005). "Understanding and sharing intentions: The origins of cultural cognition." *Behavioral Brain Science*, 28:675–735.

Topping, J. (1955). *Errors of Observation.* London: Institute of Physics.

Toulmin, S. (1990). *Cosmopolis: The Hidden Agenda of Modernity.* New York: The Free Press.

Tower, L. E. (1956). "Countertransference." *Journal of the American Psychoanalytic Association*, 4:224–55.

Trevarthen, C. (1980). "The foundations of intersubjectivity." In: D.R. Olson, ed., *The Social Foundations of Language and Thought.* New York: Norton, 316–44.

Turing, A. (1936). "On computable numbers, with an application to the Entscheidungs problem." *Proceedings London Mathematical Society*, 42(2):238–65.

Turner, V. (1969). *The Ritual Process.* Chicago: Aldine.

Tyler, B., Wegner, T., Peterson, A., and Branderhorst, P. (1990). *Fractint*, Version 15.0 (a computer program). Cleveland: Compuserve Information Service.

Valenstein, A. F. (1962). "The psychoanalytic situation: Affects, emotional reliving and insight in the psychoanalytic process." *International Journal of Psychoanalysis*, 43:315–25.

von Bertalanffy, L. (1968). *General Systems Theory*, Revised Edition. New York: Braziller.

Von Neumann, J. (1958). *The Computer and the Brain.* New Haven: Yale University Press.

Von Neumann, J. (1966). *Theory of Self-Reproducing Automata.* Urbana: University of Illinois Press.

Waelder, R. (1930). "The principle of multiple function: observations on overdetermination." In: S. A. Guttman, ed., *Psychoanalysis: Observation, Theory, Application.* New York: International Universities Press, 68–83.

Waelder, R. (1963). "Psychic determinism and the possibility of predictions." *Psychoanalytic Quarterly*, 32:15–42.

Wallerstein, R. (1964). "The role of prediction in theory building in psychoanalysis." *Journal of the American Psychoanalytic Association*, 12:675–91.

Watts, D. (1999). *Small Worlds: The Dynamics of Networks between Order and Randomness*. Princeton: Princeton University Press.

Weber, M. (1905). *The Protestant Ethic and the Spirit of Capitalism*, trans. T. Parsons. New York: Scribner's.

Weber, M. (1946). *From Max Weber: Essays in Sociology*, eds. H. H. Gerth and C. W. Mills. New York: Oxford University Press.

Weiss, S. (1981). "Reflections on the psychoanalytic process, with special emphasis on child analysis and self-analysis." *Annual for Psychoanalysis*, 9:43–56.

West, B. (2006). *Where Medicine Went Wrong: Rediscovering the Path to Complexity*. Singapore, World Scientific.

Whitehead, A. and Russell, B. (1910). *Principi Mathematica*. Cambridge: Cambridge University Press.

Whorf, B. L. (1956). *Language, Thought and Reality*. New York: Wiley.

Wiener, N. (1961). *Cybernetics: Or Control and Communication in the Animal and the Machine*, 2nd Edition. Cambridge: MIT Press.

Wigner, E. (1960). "The unreasonable effectiveness of mathematics in the natural sciences." *Communications on Pure and Applied Mathematics*, 13:1–14.

Winnicott, D. (1945–1958). "Primitive emotional development." In: *Collected Papers: Through Pediatrics to Psychoanalysis*. New York: Basic Books, 145–56.

Winnicott, D. (1949). "Hate in the countertransference." *International Journal of Psychoanalysis*, 30:69–74.

Winnicott, D. (1953). "Transitional objects and transitional phenomena." In: *Collected Papers: Through Pediatrics to Psychoanalysis*. New York: Basic Books, 229–42.

Winnicott, D. (1958). "The capacity to be alone." In: *The Maturational Process and the Facilitating Environment*. New York: International University Press, 29–36.

Winnicott, D. (1960a). "Ego distortion in terms of the true and false self." In: *The Maturational Process and the Facilitating Environment*. New York: International University Press, 140–52.

Winnicott, D. (1960b). "The theory of the parent–infant relationship." *International Journal of Psychoanalysis*, 41:585–95.

Winnicott, D. (1962). "The aims of psychoanalytic treatment." In: *The Maturational Process and the Facilitating Environment*. London: Hogarth Press.

Winnicott, D. (1963a). "From dependence towards independence in the development of the individual." In: *The Maturational Process and the Facilitating Environment*. New York: International Universities Press, 83–92.

Winnicott, D. (1963b). "Psychiatric disorder in terms of infantile maturational processes." In: *The Maturational Process and the Facilitating Environment*. New York: Basic Books, 230–41.

Winnicott, D. (1965). *The Maturational Process and the Facilitating Environment*. New York: International Universities Press.

Winnicott, D. (1968). "Playing: its theoretical status in the clinical situation." *International Journal of Psychoanalysis*, 49(4): 591–99.

Winnicott, D. (1975). *Playing and Reality*. New York: Basic Books.

Winnicott, D. (1986). *Holding and Interpretation: Fragment of an Analysis*. London: Hogarth Press.

Wittgenstein, L. (1968). *Philosophical Investigation*. New York: Macmillan.

Wolff, P. (1987). *The Development of Behavioral States and the Expression of Motion in Early Infancy*. Chicago: University of Chicago Press.

Zeeman, C. (1975). "The classification of elementary catastrophes of codimension 5." In: A. Dold and B. Eckmann, eds., *Structural Stability, the Theory of Catastrophes and Applications in the Science*. New York: Springer-Verlag.

Zeeman, C. (1977). *Catastrophe Theory: Selected Papers 1972–1977*. Reading: Addison-Wesley.

Index